Intercultural Theology

Intercultural Theology

Approaches and Themes

Edited by

Mark J. Cartledge
and David Cheetham

scm press

© The Editors and Contributors 2011

Published in 2011 by SCM Press
Editorial office
13–17 Long Lane,
London, EC1A 9PN, UK

SCM Press is an imprint of Hymns Ancient and Modern Ltd (a registered
charity)
13A Hellesdon Park Road
Norwich NR6 5DR, UK

www.scm-canterburypress.co.uk

British Library Cataloguing in Publication data

A catalogue record for this book is available
from the British Library

978-0-334-04351-5

Typeset by the Manila Typesetting Company
Printed and bound by
CPI Antony Rowe, Chippenham, Wiltshire

Contents

Acknowledgements   vii
Contributors   viii

Introduction   1
1   The Cultural Origins of 'Intercultural' Theology   11
    Werner Ustorf
2   Intercultural Theology and Political Discipleship   29
    Graham Ward
3   Intercultural Theology and Interreligious Studies   43
    David Cheetham
4   Pentecostal Theological Method and
    Intercultural Theology   62
    Mark J. Cartledge
5   Gender Issues in Intercultural Theological Perspective   75
    Kirsteen Kim
6   When Buddhist Women Go to Church: Reflections
    on the Nature of Ethical Mission   93
    Louise Nelstrop
7   Context and Catholicity: An Anglican–
    American Dilemma?   112
    Martyn Percy
8   Intercultural Theology, Walter J. Hollenweger
    and African Pentecostalism   128
    Allan Anderson
9   'Practical Christianity and Public Faith':
    Nigerian Pentecostal Contributions
    to Intercultural Theology   145
    Richard Burgess

Bibliography   169
Index   188

Dedication

To Joan and Naina

Acknowledgements

The editors of this volume would like to acknowledge the support and assistance of various academic colleagues in the compilation of this book, either through providing a text for publication or by peer-reviewing submissions for us. We are especially grateful to colleagues in the Department of Theology and Religion at the University of Birmingham and to guest speakers and postgraduate students who attended the Intercultural Theology seminars in the academic session of 2007–08. The seminar series provided the basis for this collection of essays. We are also extremely grateful to academic colleagues who were not part of that initial seminar series but nevertheless agreed to join the project at a later date. Even though this project started life as a discussion among academic colleagues and postgraduate students, we have been able to deliver some of this research to Honours-level students on the BA Theology programme. It is hoped that many more researchers and students will be able to appreciate the insights that these essays bring through their publication here.

Two essays appearing in this collection were previously published. Chapter 1 by Werner Ustorf was previously published as: 'The Cultural Origins of "Intercultural Theology"', *Mission Studies* 25.2 (2008), pp. 229–51. Permission for publication has been obtained from Brill, Leiden (licence number 2522620174045). Chapter 4 by Mark J. Cartledge was previously published as: 'Pentecostal Theological Method and Intercultural Theology', *Transformation: An International Journal of Holistic Mission Studies* 25.2/3 (2008), pp. 92–102. Permission for publication has been obtained from Koorong Publisher, Sydney, previously owned by Paternoster Press, Milton Keynes.

Contributors

Allan Anderson is Head of the School of Philosophy, Theology and Religion and Professor of Global Pentecostal Studies at the University of Birmingham. He studied theology at the University of South Africa, where he majored in Church History and Mission Studies and wrote his doctoral thesis on African Pentecostalism in South Africa. He is author of many articles on Pentecostalism and African independency, and several books, the latest being: *Zion and Pentecost* (University of South Africa, 2000), *African Reformation* (2001), *An Introduction to Pentecostalism* (Cambridge University Press, 2004) and *Spreading Fires: The Missionary Nature of Early Pentecostalism* (SCM, 2007). His work focuses on the relationship between Pentecostalism and cultures and religions, especially those of Southern Africa, where he lived and worked for almost 43 years. He is currently completing a book on the significance of Pentecostalism for the changing demographics of global Christianity during the twentieth century.

Richard Burgess is a Research Fellow in the School of Philosophy, Theology and Religion, University of Birmingham. Until 2010 he was employed on the NORFACE-funded research programme entitled 'Re-emergence of Religion as a Social Force in Europe?' He is currently conducting research on Nigerian Pentecostalism as part of the Pentecostal and Charismatic Research Initiative, funded by the University of Southern California's Center for Religion and Civic Culture and the John Templeton Foundation. Dr Burgess was previously a lecturer at the Theological College of Northern Nigeria, Jos, Nigeria. He is the author of articles on Pentecostalism in Africa and the African Diaspora.

Mark J. Cartledge is Director of the Centre for Pentecostal and Charismatic Studies in the University of Birmingham. He is an Anglican priest and has worked in a variety of jobs combining Christian ministry with academic work. He has published extensively in the fields of Theology and Pentecostal and Charismatic Studies. His publications include: *Testimony in the Spirit: Rescripting Ordinary Pentecostal Theology* (Ashgate, 2010), *Encountering the Spirit: The Charismatic Tradition* (Darton, Longman & Todd, 2006; and Orbis Books, 2007), (ed.) *Speaking in Tongues: Multidisciplinary Perspectives* (Paternoster, 2006), *Practical Theology: Charismatic and Empirical Perspectives* (Paternoster, 2003), *Charismatic Glossolalia: An Empirical-Theological Study* (Ashgate, 2002) and (ed. with David Mills) *Covenant Theology: Contemporary Approaches* (Paternoster, 2002). He is the Editor of *PentecoStudies: An Interdisciplinary Journal for Research on the Pentecostal and Charismatic Movements* (Equinox).

David Cheetham is Senior Lecturer in Theology and Religion at the University of Birmingham, UK. He specializes in the philosophy and theology of religions. He publications include: *John Hick* (Ashgate, 2003), (ed. with Rolfe King) *Contemporary Practice and Method in the Philosophy of Religion* (Continuum, 2008) and numerous articles in journals including *The Heythrop Journal, Sophia, Islam and Christian–Muslim Relations* and *Studies in Interreligious Dialogue* and other articles in the *Westminster Dictionary of Theology* (John Knox Press, 2008) and *The Blackwell Encyclopaedia of Theologians* (Blackwell, 2010). He is currently completing a new book on the theology of religions.

Kirsteen Kim is Associate Principal Lecturer and Director of Programmes in Theology and Religious Studies at Leeds Trinity University College. Originally from the UK, her interest in the intercultural dimensions of gender issues goes back to experiences of living in South Korea (1987–92) and India (1993–7). These have also formed the starting point of her explorations of pneumatology and theology of mission in publications such as *The Holy Spirit in the World: A Global Conversation* (Orbis, 2007) and *Joining in the with Spirit: Connecting World Church and Local Mission* (Epworth-SCM, 2009). Kim is also joint author with her husband, Sebastian C. H. Kim, of *Christianity as a World Religion* (Continuum, 2008), and they are currently working on a book on Korean Christianity for Cambridge University Press.

Louise Nelstrop is currently a Junior Research Fellow at the Oxford Centre for Christianity and Culture, Regent's Park College, Oxford and a Visiting Lecturer at Union Biblical Seminary, Pune, India. She combines an interest in Christian spirituality with Practical Theology and has published in the area of Christian Mysticism and the Emerging Church in the UK. Recent publications include: *Christian Mysticism: An Introduction to Contemporary Theoretical Approaches* (Ashgate, 2009) and *Evaluating Fresh Expressions: Explorations in Emerging Church* (SPCK, 2008), which she co-edited with Martyn Percy.

Martyn Percy is Principal of Ripon College Cuddesdon and the Oxford Ministry Course. He is also Honorary Professor of Theological Education at King's College London, Professorial Research Fellow at Heythrop College, London, and Honorary Canon of Salisbury Cathedral. He served as curate at St Andrew's, Bedford, and was then appointed Chaplain and Director of Studies, Christ's College, Cambridge. From 1997 to 2004 he was Director of the Lincoln Theological Institute. His main research interests are Christianity in contemporary culture, modern ecclesiology and practical theology. He is also engaged in public theology, which has included roles with the Advertising Standards Authority, the Portman Group, Direct Marketing Commission and the British Board of Film Classification. Recent books include: *Engaging Contemporary Culture: Christianity and the Concrete Church* (Ashgate, 2005), *Clergy: The Origin of Species* (Continuum, 2006) and the *Oxford University Press Handbook of Anglican Studies* (forthcoming).

Werner Ustorf taught at Hamburg and, later, Heidelberg University before succeeding Walter J. Hollenweger in 1990 as Professor of Mission in the University of Birmingham until his retirement in 2010. He is currently Emeritus Professor of Mission. His academic interests grew out of Europe's postwar situation and address issues of the decolonization of Christian historiography, Church and Fascism, and the general question of whether the kind of civilization that was responsible for imperialism (old and new) is also capable of contributing towards overcoming it. He has published research on African prophetism, West African Christian history, Mission and Fascism and on dechristianization in Western Europe. His many publications include: *Sailing on the Next Tide* (Peter Lang, 2001), (with H. McLeod) *The Decline of Christendom in Western Europe* (CUP, 2003), (ed. by R. Loffler) *Robinson Crusoe Tries Again* (Vandenhoeck & Ruprecht, 2010). He is currently working on a project tracing the theological consequences of Christianity's encounter with Aboriginal thinking in Central Australia.

Graham Ward is the Samuel Fergusson Professor of Philosophical Theology and Ethics at the University of Manchester and Head of the School of Arts, Histories and Cultures. He is the author of *Barth, Derrida and the Language of Theology* (CUP, 1995), *Theology and Contemporary Critical Theory* (Macmillan, 2000), (ed.) *The Postmodern God: A Theological Reader* (Blackwell, 1997), (ed. with John Milbank and Catherine Pickstock) *Radical Orthodoxy: A New Theology* (Routledge, 1998), *Cities of God* (Routledge, 2000), *True Religion* (Blackwell, 2002), (ed.) *The Blackwell Companion to Postmodern Theology* (Blackwell, 2004), *Cultural Transformation and Religious Practice* (CUP, 2004), *Christ and Culture* (Blackwell, 2005), (ed. with Michael Hoelzl) *Religion and Political Thought* (Continuum, 2006) and *The Politics of Discipleship: Becoming Postmaterial Citizens* (Baker Academic, 2009). He is currently working on two volumes concerned with the doctrine of God, entitled *Ethical Life*.

Introduction

This book is about a contemporary approach to theology, one that pays particular attention to the culture in which theology is set. It is hardly surprising that a topic like 'intercultural theology' should give rise to a variety of different perspectives and definitions. The term is used in many different ways and reflects a range of theological constituencies and allegiances. While most will acknowledge the close affinities between intercultural theology and contextual studies, there is a diversity of opinion in this book about what programme (if any) is suggested by intercultural theology. Many of the authors here share a kinship in thinking about intercultural theology in analytical and comparative terms particularly regarding local contextual concerns and the meeting of regional theologies. In addition, quite a few have identified similar sources for their chapters, such as Walter J. Hollenweger, Reinhold Niebuhr, Robert Schreiter and others. Nevertheless, it would be misleading to assume that such 'sources' should be regarded as canonical for intercultural theology. Even though there is a traceable historical background presented by Werner Ustorf in this volume, the very term 'intercultural' is so common that it is difficult to fix clear authorities in this field. Thus, the figures mentioned by the authors in this volume reflect their own theological preferences and views on the nature of the subject.

Differences emerge over how a focus on intercultural theology might influence the doctrinal aspects of the theological task. Perhaps least controversial, there are methodological implications for undertaking theology in light of a sheer expansion of data brought about by globalization, inculturation and non-Western theologies. In addition, to the extent that theology is perceived as a human task of reflection on God, creation and salvation, the wideness of the human testimony and witness is something that must be acknowledged. Incarnating theology, or making theology contextually relevant, has always been central to the Christian witness and, with many voices now being heard from around the globe, this feature of Christian thinking about God's relationship with the world and its cultures becomes ever more pertinent. Typically, the sources and norms for Christian theology have been defined in terms of Scripture, tradition, reason and (sometimes) experience, different theological commitments accentuating specific sources. These sources continue to be essential to the theological task, but an intercultural approach pays particular attention to the cultural embeddedness of all theological forms and displays a reflexive attitude towards it, as well as an interest in comparison, whereby other different cultural expressions are also considered important for theology. Hence in this discourse 'inter', meaning 'between' or 'among' or 'across', refers to the awareness of and engagement with different expressions of theology as they exist between different cultures.[1] But it also captures the nature of the dynamic as cultural features mutate and adapt over time and through space. This inevitably raises the question as to what we mean when we use the term 'culture'.

The way in which the term has evolved has been described by others and there is a lengthy debate about its meaning.[2] In essence, what is being addressed here is culture as a way of life rather than the 'high culture' associated with knowledge of literature and the arts (the idea of a 'cultured person' and by extension a 'cultured society'). Culture as a way of life refers to a composite and shared social reality, which gives expression to beliefs and values, attitudes and practices. These are inevitably mediated by languages and the rationalities that accompany specific linguistic paradigms. It is given shape in social institutions in government, education, economics, health care and transport systems, as well as being mediated by means of signs and symbols associated with food, clothing, architecture and the like. In short, culture provides a set of assumptions about the nature of social conventions and their expression, about how we do things here in this country and in this region. This way of life provides the glue that binds people together, thus creating a sense of identity and community. It infuses human reality and gives a sense of familiarity. But it must be stressed that culture is not static: every culture changes over time. There is always a dynamic within cultures, as they have their own internal fluidity and as they interact with others, borrowing and receiving ways of living that are subsequently integrated over time. Therefore, cultures should not be conceived in terms of sharply bounded self-contained units.[3] Using culture in this sense, intercultural theology is necessarily attentive to different expressions of Christianity as culturally mediated, and seeks to facilitate interactions between them. In so doing, it problematizes

---

1 See the discussion in Wijsen (2003), pp. 39–54.
2 See, for example, Tanner 1997 and Gorringe 2004.
3 Tanner 1997, pp. 53–6.

the familiar and advocates a critical dialogue between different culturally shaped theologies.

The central aim of this book, therefore, is *to extend the conversation concerning the contemporary cultural conditions under which different theological accounts might be given.* Intercultural theology is not just a novelty but represents an important feature in the doing of theology itself. In other words, it is a *methodological* rather than an ideological commitment and, as such, can be practised across the spectrum of theological opinion. That is, the inclusion of a wider range of cultural information and contextual reflection does not necessarily have doctrinal alteration at its heart. Indeed, intercultural theology can be programmatically construed as a project for global or interreligious theology or be wedded to interfaith dialogue in a liberal plural agenda. But this need not be the case, and not all of the authors in this volume would consider themselves theologically liberal or pluralistic; indeed, several would happily own a conservative description (in varying degrees).

Given the sheer volume of possibilities the book cannot (and does not) pretend to be comprehensive. Indeed, if the sheer breadth of possibilities associated with intercultural theology is fully grasped, it would be somewhat self-contradictory and presumptuous to suppose that an overall comprehensibility is attainable anyway. Instead it offers a survey of some of the more obvious issues as well as providing historical, theological and some contextual discussions. The chapters also reflect something of the concentration of intercultural theologians working at the University of Birmingham. This explains the amount of space that has been given to chapters dealing with Pentecostalism as it reflects one of the main research strengths of the Birmingham faculty.

This collection is concerned to illustrate the different approaches and key themes located within the ambit of intercultural theology. The approaches adopted by the essayists in this book can be classified in terms of three broad categories. First, some of the contributors have employed an analytical approach, by which they have attempted to trace conceptual patterns among writers in the field. This has been done using historical and contemporary sources, which because of the closeness of the historical period (spanning 40 years from its origin to the present day) runs into more contemporary discussion. This is demonstrated in the chapters by Anderson and Ustorf (focusing more on origins) and Burgess and Kim (focusing more on the contemporary discussion). Second, other contributors, in very different ways, seek to evaluate particular theological and cultural positions or constructs, either in terms of some form of comparison (Cartledge, Cheetham and Percy) or in terms of empirical data

3

(Nelstrop). Third, one of the contributors in this volume considers the nature of theology in a contemporary intercultural context and offers a constructive proposal (Ward). All three approaches are regarded as valid ways of addressing issues in the field and provide worked examples of how one might engage in this field of study.

Emerging from these different approaches (analytic, evaluative and constructive) are many different themes that are associated with world Christianity and its relationship to the societies in which it finds itself. They can be said to revolve around four main areas: two internal to Christianity and two external as it relates to society. The internal concerns include issues around the nature of Christianity and its spirituality, which means that discussions regarding the use of the Bible, how it is interpreted and how theology is constructed in given cultural contexts, is critical to its internal understanding. As an extension of this is the nature of Christianity in terms of its identity, the nature of Church unity (polity) and the limits of diversity (catholicity and ecumenism) in a pluralistic world. These themes will continue to require much theological reflection. The external concerns are the relationships with other religious traditions around the globe, and these inevitably vary from context to context (interreligious studies and dialogue). Associated with this is the relationship of Christianity to broader society and the concerns of politics and power, globalization, economics, the media, justice and ethics. These issues and themes are addressed in different ways throughout this book.

To begin, Werner Ustorf's chapter provides a detailed account of the historical rise of intercultural theology in the European academy. From the field of missiology, Ustorf particularly discusses the fortunes of mission studies and argues for a transformation of his field towards intercultural theology. For Ustorf, unlike Hollenweger for example, this is a full-blown transformation which is not content merely to broaden the horizon of missiological thinking within carefully staked out Christian boundaries, but to become thoroughly self-conscious of the often 'monological' character of much Western theologizing in the past and the need to face head on the challenges of secularism, doubt, decolonization and the encounter with other faiths.

Ustorf's chapter raises a number of issues that provide a useful background to the rest of the book. Expanding from the issues that he draws attention to, there are the ontological challenges that arise from Hollenweger's acknowledgement that theological work 'operates within a particular cultural framework without absolutizing it'. To what extent is abstract theologizing (perhaps 'transcendental' theology) de-legitimized by the intercultural emphasis? There will always be a place for intellectual effort and critical theorizing in theology, but for Ustorf the recognition of the cultural frameworks that underpin human thought means that universal ambitions or the pretensions of *finality* will be curtailed. Given this, one of the main methodological dilemmas for the future of theology will be the skilful marriage of contextual, and inter-contextual, insights with the quest for normativity. Certainly, this desire for normativity will be conceived differently – some will be content to see theology as a relatively unfettered and open enterprise of increasing knowledge and experiences. However, others in this book (see, for example, Ward and Cheetham) have sought to express the contextual and intercultural aspects in more universal Christian theological terms, such as via discipleship or incarnation rather than seeking to move outside Christian discourse. Indeed, it could be suggested that universality in Christian theology is only properly conceived in and through the cultural particularity of time and place.

Then there are the global challenges brought about by the presence of non-Western theologies. So the privileged status of Western theology hardly represents any special sanctity or election as such, but is a circumstantial feature of the historical and geographical rise of Christianity. It could be argued that the universal applicability of the gospel message compels us to take seriously the contributions emerging out of the places, wherever they are, in which it has become incarnated. In addition, it is probable that the future of theology will no longer be steered by Western theologians simply because the theological voices from the southern hemisphere represent regions where the growth in Christianity is most evident and may therefore enjoy greater influence as time passes.

Going further, intercultural theology does not just arise from the global influences mentioned above, but is perhaps indirectly related to a proliferation of methods and approaches to theology itself in the twentieth century and into the twenty-first. Thus, the use of the arts in theology, narrative approaches, gender issues, questions of justice and liberation as well as contextual concerns mean that contemporary theology has become decentred from its rational, philosophical and scholastic heritage. In addition to all this, there are the profound postmodern epistemological shifts in Western thinking in the twentieth century that have contested intellectual and methodological hierarchies. Moreover, mention might be made of an earlier concentration in the mid-twentieth century, highlighted by Tillich and Niebuhr, on theology and culture. As a result, theological methods have given greater priority to diverse cultural expressions of meaning, the ethical imperatives of the poor and oppressed, and the correlation of Christian thought with culture. Nevertheless, there is perhaps the danger that the pursuit of different approaches to theology may be undertaken less as a desire to give expression to local concerns, but merely for the sake of novelty. That is, globalization and the communications revolution of the past decade have resulted in such an abundance of new perspectives that one might simply relish 'diversity' as an end in itself. Ustorf's chapter wisely recommends that intercultural theologies should be 'tested' in terms of social practices and in their ability to forge links between different cultural groups. Moreover, following Hollenweger, Ustorf also cautions against what he characterizes as an uncritical 'pop-theology'. The more radical consequences of postmodern intellectual forces, post-colonial realities and global forces of the contemporary scene might mean that there is a discarding of dogmatic traditions in Christian theology and a construction of something approximating to an 'interreligious theology'. Ustorf also quotes H. J. Margull, who suggests that in the light of globalization and the rise of non-Western theologies there should be a deliberate 'transgression of traditional theological approaches and methods'. Not all theologians will be happy with this call, but it demonstrates that intercultural theology brings with it a number of issues and agendas that have to be dealt with by each theologian as they establish an appropriate way forward.

In the next chapter, Graham Ward displays just such concerns when he seeks to articulate how far he is prepared to go with the project of intercultural theology. Thus, for him it is about adopting what he calls an 'intercultural style' that emerges out of the Christian experience 'within intricate webs of interculturalism and interfaith' that is today's context. Put simply, to be an authentic Christian disciple today is to interact with an unavoidable rich diversity (Ward's own experience is the multicultural heart of Manchester in the UK). In a vivid part of his chapter he paints a picture of the Christian as someone who is caught up in a 'vast network of relationships' and who therefore brings 'into God all the concerns and connections we have with the contemporary world'. Our lives in the world are performed within an interculturally diverse context, and we soak this up into our prayer lives and engagement with God.

Along similar lines, David Cheetham argues in his chapter that a multicultural dimension is very much consistent with the Christian eschatological vision found in Revelation 7.9, which speaks of all nations, tribes, peoples and languages standing before the throne of God. With this in mind he proceeds to consider the relationship between intercultural theology and interreligious studies. Presenting a discussion about the nature of intercultural theology as a cross-cultural (rather than merely contextual) and comparative exercise, Cheetham points out that religion is very much part of the various cultures in the world, and so a study of religions, and the relationships between them, is a necessary ingredient for constructive intercultural theological thinking. Nevertheless, he is keen to stress that this does not imply that a pluralist theological position is inevitable, rather that interreligious studies is an important component of contemporary theological education in terms of providing an informed background for theologizing in the new global context. As a consequence of this, he argues that the amount of knowledge and understanding that a 'global' situation brings cannot be summed up in the work of a single systematic theologian. Instead, Cheetham asks if there needs to be greater trust of individual theologians and believers working out their own contexts and interreligious encounters in local settings.

Mark J. Cartledge's chapter is concerned to explore the extent of the possible connections between Pentecostal theological methods and those of intercultural theology. Using the work of John C. Thomas and Kenneth J. Archer, he commences by presenting a brief discussion of Pentecostal methods as a triadic conversation of the text of Scripture, the community of the Church and the person of the Holy Spirit. In unpacking the methods of Pentecostal theology, Cartledge highlights a number of key themes, such as the importance of orthopraxy and orthopathy, the affective and experiential dimensions of the tradition, and the fact that, following Archer, Pentecostal method implies an integration between practice and theorizing. Through the notion of 'testimony' and storytelling, Cartledge also highlights the narrative quality of much Pentecostal thinking and hermeneutical practice. He then moves on to compare Pentecostal approaches with Hollenweger's account of intercultural theology, finding a number of similarities. Thus, both Pentecostal and intercultural approaches to theology seem comfortable with the idea of theology as a narrative as well as recognizing the importance of local voices. In addition, both approaches ask what it means to be Church. However, Cartledge discerns real differences within these comparisons. Thus, with ecclesiology Cartledge acknowledges a wider and more inclusive scope evidenced in intercultural perspectives than in the strict five-fold Pentecostal accounts; and from an academic perspective, intercultural methods may only be prepared to study the spiritualities with academic detachment, whereas the Pentecostal method puts experience and spirituality at the 'heart of the process' of doing theology. Nevertheless, Cartledge completes his contribution by outlining an approach that seeks to integrate both Pentecostal and intercultural methods.

Although gender might be seen as a generic issue, Kirsteen Kim points out in her chapter that it is also something that is culturally defined. She provides an informative and richly sourced account of feminist theology in various contexts, showing the differences that exist between them. She begins by offering a swift overview and background to feminist theological thinking, including some of the oft-cited biblical sources in the debate. Beginning with the emergence of feminist theologies within Roman Catholicism in the 1960s, she then goes on to supply short summaries of the issues in feminist theologies as they sprang up in different regions of the globe, including the feminist work of the Protestants in the USA, the spreading of feminist thinking through the World Council of Churches and other ecumenical organizations, eco-feminism in the global South as well as Korean, African and Latin American contributions. There follows a consideration of some emphases found in the South and the East, with the focus on freedom from oppression (South) and the life-giving Spirit (East). Kim makes the important point that although feminist theologies are multicultural they are also *inter*cultural in the sense that the experience of women share affinities across cultures through encounters with patriarchy, slavery, colonization and genocide. Encouragingly, she also draws attention to the fact that there are already dialogues within feminist theological circles between different regions of the world.

Penetrating into the heart of much self-consciousness in Western thought over the last 100 or so years (the question of 'the other'), Louise Nelstrop's chapter offers a critique of the privileging of alterity to an absolute status. To focus her critique she uses the work of Cosimo Zene. Zene asks about the nature of 'ethical mission', but what Nelstrop objects to is that Zene overly stresses the preservation of otherness. Zene's Levinasian-inspired perspective, where 'one is encouraged to empty oneself out entirely in order to understand the other', is criticized and, by way of response, Nelstrop provides an interesting account of the experiences of Buddhist women who attend churches in Thailand and experience the benefit of being involved in the PIME (*Pontificium Institutum pro Missionibus Exteris* – The Pontifical Institute for Foreign Missionaries). The purpose of this is to suggest that invading the space of the other is not necessarily as detrimental as the Levinasian view would have us believe. In fact, Nelstrop astutely points out that if we submit entirely to 'the other', then any dialogue becomes almost monological because those who come to another culture are not allowed a voice. This is an odd outcome for an 'ethical' approach to mission. Moreover, it begs the question about how static we should view culture and how we should view the ethics of intercultural engagement.

Martyn Percy explores the relationship between catholicity and enculturation in the Anglican Church. His vivid essay discusses some of the dilemmas facing Anglicans around the globe, and he sets the context for this by drawing attention to the presence of Rick Warren and Gene Robinson at the inauguration of President Barack Obama. These are significant figures who represent very different theological constituencies, and they serve to highlight many of the dilemmas that face Anglicans regarding the quest for unity in difference. Thus, while there are many identities, Percy writes that there is nonetheless 'a unifying mood in the polity that rejoices in the tension between clarity and ambiguity'. Moreover, the politics of Anglicanism perhaps exhibits something that is applicable to wider society, what Percy evocatively calls 'robust models of breadth' and a 'moderate polity'. Somewhat critical of the 'Fresh Expressions' movement in Anglicanism, Percy worries about projects that distract from a broader commitment to the wider Church and the demands of local church community life. Percy identifies two threats: internally, the Church needs to be cautious about absorbing individualistic consumerist cultural fads into itself as this could undermine catholicity. Second, looking outwards, the Church should beware of becoming too like the world or modelled on its popular cultural successes (enculturation) because it undermines the 'otherness' of the Church's life. In addition, there are the constant tensions between the local and the global – between enculturation and catholicity. Nevertheless, the Anglican Church has important lessons to teach about how to cope with this, so he observes that an unordered and rather 'rumpled' institution may actually provide a suitable home for all.

Providing more examples, both Anderson's and Burgess' chapters give insights into the working of Pentecostalism in the African context. Thus, Anderson offers an account of how Pentecostalism fits the African context and mentality. Pentecostalism, with its emphasis on non-literary and spontaneous liturgy is an attractive format for many Africans. Furthermore, the open nature of Pentecostal services has 'social and revolutionary implications', which 'empowers marginalized people' and makes the worship of ordinary people acceptable. Anderson's chapter, by discussing the connections between Pentecostalism and African cultures, illustrates intercultural theology in action. Similarly, Burgess concentrates on Nigerian Pentecostalism and argues that it is appealing to Nigerians because of the way it 'resonates with the pragmatic orientation of indigenous spirituality'. Burgess sensitively articulates the virtue of using an intercultural approach to theology to contrast the singular powers wielded by individual Pentecostal leaders over their flocks. That is, the broader reference point of intercultural theology allows 'ordinary people to challenge dominant ideologies'. Reviewing the specific contributions made to intercultural theology by Pentecostalism, Burgess highlights the point that an openness to the Spirit of God reinforces the decolonization process and a 'post-secular' resistance to the secular modernism that is at the background of much Western rationalistic theology. In contrast, Pentecostal communities in Nigeria are committed to character formation, identity construction and contextual relevance.

As noted above, these essays are clearly written from very different perspectives and offer contrasting illustrations of how intercultural theology might be conceived. Despite the many differences there are important similarities methodologically, which we have outlined. It is hoped that this collection opens a window onto a multidimensional reality, the discourse about which we call intercultural theology.

The Cultural Origins of 'Intercultural' Theology[1]

WERNER USTORF

Introduction

Decolonization exposed much of Northern orthodox theological thought as unhelpful in reflecting the human realities in the South – an exposure that confirmed the inherited frustration of the Christian left with traditional theology and triggered a number of acts of theological repentance in the North, among them that of intercultural theology. From the start, intercultural theology received its thrust and energy not only from the discovery that all theologies are contextually conditioned, but also from much older Northern theological fault-lines that became active again under the pressure of the decolonization process. The term itself, though first turning up, it seems, in linguistics and international pedagogy (Kaplan 1966), was put to theological use in the 1970s by missiologists working in three European (and secular) universities. It is primarily connected with the names of the Lutheran missiologist and ecumenist Hans Jochen Margull (Hamburg; for his theological CV see Ahrens 1992, Petter 2002) and of his friend Walter J. Hollenweger (Birmingham; cf. Jongeneel 1992, Price 2002), who belonged to the Reformed tradition and, at the same time, to that of Pentecostalism. Both were, in the 1960s exponents of Church reform in the World Council of Churches in Geneva (WCC) and advocates of a new, namely a decolonized theology

---

1 The paper was originally given at the University of Birmingham. The text here is an update of a previous version published in *Mission Studies* 25 (2008), pp. 229–51. It will appear also in Friedli, R. et al. (eds), forthcoming, *Intercultural Perceptions and Prospects of World Christianity*, Frankfurt: Peter Lang. Important note: in addition to the published work cited, many of the 'historical' accounts given in this chapter have been drawn from first-hand experience and/or from emails, correspondences and unpublished material that can be found referenced in Ustorf 2008a; see 'Author's Personal Papers', p. 250.

that would include those traditions that were usually neglected by Western theology – non-Western and/or non-literary traditions (Margull 1962b, 1974a; Hollenweger 1967). In this ambition they were supported by a Roman Catholic missiologist and historian of religions from Switzerland, Richard Friedli (Fribourg), who had used American research (Luzbetak 1963, Nida and Taber 1969) to explore intercultural communication and had published a pioneering theology of religions to which Margull had written the introduction (Friedli 1974). Friedli, a generation younger than his two colleagues (emeritus since 2006), tried to rethink the future of Christianity and other religions by including two new sets of data: one, the phenomenon of a global 'cultural circulation', and two, the problem of coping with irreducible 'otherness' in terms of society, culture and religion. Both sets of data meant that believers, any believers, were aliens to the world they knew, using a transitory model of interpretation in order to put their trust into what is not transitory. In this period of transition, all traditions, including that of the Christian faith, had to reorientate themselves (for a practical application, see Friedli 1991).

From 1971 to 1981, Birmingham, Hamburg and Fribourg were in intense missiological communication. Their missiologists had little sympathy for the continuation of colonial or hegemonic mentalities under whatever guise, and they agreed as well on the bankruptcy of nationalist and ethnic ideologies. Hollenweger and Friedli were Swiss and thus coming from a multinational and multilingual background. Margull was hypersensitive to anything reminiscent of fascist thought and was deeply transformed by his encounter with Buddhism in Tokyo and Kyoto (1965–7) and by his involvement in setting up (1971) the sub-unit on interreligious dialogue of the WCC. One of the joint achievements of these years of co-operation was the trilingual book series they edited from 1975 on: *Studies in the Intercultural History of Christianity*, which comprises currently 150 or more published volumes, mostly in English, but with a number of French and German texts as well (Studies 1975; Hollenweger 1987). Though Lynne Price has argued in her theological biography of Hollenweger that he was already doing intercultural theology in Birmingham before the tag appeared (Price 2002), and though Richard Friedli had begun already in his Africa years to reflect on 'communication interculturelle', it is to my knowledge still true to say that 1975 is the first public occasion when the term 'intercultural' is used explicitly and with a theological programme in mind. Later, from the 1980s on, Heidelberg continued the exploration of this theological approach. Related but conceptually distinct attempts were made in other places. Nowadays the term intercultural theology is often used without any reference to its history in the 1970s and 1980s (for example, New-lands 2004). I will organize this chapter in four sections: a terminologi-cal observation, a closer look at the European discussion in the 1970s, a review of the attempts at conceptualizing the approach in the 1980s, and a final section I have called 'conclusions and prospects'. As the title already indicates, my hypothesis is that intercultural theology has cultur-ally particular and rather context-specific origins, and these I will try to describe. I hope to show as well that the North-Atlantic origin of this vision does not prevent it from being a rather interesting voice in the global theological discussion.

Terminological observation

Though launched publicly in 1975, the term was not immediately ad-opted in the English-speaking world. The second edition of the *Oxford English Dictionary* (1993: 863 [1095]) does have an entry 'inter-cul-tural', but simply as an example of combining the prefix 'inter' with an almost unlimited number of adjectives or nouns – even, and this is the message *ex silentio*, if there is no defined meaning attached to it. The term 'intercultural' had not yet entered the English language in any specific sense it seems, and even less so had the combined term 'intercul-tural theology'. Even the most well-known theological dictionaries and handbooks of the time are silent on this issue. The *World Christian En-cyclopedia* (Barrett 1982: VII) contains a 'contemporary dictionary . . . defining and explaining the majority of terms used in the Christian world', but the term 'intercultural' is not among them – and nor does it appear in the glossary and the dictionary of the second edition (Barrett 2001). The same is true for the *Dictionary of the Ecumenical Movement* (Lossky 1991), the *Oxford Dictionary of the Christian Church* (Cross 1997) and even for Jan Jongeneel's encyclopaedic two-volume bibliog-raphy on *Mission in the 19th and 20th Centuries* (Jongeneel 1994/97). I could expand this list.

From 1975 to the mid-1990s the word 'intercultural' was mainly to be found in the theological discussions of Europe and in the international educational discourse. The publication history of the term tells us that the two Swiss editors of the series of books *Studies in the Intercultural History of Christianity* were also involved in actively promoting the new term. Hollenweger produced a three-volume study, *Interkulturelle The-ologie* (Hollenweger 1979, 1982, 1988; see also Hollenweger 1978a and b); and Friedli used the term in his book *Mission oder Demission* (Friedli

1982a) and contributed the entry 'intercultural theology' for a German (later translated) missiological dictionary (Friedli 1987 and 1997). About the same time, in 1985, the Catholic Theological Faculty of Frankfurt University established an academic association called Theologie Interkulturell, which a year later started a series of books under this very title. And in October 1986, Theo Sundermeier, the missiologist of Heidelberg University, together with the author of this paper, dared even to think of the establishment of a Department of Intercultural Theology within the theological faculty there. A preliminary report was published (Ustorf 1989), but the institutional plans never materialized. Yet in the 1990s the Heidelberg project (see Sundermeier 1991 and 1999) had developed sufficient academic gravity to influence the conceptual design of a major theological dictionary (Küster 2001a) and, in 2005, to convince the leading academic association for theology on the European continent, the 'Wissenschaftliche Gesellschaft für Theologie', to adopt a declaration on mission studies as intercultural theology (Mission 2008). I will come back to the Heidelberg tradition and this declaration below.

Up to then, most of these publications were in languages other than English. The turning point came perhaps in the mid-1990s. About this time Robert Schreiter addressed the issue (Schreiter 1996) and the American edition of the German *Dictionary of Mission* was published (Müller et al. 1997). This does not mean of course that the issues the term intercultural theology tried to address had been unknown outside Europe. On the contrary, there was a vivid discussion, and I think David Bosch is a prominent example of this. He tried to give terminological expression to the mutual process of theological giving and receiving that characterizes the history of Christianity in its post-colonial and polycentric period. The term he chose in order to describe the step from the local incarnation (inculturation) of the faith to that of its participation in the ecumenical conversation with the other local incarnations, was already around, namely 'interculturation' (Bosch 1991). These insights rested on American research into processes of local contextualization and communication processes; Fuller Theological Seminary and other places played a role and, again, the name of Robert Schreiter may stand here vicariously for quite a number of scholars (Schreiter 1985 and 1997; on Schreiter see Hintersteiner 2001 and 2007a, Küster 2003). Bosch does acknowledge that there is a difference of theological perspective when we think interculturally, cross-culturally, or contextually. This process of searching for terms and terminological differentiation on both sides of the Atlantic was not just triggered by the insights ecumenical research and missiology had produced over the last 30 years or so, but also by the rude facts on the ground: that is, the visible and sometimes painful demographic changes in world Christianity. Reflections on these processes invaded mainstream theology only from the turn of the century, and were quickly and successfully picked up by other disciplines, for example history, as demonstrated by the notoriety the publications of Philip Jenkins have achieved (Jenkins 2002, 2006 and 2007).

Nevertheless, let us state the fact that it took some 20 or more years until the discussions in Europe on intercultural theology and the Anglo-American debate on culture, context and theological communication grew together. Today, the term has not only been widely accepted in Western theology, but in many instances it completely replaced the terms mission or missiology. A prominent example of this is the name-change at the end of 2003 at Fuller Theological Seminary, from School of Mission to that of Intercultural Studies. The reader may wish to check the description of Fuller's MA in Intercultural Studies, and may concur with me that this is a degree in mission studies in every detail – apart from the title. Another such example is the aforementioned declaration on 'mission studies as intercultural theology' of 2005. The declaration quite rightly defines intercultural theology as having grown out of missiology, religious studies and ecumenical theology, but then retreats immediately into theological orthodoxy by stating that intercultural theology is an 'explanatory term' better to describe missiology and protect this discipline from 'stereotyping', 'confusion' and 'misunderstandings'. This is, indeed, important, but just like Fuller's switch from mission to intercultural theology, the declaration seems to suggest a tactical update of the toolbox of missionary theology, without changing its basic parameters (Oborji 2008). We will see that this usage of the term intercultural theology falls short of the momentum that was achieved in the 1970s, when a 'paradigm change' was envisaged, and may even constitute what Richard Friedli called 'false labelling' (Friedli 2000, p. 190). In the meantime, the social sciences, medicine, business studies and education have adopted the adjective 'intercultural'. It is often included nowadays in the politically correct language of many city councils in Britain. In other words, the downside of the term's increasing popularity is its entropy or even disintegration. It is time, then, to find out what the term actually meant when it was first used as an explicit theological programme.

The beginning of the debate

The 1975 series of books is primarily the result of the work done in Margull's research project at Hamburg University on the 'social impact and self-awareness of the overseas variants of Christianity', which was to be carried out by an international team of up to 20 scholars, myself included. In more than one way this initiative was related to the 15 or so studies previously sponsored by the Division of World Mission and Evangelism (DWME) of the WCC, namely the project World Studies of Churches in Mission (1958–70), the analysis of which – in a time when the term pluralism had not yet acquired theological currency – had ended in 'a very humble agnosticism' (Mackie 1970, p. 101). Margull led the evangelism section of DWME from 1961 to 1964 and was well aware of the WCC study. One of the authors of the WCC series was also a member of Margull's research team in Hamburg. Yet there were also clear differences from the approach taken by Geneva.

The Hamburg project tried to hook itself into the then trendy research on development and social change in those parts of the world that were once colonized but now regarded as being in need of 'development'. Such research used to be dominated by a secular social science approach, and tended to neglect matters of religion and culture. Margull begged to differ, and declared the traditional social sciences to be 'a product of the history of western-European and North-American scholarship' and, therefore, not to be universal, but in its theories and perspectives rather a 'Kulturgestalt' of the West. Consequently, Western social theories were not to be imported lock, stock and barrel to contexts of deep change, they had rather to be formulated *in situ*, namely in response to the individual 'cultural context' there. This meant not just using an interdisciplinary approach, but also challenging the secularization hypothesis and starting from what the project called the surprising vitality and, indeed, the 'revitalization' of religion in the South. In fact the explicit prognosis was that religion would 'remain or become the means of identity formation for the masses of the people' in the 'Third World'. The project would therefore analyse in detailed field studies how religious-cultural traditions in Latin America, Africa and Asia, but also within the black immigrant churches of Birmingham and Watford, were influencing the process of development and social change. This critical approach, which identified the Third World as a political-historical, cultural and religious rather than a geographical term, did not go down well with the research establishment in the Federal Republic of Germany. After a frustrating three-year-long process of repeated negotiations, the funding bodies finally rejected the project. They believed they had diagnosed a lack of coherence, and classified the project as a sort of over-ambitious church history that had illegitimately invaded the territory of the social sciences.

However, eight of the individual research projects were already under-way or almost finished, often precariously financed, but showing results that called for quick publication. This dynamic, in combination with the lost battle for the acknowledgement of a new research paradigm, were two of the factors convincing Margull that he had to circumvent the establishment. He liaised with his colleagues in Birmingham and Fribourg, and all pegged their theological colours to the mast by publishing the research under the programmatic focus of an intercultural history of Christianity, though none of them was a trained historian. The archival records of 1971/72 show that a very specific confluence of missiological, ecumenical and religious ideas generated the critical mass out of which the term intercultural theology was born:

1 The globalization of Christianity had demonstrated that the non-Western variants of Christianity could no longer be described in theological or ecclesiological categories developed in the West. In fact the diagnosis was that there is a profound 'discontinuity with the European origin'.

2 The root cause of this discontinuity is the formative and continuing influence on the non-Western variants of Christianity of the factual, cultural, religious and contextual diversity that is to be found on the ground.

3 Non-Western forms of Christianity would develop their individual theological identities in response to the pressing issues of their social, political, religious and cultural contexts, and are part of the general 'surge of the Third World' in world politics.

4 This fundamental change in the power structures of the world, including World Christianity, is accompanied by what Margull called 'a general change of the way Christianity relates to the "world"'. This is a product of Margull's ecumenical experience and reflects the WCC's promotion of social engagement as a fundamental mode of being Christian.

5 These insights, in general, expressed a new perception of worldwide Christian experience and required now a deliberate 'transgression of traditional theological approaches and methods' – though the tag intercultural does not yet emerge on this occasion.

Several basic assumptions were implicit in these ideas. To mention the most important: Christianity was now globalized, but neither doctrine nor denominational tradition was the driving force; instead the 'world' or the historical particularities of the social, religious and cultural context had been identified as the catalyser that made local Christian faith what it was. Margull understood the diversities of faith, ecclesiology, theology, tradition, Christian engagement and the mutations of Christology as a response to – shaped by and shaping – the diversities of the contexts out of which they had grown. No theology and, as we have seen, no secular academic tradition could ever claim to be universal. The Hamburg project, however, was completely unaware that it had just rediscovered what the philosopher-theologian Johann Gottfried Herder (1744–1803) had already stated in the eighteenth century (Ustorf 2004). The degree to which the project was part of a much longer European conversation on transcendence, culture and pluralism was seriously underrated.

Conceptualizing the approach

In retrospect it appears to be a surprising flaw in the creation of the 1975 book series that, though the notion of interculturality was apparently discussed among the editors, they pursued this 'new research interest' only 'rather spontaneously and un-programmatically' and never made it explicit in the editorial presentation of the series. There was no conceptual editorial statement to accompany the individual volumes, though it is true that Friedli wrote a short paragraph in 1976 for the publisher's promotional use.[2] The first descriptive definition was published years later as an integral part of Hollenweger's research in this area (Hollenweger 1978a and b) and further systematized in his magnum opus on intercultural theology. In his 'five guiding principles', he states that intercultural theology:

1 is 'that scholarly theological discipline that operates within a particular cultural framework without absolutizing it';
2 will select its methods appropriately. Western academic theology is not automatically privileged over others;
3 has a duty to look for alternative forms of doing theology (such as non-Western and narrative forms);

2 Friedli's text reads: 'Either the church is universal and catholic – and at the same time indigenous and culturally and politically involved in its environment – or it is not church at all. This dialectical statement sums up the fundamental tension running through the scholarly publications in the series "Studies in the Intercultural History of Christianity". Starting with the cultural, social and political context – instead of the theological and political ideas of traditional denominational (catholic and protestant) church histories – the pluriformity of the Christian church and the search for its new catholicity are revealed.' Cited in Ustorf 2008a; see 'Author's Personal Papers', p. 250.

4 must be tested in social practice and measured by its capacity for bridge-building between diverse groups;

5 must not be confused with 'pop-theology' that escapes from self-critical reflection (summarized from Hollenweger 1979, pp. 50 f.; See also Hollenweger 1982, p. 145).

This description clarifies and extends some of the assumptions underlying the Hamburg project, though it is perhaps not made clear enough that the character of intercultural theology cannot be that of a 'meta-theology'. Should we detect here an inbuilt temptation to reach for finality and closure, the starting point of intercultural theology itself, namely to regard any theology as part of the weft and warp of human culture, would have to be abandoned. The actual core message of the new approach, however, is a different one: the primary question in World Christianity is no longer that of the mission and transmission of the Christian message, but that of its *appropriation*. The appropriation of Christianity, however, is not done by the missionaries, but by local people and under the circumstances surrounding their lives. Every form of theology is therefore a response to a particular Christian experience; that is, a response given under the conditions of culture and history which, in turn, makes the social and cultural disciplines indispensable for the analysis of theology. In offering this approach, intercultural theology broke away from the past of the *transmission-centred approach of mission studies*.

Yet Hollenweger defined intercultural theology primarily as an inner-Christian project. It is surprising that his guiding principles dropped the issue or rather the urgency of interreligious dialogue that Friedli pursued and that was so close to Margull's theological agenda (Margull 1974b), though Hollenweger later did in fact address the matter (Hollenweger 1988; see also Ustorf 1990). It is significant indeed that Friedli's entry for the *Dictionary of Mission* (Friedli 1987; Müller et al. 1997) reintroduced this point by insisting that intercultural theology had to open up to 'interreligious theology' and thus face the experience of dialogue that Christianity's truth claims were vulnerable and that the history of Christian understanding was unfinished and open to the future (Friedli 1997, p. 220. See also Brück 1992). This correction is justified and backed by the sources. While still working on his ecumenical project of understanding the new variants of Christianity in the South, Margull had already begun to shift his attention from missiology to interreligious dialogue. As Chair of the WCC's Commission on Evangelism, he had participated in the WCC's first worldwide dialogue not 'about' but this time 'with' Hindus, Buddhists and Muslims in Ajaltoun/Beirut (Margull 1972). Subsequently, he was appointed chair of the Commission's newly established sub-unit on interreligious dialogue (1971) and, in this capacity, he organized the Muslim–Christian dialogue of Broumana, also in the Lebanon (1972), and other activities (Margull 1973).

This shift is quite important for the matter under discussion here because Margull had identified the comparability of intercultural and interreligious communication. This comparability was because both processes (and the 'spiritual ethos' within them) were related and responding to the social context. This transfer of a primarily inner-Christian question to the area of interreligious dialogue became immediately controversial. The fifth Assembly of the WCC in 1975 is an example of symbolic quality in this regard: due to the vociferous protests by increasingly radicalized and anti-Western Muslim groups in Indonesia, the venue of the assembly had to be moved from Djakarta to Nairobi. In Nairobi, however, an equally single-minded majority of church leaders quickly exorcized the new agenda of interreligious dialogue by regressing, as Margull put it, 'to the easiest of options', namely the position of the absoluteness of the Christian truth (quoted by Friedli 1982b, p. 293). Margull detected in the appeal to the absoluteness of truth (usually a truth that is put in words, written up, and thus 'known') the presence of a deeply ingrained structure of denial that refused to open up to the call of the living God (Ustorf 1992, p. 14).

Heidelberg continued this awareness, and its leading missiologist, Theo Sundermeier, had early on opened up to the often surprising non-verbal forms of understanding, such as Christian art, not only as legitimate theological languages but as intercultural or bridging languages. The results of these attempts were usually published later or are still ongoing and therefore are outside my scope (Sundermeier 1985 and 1996 – and it should be noted that regarding the latter volume the publisher rejected the originally intended subtitle of 'an intercultural hermeneutic'; Sundermeier and Küster 1991; Küster 2001b). The group around Sundermeier also took steps to apply the philosophical critique of modernity (Adorno and Horkheimer 1944, Ricœur 1992) to the missiological discussion of culture and to construct a practical theological hermeneutic of the intercultural encounter. They were convinced that theology on its own was no longer in a position to explore fully the human condition.

This was reminiscent of the approach Joe Oldham (Clements 1999) had taken in the 1930s towards the question of rethinking the Christian message. In fact some of the practicalities of the Heidelberg programme remind us of one of the steps taken in the ecumenical past. There was for example the idea of establishing the hermeneutics for a global society by bringing together leading experts from a great number of academic disciplines and discussing (non-publicly) the epistemological presuppositions that are operative in the perception of the 'other'. The most influential text behind these attempts was Sundermeier's remarkable study on 'Konvivenz' or *convivencia* (Sundermeier 1986). This term, borrowed from liberation theology but going in fact back to the time, before the *reconquista*, when Muslims, Christians and Jews in Andalusia were able to live together, stands for a new Christian lifestyle in the global world. This style is characterized by a redefinition of mission as an invitation to a divine banquet where Christians are enabled to recognize God in the face and the religion of the other and where there is the priority of the shared experience of life over theological systematization. Priority does not mean that theological reflection is redundant – the opposite is the case, but theology must acknowledge that:

> Truth is contained in diversity. What matters is to learn, to confess, to sing and to celebrate it together to the glory of God. Truth itself calls the churches into convivencia. In it, truth wants to be discovered. (Sundermeier 1986, p. 99; see also, briefer and in English, Sundermeier 1992)

This went far beyond Oldham's incomplete project, and it may also be fair to assume that the WCC would still today hesitate to make such a statement the basis for its thinking about interreligious dialogue. However, it is also true that the next (tenth) WCC Assembly, which is scheduled for 2013, will have the subjects of migration and hospitality as its central agenda. I am not claiming that there is a direct historical line running from Oldham via Sundermeier's vision of *convivencia* to the thoughts of the WCC about hospitality. However, it is no coincidence either that the repeatedly asked and rarely fully answered question of how to share life with 'others' (people who think determinedly differently) keeps popping up in the age of globalization.

Another idea thought about in Heidelberg was that intercultural theology was not designed to 'parade the liveliness of non-western Christianity as a model in front of Europe's "dead" Christianity', but rather was meant to be an agent of change and liberation in Western Christianity by challenging the pseudo-certainty of ossified Church traditions in the West. This was a reaction against an unhealthy mode of knowing that had and still has some currency in the mission-studies approach, namely to use data of Christian growth in the South as 'evidence' in the ideological battle against secular and liberal thought in the North (Ustorf 2010).

Yet the Heidelberg team began to ask themselves whether 'intercultural theology', in the end, was perhaps a rather European agenda for liberation. There were too many signs that the approach of intercultural theology was sitting squarely on top of some major and well-known fault-lines that were running through Western culture, from cultural plurality and cognitive diversity to the entanglement of the religious with the secular and the old conflicts between the academy and the Church and between capital and labour. Was the expectation really that all these profound issues, made more difficult now by their internationalization, could be handled on one single platform of thought? Was the liminal world of the professorial imagination not a universe of idiosyncratic particularity? Was it feasible that in this universe all conflicts could be 'received' and 'resolved' because the opponents would pause in their fight and join the 'third space' (Bhabba 1994) the professors themselves were inhabiting? Did intercultural theology really have an actual practice out there in social life?

Retrospectively, I would think that the immense distance existing between the intercultural vision and the actual cultural and religious conflicts on the ground was already noticeable in the original concept of intercultural theology. Margull, Hollenweger and Friedli were/are all in their individual ways 'third space' personalities. At some stage of their lives they had all been culturally dislocated and became theologically involved in a rather contextual battle on four fronts: they struggled with:

1 what Hoekendijk had called 'morphological fundamentalism'; that is, the slowness and selfishness of their Churches as institutions;
2 differentiating Christian hope and transformation from the unpleasant historical shape mission had often acquired;
3 academic theology that kept essentializing, reifying or privileging certain modes of thought over against others; and
4 the personal experience of one's self as other; that is, the impossibility of truly knowing and being transparent to oneself.

Margull, for example, was convinced that a theological faculty in Western Europe would be incomplete without a chair in atheism. By not giving this radical challenge to theological coherence (the atheist temptation) a home, theologians would express their refusal to accept that theology was part of the human journey through history – a set of ideas that was already around (Sölle 1968), but never got much support from Margull's colleagues in the Hamburg faculty. Hollenweger's inaugural lecture in Birmingham discussed the bridging of the post-Christian or secular version that the hope for transformation had acquired in Europe, namely Marxism, with the missionary eschatology that was present in the new forms of Christianity that had grown in the South, in this case Kimbanguism in central Africa (Hollenweger 1973). Both examples demonstrate that the new paradigm of intercultural theology was directly responding to Europe's old, but specific cultural and secular-religious context; or, put in another way, the epistemological battles in Western Europe and, *nota bene*, the situation of academic marginality from which the professors of mission at the university wished to escape. Margull, whose 1959 PhD had been on mission theology (Margull 1962a),[3] published his last essay on this subject exactly at the time of his search for a new theology (Margull 1970). Mission for him no longer made theological sense, and he stopped using the term in that year. For him, the attempt to verify the Christian claim of absolute truth had not only failed historically, the religions were as a matter of principle not at the disposal of the Christians and could not be made subservient to Christian truth (Margull 1980). Hollenweger was more ambivalent as to whether or not traditional missiology was still useful. Initially he described intercultural theology as the historically appropriate successor of missiology; later – and very likely under the influence of his large clientele of international doctoral students – he still saw some mileage in using the term 'mission' (Hollenweger 1989). Nevertheless he certainly got frustrated with the Reformed Church at

---

3 'Hope in Action', thus the English title, was later also the title of an initiative launched around 1980 by Richard Friedli and others (among them John V. Taylor, previously the General Secretary of the Church Missionary Society) inside the World Conference of Religions for Peace (WCRP, 1970). This initiative worked along the lines of Amnesty International, namely as a lay movement engaged in international justice, but with a radically different methodology consisting not of accusing governments of violating human rights but of publicly affirming prophetic action; that is, those events and people that are active in the direction of greater freedom and shalom (Friedli 1982b, pp. 119–31). The initiative failed – not just because the organizational, logistical and financial basis was missing but also because one of the biggest lay movements engaged in the WCRP, the Buddhist Rissho Kosei Kai, could not be convinced to join. Quite a number of allegedly secular agencies that are globally active have an implicit missionary dimension. In fact one might even argue that many non-governmental organizations, and the zeal with which they campaign for human rights, peace, religious freedom, or ecological matters, represent a quasi-secular successor incarnation of a fairly traditional missionary motivation. This 'secular' version of the idea of mission reflects precisely the synergy that is created when a missionary motivation is based on a post- or non-Christian and often a pluralist foundation.

home and eventually resigned from it. Friedli had worked in Fribourg's faculty of Roman Catholic theology for over 20 years as missiologist, interculturally and then interreligiously, before he dropped his theological apron strings in 1992 and, in his current third phase of engagement, continued the search for truth in an 'inter-secular' way ('interworld' is his provisional term), on the platform of sociology and the social sciences. This he does, as he says, in a non-partisan way, namely as professor of the history of religions in the philosophical faculty. He is convinced that most people (in Europe at least) no longer trust the different traditions of meaning, in particular the ethical and religious answers that the Churches and religions are offering. Worldwide there are 'new compositions of the sacred' underway – perhaps 'spirituality without religion' – and therefore a much broader and non-partisan search for truth is required, and it is clear to him as to where this kind of research has to take place: outside the theological departments (Friedli 2000).

All of them mirrored in their individual theological biographies, in one way or another, the results of a profound conversation between liberal culture and Christian tradition. On the one hand, we can identify the primary vision of what David Martin calls the Christian transcendent. This vision of peace is opposed to the imperatives of power and violence and generates a kenosis-driven mode of knowing. It discovers the Passion and the Resurrection in the world, in its histories, religions, cultures, basic human needs, literatures, philosophies, art and, of course, theologies – all being stations on the journey towards truth. On the other hand, we do very much have 'Dover Beach', Matthew Arnold's dark counter-vision in the shape of a poem, composed around 1852 and, impact-wise, frequently compared to Charles Darwin's *Origin of Species* (1859): the tide of faith receding and leaving the barren sand of a profoundly iconoclastic scepticism (Arnold 1867). Balancing the Christian transcendent and post-Christian iconoclasm meant letting go the presumption of certainty about the reliability of one's self and the permanence of any attempt at constructing theological meaning. It made it impossible to feel too cosy (an alternative expression for original sin) in the second homes we call culture, faith, identity, marriage or Church. Moreover, this negation of certainty was to both the secular academy and main-line Christianity perhaps far more unforgivable than the transcendent vision that drove Margull, Hollenweger and Friedli at the time. The location between all camps, or the refusal to join any of the 'safe havens' that the systematizers of both the religious and the non-religious kind have constructed for us, introduced from the very start a strong dose of capriciousness, modern occidental agnosticism and relativism into the mix of intercultural theology.

The driving forces in the construction of intercultural theology in the 1970s were not only the post-colonial demographic changes in World Christianity, with its subsequent diversification of theologies, not just the profound encounter with the religious other, and not simply the ethical desire to let those speak who so far were prevented from being heard in theology. There were also two cultural ingredients that are clearly of North-Atlantic origin, namely (1) the shape of the iconoclastic transcendence that the Christian vision had acquired in reaction to the epistemological dilemmas of Western thought and (2) the curious and frustrating location of the professorial missiologist in the secular academic pantheon on the one hand, and on the other, within the ecclesiogenic narcissism that was rampant in the Churches. The new intercultural paradigm did indeed attack the privileges that both the Western academy and the Western Church had been enjoying for a long time – including the holy cow of the secularization hypothesis, but only by making sure that nobody else could ever again have epistemological privileges in the new world order of intercultural communication. Paradoxically, intercultural theology challenged hegemonic thinking but, at the same time, it universalized the critique of it.

Conclusions and prospects

The theological repentance of the North, if this is how the idea of intercultural theology can be characterized, cannot let go of its old (universalizing) habits it seems. Yet are the achievements made by the North Atlantic creators of the original vision of intercultural theology nevertheless useful today?

First, it is a welcome reminder that the context of any given theology includes not only the particularities of culture and history, but also the sociology and, as it were, the political economy of theological production. It is no accident that missiologists employed by secular universities were the first to raise their voices. The collapse of coherence due to the collision between the North Atlantic tribes' exclusive ways of pursuing academic knowledge, the fossilized traditions of faith in the West and the uncontrolled influx of new Christian and other experiences from the South were most acutely felt by academic-religious 'cyborgs', such as professors of mission in secular universities. Intercultural theology acknowledged that the perception of a global and post-colonial world constituted for the occidental Christian and academic discourse on truth a profound crisis of adaptation. Theologically, this meant on the one hand being able to distinguish between a religious faith willing to remember and learn,

and on the other hand the regression into the obsessive 'Heimat' of privileged religious knowledge. Margull used a term taken from the area of
personal life, vulnerability, in order to express this distinction. Sundermeier later applied epistemological language (Differenzhermeneutik). His
attempt at understanding the other without glossing over the essential
non-comparability led him to contemplate the possibility of incommensurability (Sundermeier 1996). Both languages, that of vulnerability and
that of the hermeneutics of difference, lead to a comparable level of understanding. They address primarily the professorial world of academic
discussion, but professors express only today what tomorrow is often
'common sense', therefore the academic discussion is relevant also to the
public discourse of faith.

Second, intercultural theology addressed two issues that are perhaps
specific to Western culture only, but by no means limited to it. First, there
is the 'atheist temptation' (and the creeping resignation of those who lack
the courage of having either faith or non-faith). The way intercultural theology dealt with this was, in the first place, by not writing off the very particular Northern ways to God, but trying to liberate these ways from unhelpful
roadmaps or the clutter of the pseudo-certainties that were smothering any
encounter with the divine (Cruchley-Jones 2008). Acknowledging the
mutation of the memory of Christianity in the West (Davie 2002), namely
the deep transformation of the cultural and spiritual topography, they
began to analyse its religious archaeology and reveal the often implicitly
Christian forces that condition much of the allegedly secular Western
thinking (for example the recycling of the search for the Promised Land
under a new name). The visionaries of intercultural theology addressed
also, second, the success- or growth-orientation in much of Christian
thinking and the very little conceptual space given to the study of the re-
cessions (failures, the going and even the end) of Christianity; its teacher
complex; its worries about 'reputation' and 'visibility' in the world and
its 'we have been here first' syndrome. They did this by emphasizing the
counter-vision of the Christian transcendent as clearly supranational and
anti-colonial, and by the reminder that the spadework for the enactment
of the vision of peace and justice should be done discretely (Matt. 6.4).

Third, intercultural theology contributed helpfully to the new ethos
that is required in international relations. The phrase 'contributed' signals that there are also other theological candidates, and some of them
are equally or better equipped to render this service. One of the most
promising among them is contemporary post-colonial theory that looks
into the way we handle language inequality, cultural difference and colonial (and other forms of) control (Sugirtharajah 2002). All the players

active in global communication need intercultural awareness and skills, whether we talk about the media and the academy or the states and their policies, religions and their social ethics, businesses and their strategies, or the international organizations, including military ones. This new aware- ness is the result of a conglomerate of different variants of knowledge and hence is supported by a multidisciplinary approach. For Christian theologians it requires a new set of theological skills in order to be able to say what the 'Lordship of Christ' or to walk in 'faithful uncertainty' or even to advocate a 'survival- and liberation centered syncretism' actually mean in a multipolar and multi-religious world (Kerr 1991; Price 1996; Friedli 1995). It would be a completely different matter, however, for the Buddhists to reflect interculturally on Buddha Nature, the Hindus on the Reality of Brahma and the Muslims on the Tauhid of God. Intercultural theology does not think on behalf of others, but reflects its own premises in the presence of these others and, if things go well, together with them. What the intercultural approach certainly does not imply is support for the tendency of religious institutions to have their assets agreed and rati- fied by the international community (Margull 1973).

Fourth, intercultural theology takes seriously the experiences made in interreligious communication and the more recent theologies and phi- losophies of religious dialogue and pluralism. Currently, no Christian missiology is able to avoid the pluralist challenge and yet make public sense. Missiologies that are intellectually sound do acknowledge the plural nature of human discourse – and therefore end up with a revision of the missionary mandate by assuming God's wider mission, which is be- lieved to include also the contributions of other 'co-workers for the King- dom'; that is, the efforts of other religions or non-religious traditions. In Paul Knitter's 'Kingdom-centered' approach, for example, the individual manifestations of mission are encouraged not to engage in attempts at superseding each other, but to equip themselves with the capability for dialogue and co-operation and a new readiness for having their particular knowledge of the Kingdom modified (Knitter 1996, pp. 19, 119, 165; also Pranger 2003). If other traditions have a missionary, that is a divine mandate, any idea of Christian mission as a conversion project to the one and only 'true' religion must necessarily become incoherent (Hick 1995, pp. 13–16, in particular pp. 116–19). The systematic theologian and scholar of Buddhism Perry Schmidt-Leukel states:

Conversion can mean here only to repeatedly convert to God. This does not exclude the possibility . . . that individual people find it easier or even to be the only way for them to continue their own spiritual journey in the context of a different religious tradition and, therefore, to convert to it. (Schmidt-Leukel 2005, p. 481)

Christians must be open to the call of the living God; but 'openness' means to know that one believes – not to believe that one knows (Schmidt-Leukel 2005, p. 478). It is much more difficult to dismiss such assumptions and statements today than it was in the days of Margull. The reason is that the status of theological reflection is currently shifting from the position of theological legislator to that of theological interpreter and that 'the constituting characteristics of the God of modernity – absoluteness, confidence and certainty' – are in real difficulty (Sørensen 2007, pp. 252 ff.). In today's world, any idea of mission must make sense to anybody else.

Reflecting on the promises and problems of the approach of intercultural theology, then and now, it has become quite clear that the theological discussion must competently acknowledge and make public sense of the historical situation, including the globalized context that Christians share with other religionists, humanists and Marxists (Stackhouse 2007). This is possible when and if we start decolonizing and de-imperializing the notion of what is 'true', 'global' or 'universal' and, on the other hand, let go of the romantic but erroneous predilection for the archaic, simple and non-contaminated (misunderstanding, as it were, 'inculturation' as an act of appropriating 'truth').[4]

---

4 For this to happen, the ideas on *convivencia* and hospitality should be explored further. The WCC could be on the right way. Jacques Derrida spoke of 'hostipitalité' (Derrida 1997), combining the Latin terms *hostis* (stranger, public enemy) and *hospes* (host, guest, and foreigner). Practical hospitality can only be a (necessarily deficient) conditional one, but as such it has to be constantly challenged by the notion of unconditional hospitality in the sense of unlimited generosity. The necessity for this double aspect of hospitality is not only the prohibition to reshape the 'guest' in the image of the 'host', but also to reserve the right of those who thought they were hosts to become, at any time, guests – in other words to become 'an other'. Not a bad description of the original programme of intercultural theology.

2

Intercultural Theology and Political Discipleship

GRAHAM WARD

Introduction

In this chapter I want to explore the limits and possibilities for developing an 'intercultural theology' from a Christian perspective. Recognizing that the major monotheistic faiths are international and that they have, in important ways, transcended the particular historical and cultural circumstances of their origins, to what extent can there be dialogue between the various cultural locations for theological practices today, and dialogue also between the theologies themselves? The question recalls us to a more fundamental one – the lived-out pieties themselves and the numerous everyday acts that give expression to and reproduce these pieties. Coming from a specific theological position, Christianity, I want to approach answering the question concerning the potential for intercultural dialogue from the perspective of what I call 'political discipleship'.

Foundational questions

Three foundational theological questions become paramount: What is political discipleship? Why is it so significant? Why is it theological? What I will attempt to demonstrate in answering these three questions is how any account of discipleship or the pieties of following are embedded within and correlative with the cultural contexts within which Christians live. At the level of practices of faith, the performance and dissemination of Christian theology is glocalized; that is, it operates at both local and global levels. This is nothing new. From its inception, in the resurrection of Jesus Christ and the formation of the Church as the body of Christ, the ethnic, religious and gender specificity of this man from Galilee was displaced – opening up a wider community, first in Jerusalem and then throughout the Jewish diaspora (see G. Ward

1999, pp. 163–81). Peter's Pentecostal preaching bears witness to a gathering of the nations and their cultures at the feast of Tabernacles and a dissemination of a Jewish-based faith beyond national frontiers (Acts 2.1–36). The Council of Jerusalem makes official Paul's mission among the Gentiles and their cultures. Christian churches were founded in local areas, amid local practices that the letters of Paul attempt to negotiate; and yet there remained the dominating conception of belonging to one body. From the beginning then, in the West, the localizing situates Christian discipleship inevitably within a multi-cultural and multi-faith ethos. In contemporary Britain, this ethos has been fostered by waves of immigration and migration among Jews, Muslims and Hindus most particularly. For some belonging to these ethnic movements, even the 'local' is problematized as strong family links and ethnic roots in other countries render complex the nature of national identity. Christian discipleship is performed then within intricate webs of interculturalism and interfaith. Put more theologically, if what this discipleship performs most clearly is a certain conception of being the Church, and if there are any ecclesiological issues within specific cultural contexts, then because the context today is multicultural and multi-faith, then the discipleship itself must necessarily take on an intercultural style. Subsequent reflections on this style may evoke an explicit 'intercultural theology', but at a local not a global level.

As a concrete example: I live in the northern part of Manchester, Salford, where the first language is now probably Punjabi – certainly it is arguable the extent to which it is English. English may be the common language but there are voluble proportions of the population who speak either Punjabi or Polish. My local supermarket will serve you in English, but if you took an average day the staff probably speak more Polish (to each other and their customers) than they speak English. All the local shops, whether fast-food ones serving pizzas, kebabs or tandoori or the corner shops selling pretty much anything from milk to cheap vodka, are owned by Punjabi speakers. If I walk less than 200 yards further up the road on which my house is situated, I enter an area of several square miles occupied by Hasidic Jews, who have their own schools, libraries, welfare systems and dress codes. These speak a variety of Yiddish dialects. So as a Christian living in that area I cannot live out my faith, in fact I could not even live, without being multicultural. Furthermore, because that interculturalism is, to a great extent, the product of social and cultural praxes of different faith communities, then from the same example we can see that my Christian political discipleship is performed necessarily in relation to a number of other socially and culturally dominant faiths, mainly Islam, Hinduism, Roman Catholicism and orthodox Judaism.

Whatever I say then about political discipleship will refer to, be informed by and affects this intercultural and interfaith ethos – in some way and to some extent. Two further observations, one positive and the other negative. Positively, this cultural mix of languages, traditions and faiths is enriching. In fact it makes living in a city like Manchester energizing, eclectic, diverse and interesting – a global intradependency is lived out. I enjoy eating in an Italian, Spanish, Argentinian, Turkish, Chinese or an Indian restaurant. I enjoy Polish bread and pickled herring, the exotic and ordinary fruits and veg from my local Pakistani-run market, Halal meat from my local butcher – and many of those working in these restaurants and shops are wiring money, some of it my money, across the world to their families. I enjoy that sense of belonging to both a local and an international community. Negatively, we all are – whatever our mixture of cultures, languages or faiths – fragmented and in being fragmented easily depoliticized. Government, local and national, though speaking loudly of accountability is increasingly opaque, increasingly distant. The city we share is viewed more as a place of entertainment and diversion where money earned can be money spent, where satisfaction operates at the level of the customer's needs being satisfactorily serviced (and this even happens in universities, hospitals, libraries, sports arena and police stations). The city is not seen as a shared *polis* – a place where citizens are actively engaged at a local and national level with arguing about and seeking to implement a life lived in common and orientated towards maximal flourishing.

This depoliticization has been going on for some time, as major institutions (the state included) subordinate politics to economics. It is part of a move made since the late 1970s away from state-controlled finance and redistributive fiscal policies towards accumulative capitalism and the dictates of the free market. This 'fragmented' and 'atomized' multi-faith and multicultural context actually places certain restraints on the possibilities for intercultural theologies, because what is already an encounter with the 'other' (faith, tradition, culture) is further 'othered' (alienated) through divisions in levels of income and education that perpetuate greater differences between classes, races, ethnicities and gender. At the same time the effects of open market capitalism have accelerated the globalization that delivers to me the internationalism I enjoy. Cultures themselves, and their differences, have become commodified in the advances of global trading; and insofar as there is a religious element in this commodification, it is indicative not of the liberal tolerance of religion but liberal indifference. In fact many of the products of the context I outlined above are associated with a levelling of cultural differences. So while there is evidently increasing social fragmentation and intolerance, there is also, equally as evident, an increasing religious indifference brought about by advanced, and rapacious, capitalism. For me, as a Christian theologian working professionally at the university, the social fragmentation and cultural homogenization impacts when groups of disaffected youths will call out 'you don't belong here' as I pass on my way to the corner shops to buy my international goods. The irony of heightened otherness and liberal indifference to religion, leads to the further concentration of tensions. The other will always remain to a certain extent other, there is never going to be complete social integration; but the contemporary politics that foster (perhaps even construct) these further alienations and religious indifference hamper my discipleship because they hinder the relations necessary for that intercultural theology to emerge. These further alienations freight relations with tensions, suspicions, tacit threats, xenophobias and competition with respect to the world's goods. The situation, I suggest, allows for the development of contextual theology, but resists the development of intercultural theology.

It is in this historical situation and its transnational economic climate that I want to re-emphasize the need for the practitioners of Christian pieties (who not only believe but perform their believing) to take seriously the politics of their election. We are called, as Christians, to make a difference, and in our theology we will be asked to give an account of the difference our lives have made. We make that difference today with respect to the consequences of capitalist and secular freedoms in a multicultural and multifaith world. This means for Christians (as for those of other faiths), there are three quite distinct though intermeshed politics that are lived out and negotiated one with respect to the other. The first is with respect to the secular world and the forces that govern it, the second is with respect to the other faiths that may or may not have relations with Christianity, and the third is with respect to the values and practices of the Christian faith which are at odds with either the politics of the world or the politics of other faiths. It is the living out of these three politics in the context of the Christian kingdom that constitute what I am calling the politics of discipleship.

The politics of discipleship

The language of discipleship (*mathētēs*) is the language of pedagogy. There is no disciple without a teacher. In the ancient world, as in the mediaeval, the teacher attracted pupils who would follow him or her, and the educational programme was one in which the transfer of knowledge involved moral and metaphysical instruction. It was a hierarchical relation in which the disciple submitted, and was in obedience to, the teacher. Two of the central questions Aquinas tackles in his compendious *de Veritate* concern the teacher and the nature of the mind (questions X and XI). The two questions are inseparable not only insofar as teaching is concerned with the transfer of knowledge and understanding and minds both facilitate and maintain this knowledge and understanding; but they are related principally for Aquinas because the mind or soul contains the image of the Trinity: the soul is sustained by being the *imago dei* referred to in the creation of human being in *Genesis*. God communicates interiorly to human being through the mind. Hence the question of whether only God can be understood to be a teacher arises. He answers this in his inimitable *sic et nunc* manner, claiming that while God is the first and final cause of true knowledge, reason is the efficient cause and teachers can act as an external co-operator with God. He concludes his analysis of teaching by making a significant distinction: 'The insight of the teacher is a source of teaching, but teaching itself consists more in the communication of the things seen than in the vision of them.'[1] Human teachers, then, stand in some analogical relationship to God as teacher in the same way sight stands analogically related to vision. There is similarity but there is also difference. This is important with respect to discipleship; for the primary teacher here is Christ himself. Aquinas has nothing to say about Christ as teacher in his analysis. But what is significant about Christ as teacher is the manner in which he both communicates 'the things seen' and 'the vision of them'. Furthermore, where for Aquinas the teacher is always superior to the pupil as the doctor to the patient (he frequently relates teaching to healing), Jesus subverts this hierarchy: 'No longer do I call you servants . . . but . . . friends' (John 15.15). Christian pedagogy and Christian following both begin and end with the commandment to love. And love is ultimately political; that is, it is always implicated in fields of differential power relations. Such power relations today, as I said earlier, are evidently intercultural.

The connections between teaching, following and love are ancient. From Plato there is the tradition that knowledge is a remembrance of a truth known outside of time and corporeality; a truth about whence we came and whither we will return. From Plato also is a tradition that what we desire is that which is beautiful and beyond, again, time and corporeality. Both Plato's understanding of truth and his understanding of beauty

---

1 1953, 'The Teacher and Mind', questions 10 and 11 in *Truth* (*De veritate*), trans. McGlynn, J. V. SJ, Chicago: Henry Regnery, p. 57.

is inseparable from his teaching on the Good; the Good beyond being. It is this Good that draws us, drags us like prisoners from the depths of the cave into the natural light, in *The Republic*. There is a reason for following – not just blind obedience. Education, for Plato, was the disciplining of desire; the orientation of desire towards that which was truly desirable. Augustine, as an exemplary Christian teacher will advocate a similar disciplining of desire, orientating the soul towards a greater and greater attunement with God through love. But he differs from Plato not least with respect to the fact his teaching is not his, it is Christ's. Furthermore, Christ is both teacher and what is being taught. Christians *may* follow Augustine's wise counsel, but *must* follow Christ. The politics of Christian discipleship then may bear some analogical relation to the model of teacher/pupil, and Mary attests to this in the garden on Easter Sunday when she calls Christ *Rabbouni*, but there are important differences. Jesus instructs Simon and his brother Andrew to 'follow *me*', not simply to follow his teaching. Disciples participate in the teaching that is Christ's.

The language of Christian discipleship is the language of pedagogy with a difference: it is being taught the true understanding of God by God himself, through the Spirit who 'will guide (*hodēgēsei*) you into all truth' (John 16.13). *Hodēgēo* is derived from *hodos* (way) and *hēgeomai* (to lead or to guide). The Spirit of truth travels alongside; guides in moving the disciple forward, onwards, into truth. As with all good teaching, the discipleship is fostered in a relationship with the teacher, but the Christian relationship to Christ is more profound. Discipleship is participation in God's own self-expression; rooted in the triune economy of God's grace towards creation. The disciple's love and desire, which govern the profundity of the relationship with the teacher, are not just orientated but fuelled by the love and desire of God. Jesus prays in John's Gospel 'that the love with which you have loved me may be in them, and I in them' (John 17.26). *Kagō en autois*, I in them. Elsewhere I have written about the nature of this co-abiding (2005, pp. 92–110). Here I wish to point out that the politics of Christian discipleship have one goal, namely conformity with Christ; and through that conformity, participation in the life of the triune God. There may be other by-products – salvation, the forgiveness of sin, the coming of the kingdom, the acting out of justice, truth, goodness and beauty in and through the body of Christ, the preaching of the gospel – but these are all effects of a more profound operation: 'I am in my father, and you in me, and I in you' (John 14.20). This operation and the following it enjoins go far beyond the teacher/pupil relation.

The operation of God's Trinitarian grace – that brings about that conformity with Christ – involves each Christian in a journey towards a personhood yet to be fully unveiled: an eschatological personhood. 'Beloved, we are God's children now; what we will be has not yet been revealed. What we know is this: when he is revealed we will be like him, for we will see him as he is' (1 John 3.2). We can observe again the chiasmus, the crossing over from one subject to another: what *we* will be has not been revealed, but the revelation is what *he* is, not what we are. It is the same logic of 'you in me, and I in you'. That new personhood, what might be called an eschatological humanism that stands in excess of what Charles Taylor has recently described as the Enlightenment 'exclusive humanism'(Taylor 2007, pp. 636–42), (the benchmark of the secular age), is worked out in the following.

But how do we follow? For the first disciples it was literally a matter of getting up and moving to the places Jesus travelled to. But on another level their following also involved coming to a clearer understanding of what it was Jesus had come to do and what we would have to do when he was no longer there. That second following involved listening and seeing. They were encouraged to hear the parables carefully and they were encouraged to observe the signs of the times – the miracles, the attention of the crowds and the demonstrations of power in quelling the tides on the Sea of Galilee and the withering of the fig-tree. The Gospel accounts themselves bear witness that though the disciples did not understand Jesus at the time, and neither listened nor observed the time well, eventually they were brought to an understanding. The account of Peter's first public speech, following the Pentecostal event (Acts 2.14–26) is a narrative aimed at making clear how much had been understood in the wake of events following the resurrection. In the light of the resurrection and the baptism in the Spirit, what had been listened to and observed while Jesus lived was illuminated such that a coherent picture emerged. The picture became the gospel that was preached.

John 10.1–6 provides a parable about following in which the Greek verb *akoloutheō* (to follow) is closely associated with *akoē* (hearing, the ear, listening) and *akouō* (to hear, to obey, to know). They were transformed by the knowledge of Christ they entered into, through their engagement in and then continuation of his ministry. Mark's Gospel frequently portrays the ignorance and stupidity of the early disciples, their inability to understand Christ's teaching and their misguided expectations of the messianic mission, but the Church would not exist had such ignorance not been overcome. Though, theologically, we understand our participation in Christ through the sacraments, the fact is the only Jesus we can identify, this political Jesus, is the Jesus created for us by those who followed him. The Church that grew up in the decades following the death of Jesus maintained a strong notion of imitating Christ quite literally. Saint Paul exhorts the Church to 'imitate me, then, just as I imitate Christ' (1 Cor. 11.1), for as 1 John 4.17 puts it: 'because as he is so are we in this world'. Imitation of Christ here is not copying; it is not the perfect repetition of the same act. It is not an echo. It is a re-performance albeit in another key and on another instrument. It is scandalous that we walk down our Market Streets, our Seventh Avenues or our Tottenham Court Roads as Christ walked. But that is the corollary of our eschatological humanism and the ecclesiology I am outlining. It is the corollary of our political discipleship. Following is a practice of imitation, a mimesis. It is a practice of being obedient; 'faith' is perhaps best translated not as belief but entrustment: the entrustment necessary if one is to continue following. 'Faith' is the character of living in the zone of indistinction that messianic time announces (see Agamben 2005, p.103). This faith is not the same as 'belief' in our contemporary world. Philip Goodchild has drawn attention to the way the dematerializations and virtual realities that capitalism breeds lead to a culture in which belief and desire abound.[2] Contemporary believing is cheap, in fact lazy, almost passive. Faith is following, and following is a movement forward, beyond oneself, beyond even the community within which the self is constituted. To live beyond oneself is to live the way of the cross, and it is in that living, that participation in the cross, that we deepen that primary relation to Christ and participate in Trinitarian relations.[3] This is the way of *theōsis*.

Our following differs circumstantially from that of the early disciples, but not substantially. The following still involves a listening and a watching; the engagement is one of trusting, of entrusting oneself to the future promise of what has yet to be revealed. Each of us is shaped by the practices we engage with, the other people and the institutions that facilitate those practices, even legitimate them. This is what it means to be a social animal. Not that we are completely socially determined, for we come to judgements and make choices. Nevertheless, our sense of self issues from the way we interact with our environment and the way that environment interacts with us. The eschatological personhood that issues from following Christ situates Christians in a place beyond the times and spaces of a particular environment. Christians live out, for example,

---

2 See Goodchild 2007, in which he develops the thesis that the two pillars of contemporary culture based upon capitalism today are belief and desire.

3 See Schoeps 1950, pp. 286–301, where he views following as a messianic claim, although we have to recognize following the way or path (the Hebrew word is *derek*) of righteousness is a profoundly Jewish idea.

in the practices of faith and hope, a temporality that does not conform to what has passed and what now is. We can neither be victims of history nor be condemned to the present. Contemporary globalization and advanced consumerism is obsessed with the present; the pseudo-eternity of the present that encourages a whole range of addictions from pornography to binge-drinking. To seize the day is to live the present moment to its fullest; to be satisfied. But the temporality of Christian discipleship always recognizes a remainder – where Christ is not fully revealed then the present remains unfulfilled. To live, to act out, this remainder in a culture that glorifies the buzz and adrenalin rushes of living in the present is not simply an act of resistance, but a testimony to an alternative understanding of what is the case. Christians are continually called upon to live in and beyond their cultural conditions, whether these are dominated by consumer markets or the climate of fear that is currently whipping up racism and xenophobia that are, as I said above, negative characteristics of our interculturalism. The eschatological character of the personhood Christians are working out involves them in practices that cut across or run counter to some of the ideas and ideologies in their immediate contexts. In this way following is political: because conformity with Christ necessitates the cultivation of attitudes and actions that can only align themselves to the things of this world with an eschatological remainder.

At the very cutting edge of the practice of following is prayer; for it is only in prayer that the discipline of listening is developed. The *via activa* is rooted in the *via contemplativa*.[4] We need to understand something further about eschatological personhood as conformity with Christ, and an examination of prayer will facilitate this. For it might seem so far that discipleship and following are concerned primarily with the individual person: the working out of my calling, my vocation, my response to God's grace towards me. The example Jesus gives and that is recorded late in Matthew's Gospel, of visiting the sick and imprisoned, feeding and clothing the poor, entails a discipleship and an ecclesiology performed always in the context of others. Fundamental to prayer is recognizing that as a Christian act it is not locked into any post-Cartesian and Pietist subjectivity. Prayer differs from so much of New Age religion that has this focus: self-development, self-advancement – to become better equipped to take advantage of what is about us.[5] The practice of prayer, in fact, resists the kinds of self-enlightenment and self-development that makes us more

---

4 See question 10 in Aquinas's *Truth* (*De veritate*) where he discusses the active and contemplative life with respect to teaching.

5 See Žižek's remarks on Western Buddhism in Žižek 2001, pp. 63–8.

efficient consumers. For it is both I and the Spirit within me that prays, that motivates, that moves to action. As I said above, personal salvation is a by-product, an effect of the operations of God's grace. Christ in me disrupts the atomized individual, unseats him or her from being in command, opens up the self to the infinity of what is God and the plurality of what is our world today. Following, even obedience, cannot be reduced to the exertion of an individual's will. Every Christian act is folded into the orientation of the self towards what endlessly transcends it: what Maximus the Confessor describes as 'the sheer immeasurability of God, like an uncrossable sea that one has been yearning to gaze on' (Maximus the Confessor 1955, p. 192). What we bring in prayer to this enfolding is the world itself; not simply ourselves but the multicultural and multi-faith world we are caught up in; that vast network of relationships of which we are a part: the complex corporations that our bodies are mapped on to. Specifically for me: the communities of the Polish, Yiddish and Punjabi speaking other. As Christians we bring into God all the concerns and connections we have with the contemporary world, the reduction of life to economics and consumption and the various roles religion is playing and being forced to play in the public sphere. As such, praying is the most political act any Christian can be engaged in – richly layered, nuanced and intercultural. Contemplating the world or reading the signs of the times as a practice of Christian discipleship, is to offer it up to God for transformation.

I am not reducing prayer here to intercession: prayer need not be vocalized at all. Being in the world in Christ, being in the world as Christ, as a living organism, we are continually being called upon to respond to the environment that envelops us. We respond physically, emotionally and psychologically. In fact we cannot comprehend all the levels upon which we are responding. 'The brain knows more than the conscious mind reveals', a recent neurophysiologist informs us (Damasio 2000, p. 42) and, as I have developed elsewhere (2005, pp. 95–6), the body has a knowledge that we only have an oblique insight into. There is prayer at conscious, verbalized levels – public prayer, the solitary confessions, thanksgiving, the Hail Mary or the Our Father, for example. But dwelling in Christ there is a praying at somatic and mental levels we have no direct control over. There is a praying that goes on within us, as the Spirit breathes and the soul communes. The world's events, our daily events, as they come to our attention from various sources – the media, present circumstances, the hearing of other people's stories and so on – are filtered through our ensouled flesh. They are registered within and they modify within as we attune ourselves to the manifold external. That miraculous escape we read about in the newspaper that caused us joy, those gangs of teenage girls and boys congregating at the cornershop late at night that cause us apprehension (for them and for ourselves), those scenes on the news of carnage in the wake of a bomb attack that cause us to shudder at the violence and grieve with the shell-shocked – all these events pass through us and change us. And as we dwell in Christ and Christ in us, they pass through Christ also. This is what I mean by praying: that deep inhabitation of the multicultural and multi-faith world that, to some extent, makes all our theologies intercultural, its flesh and its spirit that stirs a contemplation and a reading of the signs of the times that is more profound than we can ever appreciate or apprehend. Prayer is the living, and the reflections upon living, in obedience – where, as the Book of Common Prayer teaches, service is perfect freedom. Prayer is a glocalizing event. This activity is what in German can be described as the *Urgrund* of Christian discipleship – we live and act as the transistors for the transformation of the world through Christ. By this means it is not just the individual who is being conformed with Christ, it is the whole of creation. In fact it is only as the individual gives the world that they subsist in back to Christ that they themselves are transformed. In an observation on Aquinas, Kathryn Tanner has noted: 'one perfects oneself in imitation of the self-diffusing goodness of God by perfecting others' (Tanner 2005, p. 27). I take the act of prayer as the root practice by which such perfection is given and received. All things are brought before the feet of the cosmic king, brought to confess the lordship of Christ, through prayer as deep inhabitation of the world and contemplation that necessarily arises from that inhabitation. This is the logic of following and the politics of discipleship.

In our inhabitation of the world we are continually listening, but for what is one listening? Maximus the Confessor assists here: for part of what we listen to is our yearning; the reaching out of our desire for communion with Christ. There may be a thousand petitions, requests, voiced frustrations, cries of hurt, in prayer but fundamentally what is being spoken is our yearning. In that yearning we glimpse the yearning of the Church itself; glimpse ourselves as part of the body of Christ, extended through time and across space. And since Christ is that which is most interior to us, as the 'I in you', then part of what we listen to is Christ's yearning; that yearning in the heart of Christ to heal and transform. That desire to transform will always be restless with the status quo; it can never accommodate the world on the world's terms. The healing Christ wants can only come following the recognition of the conflict of values, of understanding; it can only follow the judgement of sin, of hubris. Our conformity with Christ will necessitate sharing in this yearning for the healing and transformation of the world; sharing also in the conflict and the judgement. As such prayer is always concerned with ushering in the Kingdom of God, even though what that Kingdom is has yet to be revealed. Every prayer reaches out towards some inchoate understanding of, even present participation in, another order, a true, just and good order being prepared, waiting to be revealed. It is the very fact that the Kingdom has not yet been revealed, and cannot now be delineated and defined, that distinguishes such a notion from utopian dreaming. For the *utopos* literally means no where, it has no place, and therefore is not a real alternative. Utopian thinking, as Paul Ricœur has shown (see Ricœur 1986, pp. 79–92), can function critically with respect to current political scenarios; it is not then without importance for it challenges the imagination to conceive differently. But the Christian Kingdom is not utopian at all because in faith and hope, and the practices of prayer and following, it has a substance – even if that substance remains eschatological. Every act of Christian living is testimony to the reality of the Kingdom as a new social and political realm. It is not the stuff of dreams because it makes possible, is the condition for the possibility of, the experienced renewal of hope.

The Kingdom operates as a horizon to all Christian acting and believing, like the hills in Psalm 121 that are constantly looked to for the advent of salvation. As I have written elsewhere, the Christian is engaged continually in practices of hope; making claims in a faith at odds with what is visible. As such the Church operates and maintains a virtual existence quite distinct from the pursuit and generation of simulacra and virtual realties that is one of the by-products of globalization. It is important to examine this difference to appreciate how another understanding of virtual reality can operate, antithetical to that produced and disseminated by advanced capitalism. For if the most political act for a Christian lies in the act of prayer, drawing what issues from the politics of election and following, into a communion of mutual yearning with God; then the political arena within which such political acts are empowered is the Kingdom.

Conclusion

We can conclude then that discipleship is political in two related senses. First, it is implicated in a field of relations.[6] The 'you in me, and I in you' relation is primary, but is given substance in the relations this relation

---

6 I am concurring here with those like Karl Barth and Stanley Hauerwas who see 'the "self" names not a thing, but a relation. I know who I am only in relation to others, and, indeed, who I am in relation with others' (Hauerwas 1983, p. 97).

fosters with others – the co-workers, the differential ministries, the languages, cultures and callings of those who also responded albeit in a different manner to the politics of election. Second, the discipleship is political because it is explicitly involved in ushering in a 'Kingdom'. The political nature of Jesus' life, death and resurrection is signalled throughout with references to the Messiah, to the new lawgiver and to the new Joshua. The Gospel of Luke is particularly sensitive to this politics. He frames his narrative with reference to Herod of Judea, the Emperor Augustus and Quirinius the governor of Syria, and Jesus' ministry with reference to the Emperor Tiberius and Pontius Pilate the governor of Judea. Mary heralds the birth of her son in a Magnificat that sings of a great social revolution: the scattering of the proud, the bringing down of thrones and dominions, the exaltation of the lowly and the filling of the hungry. Jesus begins his preaching of the gospel by reading from a scroll that tells of his anointing to bring good news to the poor, proclaim release to captives, recovery of sight to the blind and the freeing of the oppressed. The language of kingdom and kingship reverberate throughout, culminating in the scenes before Pilate and the conversations prior to crucifixion on authority. Discipleship is political because it is implicated in a messianic reversal of established values and the challenge to received authorities and principalities. It is not simply anarchic and iconoclastic, but Christian discipleship is political because it demands to know in what relation to Christ stands any other sovereignty. This discipleship began with the ministry of John the Baptist, already caught up in a political battle with Herod, and continues with Christ (see Yoder 1972, pp. 27–9). The first disciples may have been tax collectors and fishermen, but the last words of Jesus in Matthew's Gospel present a phenomenal political challenge: 'All authority in heaven and earth has been given to me' (Matt. 28.18). It is a statement in line with the calls to arms: 'Do not think I have come to bring peace to the earth; I have not come to bring peace, but a sword' (Matt. 10.34) and 'the one who has no sword must sell his cloak and buy one' (Luke 22.36). All this and the language of servanthood![7]

Now Scripture can be and has been used for any number of political agendas. All I am pointing to here is the fact that discipleship has always been a political matter because it concerns the commission to preach

---

7 Oscar Cullmann once suggested that up to half the disciples were Zealots; see Cullman 1956, p. 8. Although this can be challenged, the association between Jesus' teaching, the sedition for which he was crucified, and the work of the Zealots is the centre of two significant accounts of the Zealot movement: Hengel 1961 and Brandon 1967.

and enact the Kingdom of God. It involves choices, judgements, commitments, values and actions informed always by that ruling conformity with Christ. It also involves defeats and overcomings, and these are not at all just metaphorical: the rejection of property by Saint Francis, the stand of Luther at the Diet of Worms, the decision by Bonhoeffer to be linked with a plot to assassinate Hitler, the call to the Salvadorian army to mutiny made by Archbishop Oscar Romero, were not metaphorical acts. They challenged authority even within the Church itself – and it is always important that the space for this remains open because, as we shall see, the Church is not co-extensive with the Kingdom. Each one of these decisions and acts was done in the name of Christ; in the faith that these were Spirit-led actions in accordance with Christ. The same is true of other less dramatic, but no less effective, initiatives: the establishment of Oxfam by a Jew, an Anglican and a Roman Catholic; the founding of one of the largest NGOs, CARE, by Quakers after the Second World War, and the work of the Christian Democrats in Europe on behalf of the European Union.

I hope what can be seen by this examination is the extent to which Christian political discipleship must necessarily be intercultural, because the 'other' with whom and through whom it is being performed are culturally diverse and espoused to various other pieties. I hope we can also see more particularly the limits for developing intercultural theology. The limits are twofold. First there is an external limit imposed by the secular bodies and fiscal policies that ferment the fragmentation and alienation of the various cultures and faiths; mapping these differences on to class, gender, race and ethnic divisions. Second, there is an internal limit to intercultural theology in the Christian faith (or any faith perspective) itself. That is, the deep inhabitation I see as fundamental to the politics of discipleship means the other (the one who inhabits practices of a different piety, the cultural ethos and the traditions of that piety) will always remain other. I can learn to speak Punjabi, Yiddish or Polish fluently, but my mother language remains my mother language; I cannot (and nor should I attempt to) transcend the context I inhabit, and have been called to inhabit. The extent to which that context in intercultural is the extent to which my theology can be intercultural.

3

Intercultural Theology and Interreligious Studies

DAVID CHEETHAM

Introduction

We might start with an eschatological picture:

> After this I looked, and there before me was a great multitude that no one could count, from every nation, tribe, people and language, standing before the throne and in front of the Lamb. They were wearing white robes and were holding palm branches in their hands. (Rev. 7.9)

Given this multicultural vision of the Kingdom of God, it could even be considered a mistake to think of intercultural theology as something of a novel conception that has emerged in recent theological history. Revelation 7.9 reveals a 'multi-cultural view, not one of ethnic uniformity' (Whiteman 2007, p. 68).[1] Indeed, one of the major themes in Christian thinking has been the translatability of the gospel message and, underlying this, the crucial notion that truth is something incarnated. The opportunity globalization affords for contemporary theological method and practice is one of exploring the diverse cultural richness that is part of an eschatological *promise*. As an analysis of the factors that have led to the emergence of intercultural theology in recent times, the missiologist Werner Ustorf has provided an illuminating genealogy in which he argues that intercultural theology 'received its thrust and energy not only from the discovery that all theologies are contextually conditioned, but also from much older Northern theological fault-lines that became active again under the pressure of the decolonization process' (Ustorf 2008a,

---

1 Whiteman discusses Revelation 7.9 in the context of globalization and the multicultural kingdom of God (Whiteman 2007, p. 68), the theme is also picked up in the same volume by Craig Ott (see Ott 2007).

pp. 229–30). Nevertheless, although by dissecting the various influences operating in the theological academy we can rightly say that contextual theology is largely a contemporary movement, one might also claim, as a judgement about the nature of the Christian gospel, that it has always been a theological necessity – that is, Christian theology is properly contextual. Major theological themes such as 'incarnation', 'sacrament' or even 'resurrection' testify to the *embedded* nature of Christian theological discourse (see Cheetham, forthcoming).

Nevertheless, attention to the multicultural variety (or potential) in theological method is something that has been more evident in liberal outlooks than conservative ones, and the agendas for an intercultural theology (as a discipline with links to the 'history of religions' or 'comparative religion') seem to have been defined more by this kind of theological perspective.[2] Additionally, when we consider the concerns of this particular chapter there might be an unconscious assumption that intercultural theology is something naturally wedded to interfaith dialogue. This is not necessarily the case, and we should resist this conclusion as it will have a tendency to close down a wider range of options.[3] There are various theological constituencies that will have different expectations with regard to intercultural theology and its relationship to interreligious studies. Further, the subject matter presents a different set of challenges for each. So if the challenge to (and critique of) liberals is to devise more biblically based schemes of thought, the call to conservatives is to realize a vision for theology that is truly global and intercultural in scope.

This chapter seeks to present a discussion concerning the relationship between intercultural theology and interreligious studies by first considering the nature of intercultural theology itself. Intercultural theology is not just concerned with context but also with the exchange and comparability between cultures and, as such, it provokes a broader discussion about the

---

2 For example, Eric Sharpe – writing in the mid-1980s – remarks on the 'wide overlap between comparative religion and liberal Christian (and other) theology. From the "founding fathers" of comparative religion, C. P. Tiele, Max Muller, Nathan Soderblom and W. Brede Kristensen in the years around the turn of the century by way of Rudolf Otto and Friedrich Heiler down to Wilfred Cantwell Smith in our own day, the involvement of liberal religion in the comparative exercise has been fairly constant.' Sharpe 1986, pp. 294–5.

3 An example of different assumptions concerning the focus of intercultural theology can be seen in the work of George Newlands. In Newlands 2004, he seeks to embark on a study of intercultural theology that eschews interfaith concerns altogether as its primary agenda, preferring to develop 'a programmatic approach to theology in dialogue' (p. 3), which is something 'concerned for the relation of faith to whole created order' (p. 4).

various *ingredients*, including religious, that form part of different cultures and thus the necessity for interreligious studies to be part of its remit and methodology. The chapter moves on to consider 'comparative theology' as an example of intercultural theology operating together with interreligious studies. Finally, whatever the theological positions adopted, interreligious studies is an important component of contemporary theological education in terms of providing an informed background for theologizing in the new global context. However, given the sheer quantity of knowledge that is made available to the global theologian, the chapter concludes by asking questions about who can undertake such a project. Perhaps, in the end, there needs to be greater responsibility handed over to individuals to work out their own theological engagements and encounters.

Intercultural theology: both context and exchange

The importance of context is of crucial importance to Christianity for, in the end, it is not the grand schemes or metanarratives that seem to count but those things that are small and despised. This ought to have an influence on the way in which we undertake theologizing and also provoke a seriousness with which we attend to different cultural expressions of Christianity. The contemporary emphasis on the importance of context for theology is the result of a combination of influences. In the Western academy there was a paradigmatic move during the last century towards a greater stress on the historical and cultural contexts of thought and practice.[4] Whether or not this is a temporary phase or an adjustment or even a more fundamental shift is yet to be seen, but such perspectives have contested the idea of a universal rationality that permitted more abstract or ahistorical theology to be undertaken. A further encouragement towards more contextual studies was the influence of 'religious studies' that now routinely exists in various forms alongside theological faculties in universities and has instigated a much greater methodological emphasis on the social sciences.[5] In addition to this, there is the testimony and scholarly activity of Christian missionaries that has been chiefly preoccupied with the process of the translation and the *indigenization* of the gospel message. This has resulted in a great deal of highly accomplished

---

4 It would, of course, be presumptuous to suggest that what follows is a universal account.

5 The relationship between 'theology' and 'religious studies' has been the subject of considerable debate in recent times. Some good discussions are to be found in Warrier and Oliver 2008, and Ford, Quash and Soskice 2005.

non-Western theological literature that has brought new insights to
Christian thinking that were previously absent or hidden from (or latent
within) the Western tradition. In this connection, the acknowledgement
of colonialism (and the Western guilt that has been associated with this),
or the need for the liberation of the oppressed, has given momentum to
the questions of *power* in theological discourse and hermeneutics. Additionally, within Western cultures in particular, the influence of post-
modernity as a cultural descriptor and as a philosophical bricolage has
contested notions of hierarchy, and this has meant that more attention
has been given to less systematic or dogmatic approaches to theology like
those found in the arts, literature and media.

Drawing stark distinctions between contextual theology and a more
'straightforward' biblical approach is not unproblematic. For it is quite
clear that the world that is presented in the Bible is also one of multiple
cultures and contexts. Commenting on the biblical testimony, H. Richard Niebuhr writes: 'Those critics of cultural Protestantism who urge a
return to Biblical ways of thought sometimes seem to forget that many
cultures are represented in the Bible . . .' (Niebuhr 1951, p. 104). Thus
the establishment of a biblical perspective does not necessarily promote a
mono-dimensional picture or lend support to a defensive posture against
diverse hermeneutical insights. Similarly the Pentecostal theologian
Walter J. Hollenweger writes that 'Intercultural theology starts from the
insight that all theologies – including the biblical ones – are contextually
conditioned. There is no pure gospel. The gospel appears to us as *per
definitionem* in an incarnate form' (Hollenweger 2003, p. 90). This is, as
Hollenweger admits, only a starting point because intercultural theology
obviously means more than this. Intercultural theology does not just draw
our attention to context per se but also to the exchange that takes place
between cultures and their different theological traditions. Moreover the
term is appropriated differently as we move along the theological spectrum. Niebuhr provides an excellent summary of Christian perspectives
on culture and history (reflecting his own fivefold division) that might
assist us in our approach to intercultural theology:[6]

> For the exclusive Christian, history is the story of a rising church or
> Christian culture and a dying pagan civilization; for the cultural Chris-
> tian, it is the story of the spirit's encounter with nature; for the synthe-

---

6 In Niebuhr's text he presents five models: Christ against culture, the Christ
of culture, Christ above culture, Christ and culture in paradox, Christ the trans-
former of culture.

sist, it is a period of preparation under law, reason, gospel and church for an ultimate communion of the soul with God; for the dualist, history is the time of struggle between faith and unbelief, a period between the giving of the promise of life and its fulfilment. For the conversionist, history is the story of God's mighty deeds and of man's responses to them. (Niebuhr 1951, p. 195)

It seems clear that the study of intercultural theology in the context of interreligious studies is going to seem more or less appealing according to the theological position being adopted and the priorities that such positions prefer. This inevitably connects to the much greater issue of the relationship of Christ to culture. Thus it really is going to be a non-starter if we adopt Tertullian's exclusive perspective that all culture is sinful and that a clear distinction needs to be drawn between Christian and pagan thinking.[7] However, looking beyond the Christ *against* culture option, the various shades of theological opinion that are outlined in Niebuhr's survey allow the inclusion of contextual influences and cross-cultural conversations. Indeed, it seems that as soon as we move away from a sense of *discontinuity* between Christ and culture, a dialogue with culture and, further, a horizontal dialogue *of cultures* becomes possible. Such connections might take many different forms: cross-cultural dialogue, an explanatory narrative of preparation or fulfilment, the unfolding of the Christian mystery across cultures or even some all-encompassing vision concerning the eschatological consummation of nations and races under Christ.

One of the questions that has to be considered is how far intercultural theology and interreligious studies are linked. Can the two areas be considered as separate concerns or does the competent study of one require the other? Further, if we accept that the two are linked, then what kinds of theological account can be offered for this? The term 'intercultural theology' itself is appropriated differently. For example, it can be interpreted as a term that has emerged as a development of mission studies.[8] Thus for

---

7 See, for example, this striking quote from Tertullian: 'we want no curious disputation after possessing Jesus Christ [. . .] With our faith we desire no further belief.' *Prescription Against Heretics*, vii, *Apology*, xlvi. Cited in Niebuhr 1951, p. 54. Alongside Tertullian, Niebuhr uses Tolstoy as an example of the 'Christ against culture' posture.

8 In this connection, see 'Mission Studies as Intercultural Theology and its Relationship to Religious Studies' issued by The Religious Studies Section of the Academic Association for Theology and the Administrative Board of the German Association for Mission Studies, in *International Review of Mission* 97 (2008), pp. 149–53.

Fuller Theological Seminary, intercultural studies is something undertaken in order to grow 'innovative missiologists who can effectively communicate the Gospel in crosscultural contexts'.[9] Alternatively, for those with more interfaith leanings like Wesley Ariarajah, intercultural encounter is a necessary ingredient for the contextual enrichment of interreligious dialogue (see Ariarajah 2003). Once again Hollenweger acknowledges that 'there are authors who widen the term by including interreligious theology' and that 'dialogue with other religions is part and parcel of mission'.[10] Here a distinction needs to be drawn between a full-blown interreligious theology as a pluralistic (or postmodern) project and the more limited agenda of widening the content and scope of theological reflection in light of a conversation with other faiths and cultures. With the former there may be a disengagement with tradition and a discarding of Christian normativity (for example, the status of Christ). With the latter it is more a matter of sustaining a commitment to the Christian message while properly acknowledging that there exist plural contexts for Christianity in the world and that those contexts need to be properly integrated and included as full participants in theological discussion.

As we have suggested, intercultural theology could easily be described as merely a global intra-Christian discourse. Indeed, the need for Christians to listen to and consider the theological insights of other Christians from different cultural backgrounds is a timely project in its own right. Western theology has for so long been the normative standard for Christian theology in general, but there needs to be a recognition of the polycentric character of theology in today's global reality.[11] Perhaps the polycentric character of theology is something that has always been implicit in the gospel but, putting a historical twist on this, Kevin Vanhoozer asks: 'How do we do theology "after the West"?' And he adds: 'It may be that theology in an era of world Christianity inhabits a situation in which

---

9 http://www.fuller.edu/academics/school-of-intercultural-studies/masters-degree-program/maics.aspx (accessed 15 September 2009). Werner Ustorf is critical of Fuller's current position. He suggests that Fuller's use of the term 'intercultural' is merely 'a tactical update of the toolbox of missionary theology without changing its basic parameters' (Ustorf 2008a, p. 233).

10 Cited in Ariarajah 2003, p. 91

11 Thus Tite Tienou writes: 'Polycentric Christianity is Christian faith with many cultural homes. The fact that Christianity is at home in a multiplicity of cultures, without being permanently wedded to any one of them, presents for Christians everywhere a unique opportunity for examining Christian identity and Christian theology.' 'Christian Theology in an Era of World Christianity', in Tienou 2007, p. 38.

no one method dominates.'[12] How this is put together as a systematic exercise is a moot point, but an initial place to begin would be to recognize the distinctive aspects that are brought to theology from different regions of the globe. Here the list might include such obvious examples as the theologies developed in the midst of the religiously diverse contexts of South Asia, the questions of theological contextuality in Africa, perhaps the matter of dual or multiple religious belonging in parts of East Asia, the liberation theologies of South America (and, again, Asia), the post-colonial perspectives from around the globe and so on. These contexts bring new perspectives to theology beyond the concerns with systematics or dogmatics found in the West.

However, the most vexing issue must concern how *profound* such new perspectives are in their ability not only to supplement Christian theological tradition but also to initiate changes in method. That is, new perspectives from around the globe are unlikely merely to suggest new adornments on fixed themes. They will contain 'thick-descriptions' – the entanglements of their own cultural contexts – that prevent them from being hastily assimilated. Thus the task of intercultural theology – at least one that seeks to be faithful to the gospel while being expansive and inclusive – involves not only the enrichment of the Christian theological heritage by a comparative study of contextual theologies, but something considerably more demanding: attentive *discernment* and contextual evaluation. The practice of discernment is a complex matter, but I am intending to suggest something like the exercise of an attuned theological 'recognition' by those thoroughly trained in the Christian tradition. Similarly, it may also be something like the kind of spiritual discernment that the Pentecostal scholar Amos Yong explores in his own theology of religions (see Yong 2003). Or differently, when Robert Schreiter considers the relationship between local theologies and Christian normativity he indicates various criteria that, taken together, require that the various cultural expressions of Christianity still permit a coherent 'performance' of Christian beliefs and practices that relates constructively to the wider Church across the globe.[13] Perhaps this actually represents a post-Western descriptor of theologizing that is growing up into a broader horizon. Moreover, relating back to our quotation from Revelation at the beginning, such a broadening-out of theological practices and methods should be viewed not so much as a new departure for Christian thinking but as

---

12 K. Vanhoozer, "One Rule to Rule them All?" Theological Method in an Era of World Christianity', in Vanhoozer 2007, p. 91.

13 See the five criteria described in Schreiter 1985, pp. 117–21.

a movement towards the fullness of the Christian vision of the kingdom of God.

Methodologically speaking, intercultural theology in relation to interreligious studies presents us with a daunting complexity. This is, not least, because of the sheer volume of information that it introduces and the multiple new contexts and encounters that come into view. It is impossible for any single theologian to encompass this amount of material in any systematic way, but maybe it forces us now to trust the individual believer in his or her own context to theologize *in situ*. Moreover, there is a sense of *letting-go*. It is not as an abdication of theological responsibility but as a new way of apprehending diversity within, and surrounding, the Christian tradition. In the final chapter of his book, *Self and Salvation*, David Ford relates an eschatological vision of the 'joy of the saints' by using the image of *feasting*. In a provocative passage he writes about the 'metaphysics of feasting'. This is something that concerns 'the "logic of superabundance" which might be discerned in creation and history' and, more significantly, it refers to 'the orientation of the divine economy that is appropriately described in, among other ways, the figure of feasting' (Ford 1999, p. 271). Thus there is an 'ultimate feasting', and '[w]e can imagine a "great feast of languages" (Shakespeare), with cultures and traditions in conversation' (Ford 1999, p. 271). Ford's suggestion of 'feasting' being part of the divine economy is a useful image. For as we seek to consider the implications of a globally diverse Christianity and how we can approach intercultural theology methodologically (with its various ingredients, both religious and cultural), we might consider the figure of 'feasting' as an appropriate orientation.

Christian thought has been influenced and formed by interacting with the prevailing cultural voices and trends throughout history – but, of course, perhaps the fact that this has largely been *Western* cultural voices and trends has meant that it has passed under the radar of those who think of Christianity in purely intra-textual terms. Given that the contemporary shift of emphasis, in terms of the crucible of Christian growth and activity, is moving towards the southern hemisphere of the globe, it seems inevitable that greater attention is going to have to be given to voices that emerge from these contexts.[14] Linking with the concern to develop more polycentric or post-Western theological methods, Hollenweger presents an imperative for intercultural theology: 'All the more important it is that Christians remain in constant exchange with other Christians in order

---

14 In this connection, see Jenkins 2002. See also Yates 2005 and Wijsen and Schreiter 2007.

not to consider their form of the gospel as the only authentic version of the gospel. That is the task of intercultural theology' (Hollenweger 2003, p. 92). In an important observation, he makes it clear that intercultural theology is not necessarily a practice that only takes place in an overseas missionary context: 'No longer do we have to cross the oceans in order to meet Christians of other cultures. We can save the ticket. God has sent them right before our doorsteps' (Hollenweger 2003, p. 94). In the Western context the approach of intercultural theology is very much consonant with the experience of people living in today's cyber-mix and multi-ethnic culture, with its global interconnectivity, and it should be a timely addition to the theological curriculum in Western institutions. However, notice that Hollenweger is talking about meeting 'Christians of other cultures'. For him, intercultural theology is not an inter*religious* theology but the dialogue of Christian cultures. But this brings us back to the question posed a moment ago about the 'profound' nature of new perspectives that might be introduced by different cultural expressions of Christianity. That is, how *thick* are the descriptions of these different cultural expressions such that we acknowledge the religious ingredients that have formed the background of their make-up?

This is hardly a new issue in Christian thought. If we select an obvious example, it is taken for granted that Judaism is vital for our understanding of key Christian doctrines,[15] and the knowledge of early Christian thought cannot be fully comprehended without reference to Greek philosophy. Nevertheless, are such early historical ingredients providential or coincidental? If they are providential, then the Judaic and Greek background is an exceptional context that has been 'anointed' or 'baptized', so to speak, as a special contextual vehicle for the proper conceptualization of the Christian message. If the latter (that is, *coincidental*), one might expect to absorb various cultural elements into the fabric of Christian thought and practice. Nevertheless, whatever the position taken on this, it seems that the incarnational nature of Christian theology necessitates some kind of immersion within, or adaptability to, the cultural contexts in which the gospel is placed and expressed. And so a further question must be: How much is to be included from the cultural ethos of these Christians? For example, with regard to the Indian context, Klaus Klostermaier writes:

---

15 Keith Ward points out that our understanding has to go back further to earlier Judaism and the influence of Canaanite religion and Middle-Eastern cults. See K. Ward 1994, p. 37.

Greek Christology has not exhausted the mystery of Christ, though it has helped the Church the better to see some aspects of Christ. Indian wisdom, too, will not exhaust the mystery of Christ. But it would help the Church in India to understand Christ better and to let Him be really understood: the knowing of Christ as the revelation of the mystery of *Brahmavidya* – Christ, the desire of the eternal hills . . . (Klostermaier 1993, p. 125)

If there is a necessity to absorb some of these contexts, there are also some who express reservations about doing so. Staying with the Indian example, Y. D. Tiwari seeks to make clear distinctions. He writes cautiously:

I shall use the literary vocabulary of Sanskrit language, its idioms, figures of speech, its literary allusions, so far as they harmonize with our present day usages and needs, *but*, as far as possible, *not the Hindu philosophical terms*. Words like *Avatar, Jagadguru, Rishi, Diksha* are better avoided. Some words we should adopt (viz., *Mukti)* but in general it is good not to borrow technical terms from other faiths. A wide use of Hindu terms will weaken the Christian message. The Hindu will say, 'Well, you are saying the same thing which our philosophers and sages have said. Only, you say haltingly and in bad idiom what we have said in a charming and effective manner.' Any indiscriminate use of such language will produce vagueness. We cannot be theologically accurate if we use these terms. (Tiwari 1993, p. 137)

Many others would disagree with Tiwari's reticence here; thus by contrast the Roman Catholic convert, Brahmabandhav Upadhyaya, enthusiastically recommends that:

[t]he truths of the Hindu philosopher must be baptized and used as stepping stones to the Catholic faith . . . The European clothes of the Catholic religion should be laid aside as soon as possible. It must assume the Hindu garment which will make it acceptable to the people of India.[16]

What such comments highlight are differences of opinion regarding the practice of intercultural theology with its emphasis on cultural context and, more specifically, the degree to which theological orthodoxy across cultures can be sustained while also permitting the distinctive theologies

---

16 Cited in Chandran 1993, p. 8.

to emerge. Thus there is the fear that important aspects of the Christian doctrinal heritage may become compromised or obscured for the sake of intercultural exchange. Again, Niebuhr flags up the problems surrounding the different cultural appropriations of Christ. The main caveat for the 'Christ of culture' is that Christ:

> becomes a chameleon; that the word 'Christ' in this connection is nothing but an honorific and emotional term by means of which each period attaches numinous quality to its personified ideals. Now this word designates a wise man, a philosopher, now a monk, now a reformer, now a democrat, and again a king. (Niebuhr 1951, p. 107)

Nevertheless, Niebuhr's wonderfully balanced treatment means that he offers a defence: 'Jesus Christ has indeed many aspects' and 'even caricatures sometimes help to call attention to features otherwise ignored' (Niebuhr 1951, p. 107). It is as if, once again, there is a richness to be grasped about the meaning of Christian doctrines that gradually emerges from, but is not exhausted by, a global diversity. If we suspend the objections of incommensurability, Niebuhr suggests that the fact that people have drawn parallels between Christ and great cultural figures in history could be 'less indicative of Christian instability than of a certain stability in human wisdom' (Niebuhr 1951, p. 107). This is not necessarily a bald philosophical claim concerning a global epistemological parity, but it arises out of a theological insight concerning the idea of the *logos* that inhabits human reasoning.[17] Thus we are being asked to make a judgement concerning theological method here. Is it our task as theologians to seek to sustain or guard orthodoxy, or can we in fact rely on the 'stability of human wisdom' to interpret appropriately the 'Word made flesh' in different contexts?

In further response, the task of discerning orthodoxy within the different contextual theologies might be achievable by evaluating their overall consistency and continuity with the Christian tradition – paying particular attention to the spirituality, ethical practice and constructive exchange with other Churches and theologies.[18] However, another problem is the potential danger that the indigenization of theological discourse will be

---

17 Niebuhr does not explicitly make this connection, but seems to hint at it when he writes: 'Though apart from Christ it is difficult to find unity in what is sometimes called the great tradition of culture, with his aid such a unity can be discerned' (Niebuhr 1951, pp. 107–8).

18 For an elaboration of this view, see Schreiter 1985, pp. 117–21; and Bevans, 1992, chapter 2.

accompanied by an over-indulgent cultural immersion[19] that becomes an end in itself and may actually obscure important theological themes that ought to have greater prominence. For example, it is possible that issues of identity or liberation can sometimes take centre stage. Kevin Vanhoozer cautions against too great an emphasis on questions of identity and ethnicity. Thus he poses an important question: 'Should every theology be an ethnic theology, or is theological ethnification an example of a bad local? Can ethnic theologies resist the temptation to become ethnocentric?' (Vanhoozer 2007, p. 104). When he speaks of a 'bad local', he is referring to the potential for ethnic theologies to be too introverted. Instead, a 'good local' would be an ethnic theology that looked outwards and sought to relate itself to Christianity as a whole, hence Vanhoozer's recommendation to see 'ethnic theologies as local instantiations of the faith of the church universal . . .' (Vanhoozer 2007, p. 107). Tackling the issue of sustaining orthodoxy in the midst of intercultural variety, Vanhoozer maintains that alongside the diversity of cultural Christianities there also needs to be the recognition of 'textual sameness' (Vanhoozer 2007, p. 105).[20] That is, reference to the authoritative biblical text itself. The challenge facing the contemporary and future practitioners of intercultural theology will be to relate the Christian message to peoples' cultural contexts while being attentive to normative scriptural reference points.

Comparative theology

As we have said, an important aspect of our discussion of intercultural theology and interreligious studies must be the *methodological* relationship between the two fields. There may also be the matter of priority, and this relates to the broader question concerning the relationship between theology and religious studies. Thus the perennial debate concerns whether theology is considered to be *part of* religious studies or vice versa. In the case of religious studies as the overarching approach, intercultural theology relates to the broader phenomenological project of comparative religion looking especially at questions of belief, truth, doctrines, or the different 'theologies' of various faith traditions without privileging one faith in particular. With theology as the overarching approach, intercultural

---

19 Robert Schreiter cautions against 'cultural romanticism' in Schreiter 1985, p. 14.

20 Of course, this largely presupposes (as Vanhoozer recognizes) that the biblical text is seen as something through which God *speaks* rather than being solely a fusion of horizons (for example, Gadamer) between reader and text.

theology is a project that, compelled by the global diversity of Christian experiences and encounters (religious or otherwise), draws upon the wealth of diverse religious and cultural contexts of Christians in order to increase understanding about Christian beliefs and practices.

Nevertheless, these general distinctions do not tell the complete story. For example, the liberal Anglican theologian Keith Ward is clear that his own project of comparative theology is neither religious studies nor confessional theology. It is not to be seen as 'a form of apologetics for a particular faith but as an intellectual discipline which enquires into ideas of ultimate value and goal of human life, as they have been perceived and expressed in a variety of religious traditions' (Ward 1994, p. 40). Showing his commitment to a global vision (evidenced in his four-volume work on comparative theology),[21] he seeks to expand the boundaries of theology beyond its normal Christian remit, pointing out that 'it is quite common now for Muslims, Jews, and Hindus to speak of theology, and there is no reason at all why there should not be a Muslim or Hindu theology'.[22] Given this, global theology (as an enterprise of truly interreligious theology) assumes an interrogative task that, through its practice, 'asks whether there is any reason why theology should be confined to a particular religious tradition in principle'.[23] For Ward, global theology is not necessarily a Christian task at all, but rather a huge exercise for the theologian committed to free intellectual and ever-changing enquiry who endeavours to consider the ultimate realities and value systems that have existed throughout human history and, as such, Ward believes that those who study it are not obliged to possess any set of religious or anti-religious views of their own as a prerequisite.

Ward's project of comparative theology appears to be similar to the description provided by David Tracy in 1987 when he wrote of a theological enterprise 'which ordinarily studies not one tradition alone but two or more, compared on theological grounds'. Nevertheless, Tracy regards the idea of undertaking comparative theology 'without a particular theological commitment' as rare.[24] Indeed, although it seems that Ward aspires towards a greater degree of neutrality for comparative theology, he also readily acknowledges that this can only be achieved in a limited way. Nevertheless, he states that comparative theology must be 'a self-critical discipline [. . .] a pluralistic discipline [. . .] and an open-ended discipline, being prepared to revise beliefs if and when it comes to seem

---

21 See Ward 1994; 1996; 1998; 1999.
22 Ward 2007, p. 378.
23 Ward 2007, p. 378.
24 Tracy 1987, p. 446.

necessary' (Ward 1994, p. 48). In Ward's project we can see that one particular approach to intercultural theology and interreligious studies is to combine them within the practice of a liberal global theology project that endeavours to adopt a non-confessional open-ended stance. In addition, there can be a more programmatic brief for such a project. That is, an interreligious and intercultural theology becomes a comparative effort to conceive a multi-faith 'systematic theology'. Along with Ward's significant contribution, other examples of this approach include the work of Wilfred Cantwell Smith,[25] Ninian Smart and Steven Konstantine (1991), Ross Reat and Edmund Perry (1991).[26] John Hick, who is popularly bracketed as a global theologian, is more properly characterized as a philosopher of religion who has constructed an explanatory pluralistic hypothesis (see especially Hick 2004).

However, there are other versions of comparative theology that adopt a more explicitly tradition-focused stance. These other versions (for example advocated by Roman Catholic thinkers such as Francis Clooney and James Fredericks)[27] seek to draw a distinction between comparative theology and what is called the 'theology of religions' by placing greater emphasis on *local* comparisons without seeking to supply an explanatory meta-theology. Thus for Clooney and Fredericks,[28] whereas comparative religion looks at the phenomenon of religion generally (and those engaged in it may well indulge in explanatory hypotheses concerning religion as a universal concept), comparative *theology* will engage in comparison from the perspective of a particular tradition. Practitioners like Clooney speak less of finding an 'overarching' or common religious purpose (or essence) within religious plurality, and more about the limited goal of enriching the understanding of their own faiths through such comparative encounters. He proposes a methodology that advocates a deep scholarly dialogue with, and study of, other faiths *in advance* of constructing any theological reading or appropriation of those faiths.[29] Clooney is critical

---

25 W. Cantwell Smith, *Towards a World Theology: Faith and the Comparative History of Religion*, London: Macmillan, 1989.

26 This work is cited in Vanhoozer 2007, pp. 101–2.

27 It is these versions of comparative theology (especially Clooney's) that have become 'representative' in current debate and serve as reference points for critics such as Knitter and Schmidt-Leukel.

28 See Fredericks 2004, pp. 97–8; Clooney 1995. See also Clooney 2010.

29 In this sense, Clooney's approach shares a certain kinship with the contemporary movement of Scriptural Reasoning, which promotes a deep scholarly reading of (Abrahamic) Scriptures in the presence of those to whom the Scripture 'belongs'.

of methodologies that conduct theological constructions of *the other* based solely on a priori principles, and this means that ambitious and 'universal' theological metanarratives that are related to the construction of paradigmatic thinking in the theology of religions (like the popular 'exclusivist, inclusivist and pluralist' model) are viewed as too preemptive. Defining comparative theology, he writes:

> Comparative theology thus combines tradition-rooted theological concerns with actual study of another tradition. It is not an exercise in the study of religion or religions for the sake of clarifying the phenomenon. It reduces neither to a theology about religions, nor to the practice of dialogue. (Clooney 2010, p. 10)

Although comparative theology, as described by Clooney, seeks to move away from grand theological scheming, its ambitions are characterized by a focus on local contexts and limited comparisons. Thus rather than undertaking a Christian perspective on other religions *generally* that we find in the theology of religions, comparative theology might have a regional focus or else there could be particular exchanges concerning selected theological themes. Defenders of comparative theology argue that such a restriction of scope facilitates a more effective and authentic dialogue that eschews abstractions and prefers closer comparisons. Moreover, by suspending theological metanarratives or caveats, it may be possible to pursue limited dialogues between people of different faiths more easily. Nevertheless, from a theology-of-religions perspective, one of the weaknesses of comparative theology is that it is hard to see how it can succeed in avoiding an interpretation of other religions that involves at least some theological presuppositions. This criticism has been raised by the likes of Paul Knitter and, more recently, Perry Schmidt-Leukel.[30] Schmidt-Leukel argues that sooner or later the comparative pursuit 'if it is carried out theologically' will 'lead to a point where the question of the relationship between the non-Christian and respective Christian belief becomes unavoidable' (Schmidt-Leukel 2009, p. 99). Thus despite their desire to move away from the more theoretical theology of religions, comparative theologians will inevitably have to enter this field when they seek to draw theological conclusions from their comparisons. Additionally Schmidt-Leukel maintains that it is complacent to follow James Fredericks' suggestion

---

30 See Knitter 2002, pp. 235–7; and Schmidt-Leukel 2009, especially chapter 5.

'that we should live with unsolved tension between confessional commitment and inter-religious openness . . .' (Schmidt-Leukel 2009, p. 100).
However, although Schmidt-Leukel's critique is persuasive, it is possible
that he is insisting on a greater resolution to theological issues than is
actually necessary, and he is doing this by defining theology as an activity that is only legitimately theological when it is ultimately concerned
with truth. Schmidt-Leukel maintains that the mere consideration of local
comparisons without asking where these comparisons fit into a greater
theological scheme is to stay within the phenomenological parameters of
'comparative religion' rather than comparative theology. But why must
all genuinely theological comparisons lead inexorably towards the *big
issues* associated with the theology of religions? This is a classic 'slippery
slope' argumentative strategy. Clooney and Fredericks are more concerned with particular places and 'close conversations', and this might in
fact be an approach to theologizing that is simply content to recognize
human finitude in its method and procedure. Thus in its defence it is possible to suggest that the practice of comparative theology is less ambitious
(or presumptuous) than the theology of religions: merely content to work
on a small scale and postpone the larger issues. Nevertheless, although
the chief claim to distinctiveness for comparative theology would appear
to be mostly a matter of *procedure* – as we have seen, there is a greater a
posteriori emphasis on letting the 'other' speak first and on undertaking
theology afterwards (and closer to the ground or grassroots) – it is not
clear that this is greatly different from the methods of some theologians
of religions.

Moving on, whatever the theological implications of the practice of intercultural theology in light of interreligious studies, there is also a basic
pedagogic necessity. On one level we might think of this as the need to
learn about contexts simply for the purposes of translation, exchange and
relevance. On another level there might also be an ambition for *compre-
hensiveness*. Ward writes:

> A genuinely global theology will seek to expound the whole range of
> human beliefs about the objects of religious faith as far as is possible,
> and its various teachers may advocate a range of diverse positions with-
> out presenting their own beliefs as unjustly privileged. (Ward 2007,
> p. 379)

Regardless of whether or not one adopts an exclusivist, inclusivist or
pluralist perspective, I think Ward is correct when he suggests that those

committed to the uncovering of truth must also be committed to considering as much *data* as is available.[31] Again, he writes:

> If religion is serious about truth, we must test our claims to truth ruthlessly against our competitors. If we are to see the limitations of our own viewpoints, we must have the courage to contrast them with the viewpoints of others. If we are to understand ourselves, we must see how and why others understand us. (Ward 2007, p. 388)

Thus as we have said, we might consider the question of the relationship between intercultural theology and interreligious studies to be a matter of a pedagogic imperative to provide a broad and informed theological curriculum and education. Put simply: interreligious studies becomes an important and necessary component for the study of theology in a global, intercultural context. Or else, speaking more theologically, there is a Christian virtue in interreligious studies that is linked to Anselm's *faith seeking understanding* imperative.[32] The striving for truth is both an academic/pedagogic and a religious goal. This obligation is about acquiring an attitude that seeks to comprehend the historical and conceptual context of belief in God in relation to how this compares or contrasts with other global contexts.

Towards a conclusion

Any theologian concerned with universal or transcendent issues will have to consider these in contextual and global perspective if s/he is to make sense – at the very least – of the translatability, or the incarnational nature, of the Christian gospel. If the Christian theologian is conscious of his/her public role, then this must beg the question of how large that 'public' arena is and how universal is the Christian message. The scope of information available has grown massively over the past several decades, and the theologian is now faced with multiple voices (Christian and otherwise). In the future, theology will have to adopt a far greater epistemological humility than it did before as it considers these voices, and it may be that new methodologies will have to be crafted to take account of a global diversity.

---

31 For my argument about this in the context of comparative philosophy of religion, see Cheetham 2008.

32 This is discussed by Norbert Hintersteiner in Hintersteiner 2007b.

Being an intercultural theologian who is serious about interreligious studies does not necessarily imply that one is committed to a pluralist perspective as a consequence. Of course, this is a serious option and many contemporary theologians will wish to pursue the possibilities of constructing global theologies in the context of interreligious dialogue. Alternatively, I have suggested that within a Christian theological framework, an intercultural theologian is one who is simply committed to a *larger context* for undertaking theology – recognizing the necessity of this brought about by the new global awareness to consider the contributions and contexts from around the globe. Moreover, this resonates with something already ingrained in Christian understanding: the nature of Christian reasoning itself and its eschatological vision – committed to a gospel message that while being fully incarnational also transcends cultures and contexts and speaks of an ultimate consummation involving all nations and races.

Given the sheer volume of information (a truly global scale) that opens up before us, I would suggest that there will be a shift away from the 'grand systematician' and a greater emphasis on the individual responsibilities of Christians and theologians to engage faithfully with their particular contexts. We have referred to H. Richard Niebuhr's work throughout this chapter, and his classic book, *Christ and Culture*, presents a series of options or perspectives; but he ends (deliberately) with an inconclusive conclusion: giving decision-making to individual believers in their various contexts. On the face of it, this seems like a recipe for hermeneutical chaos, but Niebuhr does not fail to suggest theological checks and balances, because:

> to believe is to be united with both the one in whom we believe and with all those who believe in him. In faith, because we believe, we are made aware of our relativity and our relatedness; in faith our existential freedom is acknowledgedly as well as actually exercised in the context of our dependence. To decide in faith is to decide in awareness of this context. To understand that context as best he may is as much the duty of the believer as to do his duty *in* the context. (Niebuhr 1951, pp. 233–4)

Although Niebuhr was addressing the generic questions about the relationship of the Christian to culture, what he outlines is even more pertinent in our global *inter*cultural and *inter*religious age half a century after he penned these words. Nevertheless, looking for a more contemporary version of this, it could be suggested that Niebuhr's option for a free but faithful existential faith is similar to the kind of improvisational theo-dramatic model that has recently been proposed by Kevin Vanhoozer (see Vanhoozer 2005). Thus Vanhoozer portrays the Christian gospel as 'essentially dramatic' and proposes that theo-dramatic reason is 'as imaginative-intuitive as it is analytic-conceptual and that theology's primary aim is to help disciples discern how best to "stage" the gospel of the kingdom of God in concrete situations' (Vanhoozer 2007, p. 109). In terms of devising new methodological strategies for the future of theology in a multi-faith world, combined with the sheer quantity of knowledge and variety that this entails, it may be that the picture of the 'improvisational believer' (Vanhoozer) or the Christian operating in 'existential freedom' (Niebuhr) represents the most likely, or feasible, way forward. Improvisation, as Vanhoozer stresses, does not imply hermeneutical laxity. Instead there is a 'disciplined spontaneity' that is nevertheless 'fitting' or appropriate to the circumstances (Vanhoozer 2007, p. 114). That is, the best improvisers do not just arbitrarily make things up on the spot but interpret, or contribute to, situations building upon their training, background knowledge and skill. In the case of the Christian, Vanhoozer calls upon them to use their 'canon sense' (Vanhoozer 2007, p. 115). At this point we might also revisit the eschatological image of 'feasting' that we saw David Ford use earlier. Thus the intercultural theologian is a faithful and discerning improviser who *revels* in the opportunities that intercultural theology, combined with interreligious studies, creates for new insights and for a broadened and deeper understanding of Christian truth.

4

Pentecostal Theological Method and Intercultural Theology[1]

MARK J. CARTLEDGE

Introduction

It could be argued that Pentecostal theology has come of age. It now has its own academic societies, journals, monograph series and biblical commentaries. However, there is still some debate regarding its place within the academy and its global and multicultural approach to theology has not always been appreciated. It has even been suggested that 'Pentecostal theology' is in fact an oxymoron – as if Pentecostals actually did theology! Of course, times have changed and now there is such a great diversity of approaches in the contemporary academy that different perspectives are accepted to a limited extent, even if they might not be fully valued. But if we were to articulate a Pentecostal approach to theology, what might it look like? Is there a distinctive method or approach to help us understand its nature? In this chapter I address these questions by bringing together two distinct but historically related areas in the field: theological method and intercultural theology. I intend to explore recent Pentecostal scholarship in its attempt to articulate a Pentecostal theological method. In order to appreciate the roots of the academic study of Pentecostalism more broadly, I connect this material to the field of intercultural theology as expressed by Walter J. Hollenweger. I have chosen Hollenweger because he has led the way in the academic study of Pentecostalism, allowing it to be appreciated as an important field of study. As a missiologist, his work has always been open to horizons

1 This chapter was originally published as 'Pentecostal Theological Method and Intercultural Theology', *Transformation: An International Journal of Holistic Mission Studies* 25.2–3 (2008) pp. 92–102. It appears here with minor alterations.

beyond his own, and his approach to theology has both affirmed Western theology and critiqued it through his appreciation of oral cultures and non-Western Christianity. I shall place these approaches side by side in an attempt to appreciate how they can illuminate each other and offer insights.

The term 'Pentecostal' is a designation that has been used in a variety of ways to classify particular Christian groups and denominations in the twentieth century. For many it denotes those groups who have used glossolalia, and has its origins with Charles Parham and William J. Seymour, especially in the Azusa Street revival. For others Pentecostalism has multiple and global origins that cannot be reduced to 'made in America', and it includes not just 'speaking in tongues' but the manifestation of all of the *charismata* (see Anderson 2004, pp. 166–83). My own view is that the terms Pentecostal, Neo-Pentecostal and Charismatic will continue to be applied unevenly in the literature, and that it is always important to distinguish the kind of Pentecostalism that is in view. For me there is something that I have called the 'charismatic tradition', which has transcended particularities across time and place in the history of the Church. It has manifested itself differently across the centuries, but established itself uniquely at the beginning of the twentieth century through various global expressions (see Cartledge 2006). From the early alignment of this tradition with the Wesleyan and Holiness traditions in the West, and forms of Evangelical Christianity elsewhere, there emerged different forms of Pentecostalisms. What I normally refer to as Pentecostalism is the expression of this spirituality as it became institutionalized in what is usually called classical Pentecostalism. This expression of Christianity is associated with particular denominations that have codified beliefs through statements of faith and specific doctrines, usually 'subsequence' and 'initial evidence'.[2] Charismatic Christianity in general is more fluid and aligns itself with other Christian traditions more readily, such as forms of Protestantism and Roman Catholicism, because it usually stresses the experience of the *charismata* rather than particular doctrines associated with them. In this chapter I am focusing on one form of American classical Pentecostalism, namely the Church

---

2 The term 'subsequence' normally refers to an experience subsequent to conversion entitled 'Baptism in the Spirit' through which the believer experiences the power of the Holy Spirit and is empowered to witness. The phrase 'initial evidence' refers to the sign that Baptism in the Spirit has occurred and normally refers to glossolalia. See Anderson 2004, pp. 190–2.

of God (Cleveland, Tennessee) and theologians associated with it (for a Declaration of Faith, see Hollenweger 1972, p. 517).

The phrase 'intercultural theology' is one that is associated with mission studies and interreligious dialogue. It was coined in the 1970s and was usually associated with a liberal and pluralistic approach to theology. It is normally taken to mean that theology should pay attention to the cultural embeddedness of all language, thought and practice, and by doing so achieve greater openness and dialogue because of the relativity that such recognition obtains. With the development of local theologies (see Schreiter 1985), it refers to the dialogues that these local theologies have one with another, and as a comparative approach it stimulates critical and creative thinking.[3] It has recently been revived in British scholarship by George Newlands, who argues for a progressive orthodoxy in the liberal tradition (Newlands 2004). However, his position, while acknowledging something of its heritage, fails to appreciate the nature of intercultural Christianity as Western and non-Western perspectives dialogue. Instead he assumes that the 'cross-cultural' and the 'intercultural' in relation to the non-Western usually mean the interreligious. He thus domesticates the term to an exclusively Western conceptualization by construing 'culture' largely in terms of Western subcultures and interdisciplinary dialogue. While this may be necessary for a Western liberal theology to find its place, it simply does not connect to other forms of Christianity, especially Pentecostalism. Therefore I shall use the term in its broadest cultural sense as defined by Hollenweger (see below).

Pentecostal theological method

I want to suggest that Pentecostal theological method in recent scholarship can best be understood by focusing on the Church of God (Cleveland, Tennessee) theologians who have pioneered reflection on the subject. This is not to suggest that other Pentecostals have not been active in the field,[4] but that it is useful to identify a particular tradition of thought within Pentecostalism for our purposes. Therefore I have chosen the work of John Christopher Thomas and Kenneth J. Archer as representative of this constituency. As an illustration of how this kind of method is being

---

3 Frans Wijsen, 'Intercultural Theology and the Mission of the Church', http://www.sedos.org/english/wijsen.htm (accessed 3 August 2007).

4 Amos Yong is another Pentecostal theologian who has picked up this trialectic, and offers an approach in dialogue with the philosophical tradition of American pragmatism; see Yong 2002.

applied, I have summarized the vision for a Pentecostal Bible commentaries series.

Spirit – text – community

These American Church of God (Cleveland, Tennessee) theologians have argued for a method of doing theology that works with a triad of sources: the text of Scripture, the community of the Church and the person of the Holy Spirit. All three sources are expected to work together in order to generate theological reflection and inform ecclesial decisions in relation to missiological praxis. The key illustration of how this method works has been articulated by John Christopher Thomas in relation to Acts 15 and the decision by the Jerusalem Council to include the Gentiles in the household of faith. First, attention is given to what had already taken place among the Gentiles: they had heard the gospel, believed, received the gift of the Holy Spirit, had their hearts purified by faith and experienced signs and wonders (vv. 7–9). Second, attention is given to Scripture and James' choice of Amos 9.11–12 to argue that there is continuity between David and Jesus as David's fallen tent is both rebuilt and expanded to include the Gentiles. In other words, the experience of the Spirit and the response to the gospel can be explained by this text. Third, in the light of these two aspects the whole group makes a decision together to include the Gentiles without requiring that they pass through Judaism (vv. 24–26). Testimony is given and received and this enables a group decision to be discerned. In the context of Acts 15 the Gentiles are allowed into the fellowship of the Church, provided that table fellowship is maintained, and in order to do this they are required to adopt specific attitudes towards Jewish food laws and sexual codes. The Holy Spirit is seen as acting through the text of Scripture, experiences such as signs and wonders and the testimonies in the group (Thomas 1994, pp. 41–56).

Kenneth J. Archer has built upon this proposal in his work on Pentecostal hermeneutics. He agrees with Thomas' reading of Acts 15 that there must be a dialogical and dialectical relationship between 'Scripture, Spirit and reader/readers' (Archer 2004, p. 147). He argues for a contemporary Pentecostal hermeneutical strategy that embraces a triadic negotiation for meaning, borrowing from semiotics and reader-response criticism. He integrates these insights within the Bible-reading method of the early Pentecostals in the context of the community. The voice of the Holy Spirit is heard through the community and Scripture, and permeates the hermeneutical process (Archer 2004, pp. 156–91). Archer has recently extended his argument from biblical hermeneutics to theological method, to which we now turn.

Method and manner

Archer contends that there is such a thing as a Pentecostal way of doing theology (Archer 2007, pp. 1–14). This approach takes the 'world of Pentecostalism' as its starting point and appropriates insights from other traditions. This means that orthodoxy cannot be separated from orthopraxy and orthopathy. Instead of seeing Pentecostalism as a form of Evangelicalism, it is understood as a distinct and authentic Christian tradition and its theological manner and method is equally distinct. Commending the insights of Hollenweger, he notes how early Pentecostal sources suggest that theology is done via testimonies, songs, trances, sermons and dances. This builds on the work of Deborah McCauley, who has shown how oral communication and narrative are the primary modes of expression for the American Christians of the 'Mountain Region'. These Christians are largely Pentecostal, marginalized and are predominantly oral/aural learners. Similarly Frank Macchia refers to the 'non-academic' theology of Pentecostals through prayers, commentaries, devotional writings and disputations. However, Archer wonders whether Macchia has given too much away by using the language of 'non-academic', suggesting inadvertently that such theology lacks academic credence.[5] Therefore the word 'pietistic', Archer suggests, might be a better adjective for Pentecostal theology. Whatever, we call it, the Pentecostal tradition requires that the affective and experiential aspects be included, which he suggests come primarily through worship.

The method that Archer advocates is 'integrative', by which he specifically means the integration of orthopraxis and orthopathos. Praxis embraces the idea that theology and practice are inseparable and mutually informing as theory arises from a reflection on practice and returns to inform further practice. Praxis needs to be supplemented in order to nurture Pentecostal theology, and it does this by attending to orthopathos; that is, an identification by theology with the suffering community, allowing a 'firsthand, direct existential engagement' among the marginalized

---

5 Frank D. Macchia elsewhere refers to this distinction by using Karl Barth's terms 'regular' and 'irregular' theology, and makes a plea for the acceptance of *both* an 'enacting theology', as in the case of African Pentecostalism, *and* the value of abstract Western theology; see Macchia 2002, pp. 105–9.

(Archer 2007, p. 10). Both personal and communal experience is affirmed, and cognitive doctrine is never detached from the pathos of God. This 'conjunctive methodology' 'takes seriously orthopathos as the integrative centre for our Pentecostal theology without setting aside either praxis or dogma' (Archer 2007, p. 10).

For Archer, the manner of this Pentecostal theology is narrative. This proceeds by understanding Scripture as the grand metanarrative, with the Gospels and Acts as the centre of the story. The social doctrine of the Trinity is the central character, with Jesus Christ at the very heart, thereby emphasizing the gospel of Christ and its significance for the Church and the world: the hub around which other theological themes revolve. Pentecostals have articulated this gospel in terms of the 'full gospel', or 'five-fold' gospel: Jesus as saviour, sanctifier, Spirit baptizer, healer and coming king, giving what Archer calls central narrative convictions. These convictions flow out of the doxological community, bestowing identity and affording guidance in the Christian life. Therefore if this gospel is the hub, the Pentecostal doctrines, beliefs and practices are the wheel connected to the centre: Jesus Christ. Each dimension of the gospel is linked to the others and provides a way of reflecting on other themes such as ecclesiology and eschatology, being 'held together around our missional story of the Social Trinity' (Archer 2007, p. 13).

Pentecostal Bible commentaries

In 2004 a new Bible Commentary series was launched by T & T Clark, edited by the New Testament scholar John Christopher Thomas. The first two commentaries appeared in that year by the editor on the Johannine epistles, and by Rebecca Skaggs on the epistles of Peter and Jude (Thomas, 2004; Skaggs, 2004). These commentaries provide an interesting insight into how the Pentecostal theological method noted above has been used in a creative way to provide resources for pastors, lay people and students through popular, non-technical language. In the Editor's Preface to the series the nature of the commentary and the process of writing is outlined. A number of points are worth noting.

First, Thomas points out that contrary to those who understand Pentecostalism as either fundamentalist Christianity with Spirit Baptism and *charismata* or an experience capable of fitting with any spirituality or theological system, it is a distinct theological tradition. At the heart of the tradition is a message of the five-fold gospel: Jesus as saviour, sanctifier, Holy Spirit baptizer, healer and coming king. This message reveals the heart of the tradition and displays aspects that are similar and dissimilar to other Christian traditions. Writers of the commentaries should therefore be people who do not just speak in tongues but who represent this tradition's ethos. The writers should represent the diversity of the constituency coming from different continents, races and communities.

Second, the writing process has been designed in order to represent this tradition. Each contributor is 'urged' to include a number of spiritual disciplines in his or her work. They are encouraged to pray for the project both individually and as members of Pentecostal communities, asking specifically for the guidance of the Holy Spirit and for the leadership of the Spirit in interpretation. It is expected that there will be specific times of prayer when the community intercedes on behalf of the writer and seeks to hear from the Lord through prophetic words. As part of this engagement with their Church community, it is expected that commentators will explore ways in which their scholarship might be contextualized within their own local setting, thus strengthening the interaction between the Spirit, the body of Christ and the Word of God. As part of this contextualization, writers are encouraged to covenant with their churches regarding spiritual support, and where possible lead a group Bible study on the book they are writing about. Writers are also encouraged to seek the advice and critique of a gifted colleague, so that their work would not be done in isolation.

Third, the physical format of the commentary is designed to reflect the dialogical manner in which the tradition approaches the text. Each commentary begins with a set of questions aiming to draw attention to the corporate and individual issues addressed in the book. The reader is invited to interpret his or her context in a 'confessional-critical' manner. This means that the commentary is contextualized within the life of the Church from the beginning. From this initial section the introduction to the commentary proper informs the reader regarding the composition of the book, but avoids unnecessary and irrelevant questions. It includes topics of interest to Pentecostals as well as discussing genre, structure and organization of the book. A section on the book's teaching on the Holy Spirit is included. The commentary proper provides a running exposition of the text, interacts with major interpretive options and provides periodic opportunities for reflection on the text via the use of questions and a section guiding personal responses to issues arising, with possible concrete responses being offered. This is regarded as the literary equivalent to an altar call.

Therefore it is through this approach that these Bible commentaries give expression to the Pentecostal theological method in a tangible form. I now turn to the subject of intercultural theology by way of a comparison.

Intercultural theology

The father of the academic study of Pentecostalism and the former Professor of Mission at the University of Birmingham, Walter J. Hollenweger, began to argue from the late 1970s for what he called 'intercultural theology' (Hollenweger 1978b, pp. 2–14). By this he meant the appropriation of 'cultural media' outside the theologian's own tradition that can serve as raw material and tools for doing theology, in particular missiology. Intercultural theology does not jumble together languages and cultures but rather chooses a cultural framework and sticks to it without assuming that the theologian's cultural background is universal. It searches for 'a body of Christ', contributing to the body without assuming that it is the most important or the most academic. It is a way of doing theology that escapes the Western religious and academic ghetto and places it in the world in which we live (Price 2002, p. 64).

He offers five main points in order to define his approach. First, intercultural theology operates within a given culture but without absolutizing this particular culture. It reflects or mirrors the sacramental body of Christ, open to the universal and sacramental dimension of the Christian faith. Second, the methods by which this is achieved are chosen on the basis of their suitability. No one tradition should be ruled out or taken for granted as the only or most important. 'In this "body of Christ"-approach, theology has to hold its ground against all pagan and sectarian schools of learning (and in the churches!). It cannot conform to the *stoicheia tou kosmou*' (Hollenweger 1978, p. 12). Third, it is suggested that narrative theology is one of the possible approaches towards a theology of one culture that is open to other cultures. Fourth, experiments in intercultural theology can be tested for their suitability and thereby build bridges of communication lacking in normal Western academic theology. Fifth, intercultural theology is not a form of 'pop-theology', and makes the task of theology more difficult, not easier. Critical scholarship continues, but it is also applied to the process of communication, not just the content. Doing theology interculturally within the body of Christ pays attention not just to what is 'broadcast' but equally what is 'received', thereby 'demonstrating theology's place in the world in which we live' (Hollenweger 1978, p. 13).

By the mid-1980s Hollenweger's ideas about intercultural theology had become clearer and he was able to articulate seven presuppositions: (1) all theologies are contextually conditioned; (2) there is nothing wrong with theology being contextually conditioned; (3) it may take others to show us how conditioned, parochial, or ideologically captive our own theology is; (4) even if once we could ignore such voices, now we can no longer do so; (5) the point of contact between our traditions and the new theologies of the Third World is Scripture; (6) only in creative tension with the widest possible perspective can we develop theologies appropriate to our own particular situations; and (7) since within the Church the ultimate loyalty is not simply to nation, class, culture, the universal Church is uniquely suited to provide the context in which the task of creative theologizing can take place (Hollenweger 1986, pp. 28–35).

At the time of writing, Hollenweger explains that he is involved in training theological teachers for the Third World and that in their research work he looks for three things: (1) originality; (2) work that is relevant to *their* context, country, culture and society; and (3) familiarity with the research conventions of a European university (Hollenweger 1986, p. 34).[6] Quite often there is a clash between (2) and (3). So he offers a plea for an intercultural theology that uses both the tools of classical Western theology as well as attending to the oral spiritualities of Third World religious communities and the narrative structure of their theology, so akin to the first generation of Christians (see Hollenweger 1997, pp. 81–82). Therefore we need to combine story *and* analysis, dream *and* critical interpretations in our theological articulation. However, it is through the basic category of narrative that theology has the possibility of becoming universal (Hollenweger 1997, p. 131).

Lynne Price, in her theological biography of Hollenweger, notes how he engages in all three 'publics' of theology: academy, Church and society by experiential, dialogical and reflective modes but always attending to context (Price 2002, pp. 26–8). His theology is both global and ecumenical and relies significantly on the narratives set within particular cultural settings (Price 2002, p. 36). His use of 'narrative exegesis' allows him to share the fruits of critical scholarship with non-academic and cross-cultural audiences, as he playfully rescripts biblical stories to elucidate their messages for different settings.[7] Price observes that while Hollenweger defends the use of critical scholarship, he did not support its claim to objectivity or neutrality. As she says:

> For him, the Bible remains foundational – not as a source of proof texts
> to support particular dogmatic positions, but in a much more complex

---

6 Many of these theses were published by Peter Lang, Frankfurt am Main, in the series he initiated with others entitled 'Studies in the Intercultural History of Christianity'.

7 Price 2002, pp. 42–63, but note Hollenweger's 'midrash' of Dietrich Bonhoeffer's visit to a Black church service in New York in the 1930s; see pp. 79–83.

way a truly universal collection of inspired writings whose meanings become clear only as succeeding and diverse communities engage with them in the midst of present realities and share their insights with each other. In answer to the question: 'Who interprets Scripture correctly?' his reply is: 'no one person interprets Scripture correctly on his [sic] own. It is only in conflict, debate, and agreement with the whole people of God, and also with non-Christian readers that we can get a glimpse of what Scripture means. (Price 2002, p. 63; citing Hollenweger 1997, p. 325)

It is this desire for an ecumenical and multicultural conversation that drives Hollenweger's model of intercultural theology. Indigenous non-Western theology should be developed in dialogue with European Church history in order to advance ecumenism (Price 2002, p. 74). However, such a theology is, according to Hollenweger, necessarily pluralistic, partial and transitional, with truth emerging from out of different times and places. Thus the oral and narrative categories of non-Western cultures are given priority in Hollenweger's theological method because these forms allow 'the "ruling language" to be brought into intercultural dialogue as one possible language next to other possible languages'.[8] The non-Western 'other' is necessary for both insight and correction and should not be domesticated or overruled by the Western academy, Church or culture. In his intercultural theology Hollenweger mediated between the Western academy and the non-Western world: to the West he argued for diversity and oral/narrative modes of theological discourse, to the non-West he promoted analysis, reflection and the need to relate to the wider history of the Church. To all 'he stressed the need for sensitive, appropriate and critical Christian response to the concrete realities of local and global, historical and contemporary, contexts' (Price 2002, p. 91).

Theological and methodological reflection

The juxtaposition of Pentecostal theological method and intercultural theology outlined above raises a number of interesting and important points for the broader discussion of how we do our theology. There are

---

8 Price 2002, p. 79. This is also reflected in Hollenweger's prioritizing of William J. Seymour over Charles Parham as the founder of American Pentecostalism precisely for the theological reason that he represents 'oral black modes of communication' rather than the doctrine of initial evidence; see Hollenweger 1997, p. 23.

similarities and differences between the two approaches. I make four main points by way of a theological and methodological comparison.

First, both approaches stress the nature of theology in terms of narrative, and this is a category that is now being fully recognized as important; but it will always need to be supplemented by dogmatic statements, metaphors and models that assist in the explication of theology. Of course, these metaphors and models may vary across time and place, but will certainly need to be constructed for the communication of the gospel. This is exactly what Archer does in terms of his five-fold gospel, which provides a Christological centre, and his appeal to the social doctrine of the Trinity, which provides an overarching 'theological framework', even if he does not call it that. It is not entirely clear from the work of Hollenweger what the role of a dogmatic core plays in intercultural theology. He has in the past criticized Pentecostals for a Western Calvinist view of the Trinity that subordinates pneumatology to Christology, which he traces to the *filioque* clause (Hollenweger 1997, pp. 218–22).[9] His answer is to use the Barthian language of *Seinsweise* (modes of being) in order to overcome this problem. But a social doctrine of the Trinity would, theoretically at least, remove such subordinationism, even if it has other problems; and after all, many Pentecostal theologians are influenced by Moltmann rather than Barth (the most notable exception is Frank Macchia). The critical question that the Pentecostal theological method offers the intercultural theology of Hollenweger concerns the role that Christian doctrine plays in relation to narrative theology. On this point they appear to diverge considerably.

Second, both approaches wish to give priority to local voices, although it is expressed differently. The Pentecostal method offers this through community testimony and group prayer meetings, while the intercultural method uses indigenous categories to critique and challenge Western categories (see also Sugirtharajah 1999). In this attention to the local, both approaches, it could be argued, are forms of postmodern theology, although expressed differently. The Pentecostal method uses an 'in front of the text' reading while nevertheless seeing the Bible as the judge of contemporary praxis. Hollenweger's method uses the insights of 'behind the text' historical-critical scholarship and assumptions about plurality and conflict in the canon, which are then used to engage with contemporary forms of conflict and plurality through rescripted narrative and drama. In this sense both approaches resolve the issue of universality versus particularity, but in different ways. Both align experience with the text, but

9 Also see my discussion in Cartledge 2004, pp. 76–84.

again in very different ways. Ultimately, for the Pentecostal theological method the Bible is the norming norm (*norma normans*) around which experience is tested and interpreted, even as it is used to interpret the Bible: it is the final form of the text in the hands of the community that inspires. For Hollenweger, the assumptions of modern critical scholarship are not challenged but simply communicated via a narrative medium. It is not the final form that is important but the perceived issues and processes in the texts that inspire a re-reading in new contexts. Although apparently similar, these approaches could not be so different.

Third, both approaches are interested in the Church but ecclesiology appears to be understood very differently by them. The Pentecostal method never really defines the community. One is bound to ask: Which community? Whose community? One suspects the community is a fairly small one that believes in an American version of the five-fold gospel! Global Charismatic Christianity in all its diversity is apparently excluded by a narrow definition of Pentecostalism and Pentecostal tradition. By contrast, intercultural theology is ecumenically open, although this perhaps reflects the period in which Hollenweger was involved in the World Council of Churches. In this ecumenical winter the possibilities of ecumenical theology look somewhat different. Nevertheless the openness of such an approach is certainly more appealing to someone standing outside classical Pentecostalism. In this regard a number of the key presuppositions of intercultural theology are pertinent. Given that all theology is contextual, listening to others outside our tradition is necessary in order to highlight the 'blind spots'. It is in creative tension with the widest possible perspectives that theologians can best understand their own context, and this is best achieved ecumenically as global Christianity engages in dialogue.

Fourth, both are interested in spirituality but only one puts it at the heart of the process of doing theology; the other puts it as the object for research. This may be a crucial difference between the seminary model of the Pentecostals and the university model of intercultural theology. But in an age in which different perspectives are accepted and even a Tübingen professor can argue for the epistemological advantage of contemplation and 'spiritual gaze' for theology (Moltmann 1992, pp. 202–8), it seems an unnecessary and unfortunate divide. This difference may well relate to the question of who does theology. Both see theology as conducted by the professional and by the ordinary person in the Church. But it is not entirely clear how these different roles are to be worked out and where the balance of power lies despite the support for the marginalized and powerless. The university theologian may well be asked to put matters of 'faith' to one side for the sake of academic credibility, but increasingly it is accepted that spirituality and worldview issues cannot be divorced from intellectual pursuits. (Indeed, it could be argued that faith is never ever put to one side because that is an impossibility – even atheism is a position of faith!) The integrated Pentecostal theological method is one that has the capacity to travel. Yet it is not without its difficulties. Theologians are not always comfortable people to be around because they often raise the hard and difficult questions, however committed they are to 'the faith once received by the saints'. A communitarian approach to theology can also domesticate insights that are new and different because the power of the reading tradition and the pressure of spiritual enactment stifle creativity while ironically claiming to promote it.

Conclusion

It has been interesting and useful to consider afresh two very different approaches to theology, both of which have engaged with the Pentecostal tradition. On balance I suspect that most Pentecostal theologians will gravitate towards the Pentecostal theological method outlined above, and with some good reason. However, intercultural theology has much to offer, not least a wider appreciation of issues of cultural and global Christianity that overcomes the label 'made in America'. As a practical theologian, I can see advantages and disadvantages with both approaches. However, neither appears to engage in a multi/inter-disciplinary approach to theology, which is surely an important aspect of twenty-first-century theology;[10] and neither explains the processes by which oral and local data is identified, gathered and analysed. My answer is to integrate Pentecostal-charismatic spirituality, as per the insights of Pentecostal theological method, within the process of practical theology as an intercultural and comparative empirical discipline, thus addressing the weaknesses noted above (see Cartledge 2003). In this way the three publics of Church, academy and society may be mutually informed for the benefit of all.

---

10 For a Pentecostal proposal that does attempt to do this, see Yong 2005, pp. 27–30.

5

Gender Issues in Intercultural Theological Perspective

KIRSTEEN KIM

Introduction

While gender is universal, it is always culturally expressed. Whereas women and men are differentiated by sex at birth, the categories of male and female, although universally recognized, are differently perceived across cultures. The fact that gender roles and relations are worked out differently across cultures is a motivating factor in leading women to question the roles and status ascribed to them in their traditional culture and to envision new ways of being and behaving.

This chapter will focus on Christian feminist theology, primarily because Christian theology is the expertise of the author. It must be recognized at the outset that the discipline of gender studies is much wider than women's perspectives and feminism. Gender, and its role in human relations, is the issue, not women (Gross 2005, p. 20). Recently intercultural attempts have been made in Christian theology to broaden the discussion and situate feminist theology within gender studies (for example, King and Beattie 2005) and also to deal with issues of sexuality that have become particularly pressing in some parts of the Church (for example, Brown 2006). However, it is largely owing to women's struggles against what they identify as their exclusion or domination in religion, especially in the context of growing gender equality in movements of modernity, that the importance of gender issues has been brought to the attention of contemporary theology.

Gender and feminist movements are not unique to Christianity but are found in most of the major world religions (see, for example, Sharma and Young 1998; Becher 1990). Although Christianity will be the main focus of this chapter, since culture cannot be separated from religion, where other religions dominate, Christian thinking on gender also addresses conceptions of gender relations from those traditions, as we shall see. The 'first wave' of feminism in the West in the nineteenth century called for women's rights – particularly to vote, own property and gain education – and was inextricably linked to Christian-inspired movements. Christian women were leading figures in movements for social change, such as abolition, prison reform, education, health care and so on, and they outnumbered men in the missionary movement (see, for example, Byrne 1995; 1993). Their leadership was recognized and enabled in newer Christian movements – such as Quakers and Congregationalists – but women's ordination to ministry was, and is, generally resisted in older Churches, particularly the most traditional (Orthodox and Roman Catholic, who tend to cite theological and ecclesiological reasons for women's exclusion from the priesthood), and the most conservative – especially fundamentalist and many Evangelical Protestant groups, who give biblical grounds for limiting women's ministry (see, for example, Martin 1994; Köstenberger and Schreiner 2005). Where theology is an activity of the Church leadership, it is also largely the preserve of men.

The opening of ordination to women candidates in more liberal Protestant denominations that dominated after the Second World War led to increases in the numbers of women studying theology. Though the prospect of ordination was more remote, Roman Catholic theological education was opened to women in the 1960s, following the reforms of Vatican II (Ruether 2002). During the 'second wave' of feminism in the 1960s and 1970s, there were the first systematic attempts by women to apply feminist perspectives and theory to theology. Since Christianity is spread across the globe and because feminism became a global movement, feminist theology soon spread. However, it also diversified in local contexts into a variety of feminist theologies – Western, Asian, African, *Mujerista* or Latina, Womanist (Black American) and so on. As Rosemary Radford Ruether explains:

> Christian women theologians across the globe are concerned with common themes of critique of sexist symbols in Christianity and the reconstruction of the symbolism for God, Christ, humanity and nature, sin, and salvation, to affirm women's full and equivalent humanity. But women theologians in each context take up issues particular to their societies and histories and draw on cultural resources before and beyond Christianity to envision a more just and loving world. (Ruether 2002, p. 18)

The common resources that Christian women share and both criticize and utilize for theologizing are the Bible and Christian theological tradition.

In interpreting the Bible, women have to contend with verses, mostly from Saint Paul, that appear to limit their participation and status in the Church (especially 1 Cor. 11.2–16; 14.34–35; Eph. 5.21–33; 1 Tim. 2.8–15). On the other hand, women can point to liberative traditions in the New Testament. For example, the Gospel writers record that Jesus Christ showed an attitude towards women that was counter-cultural at the time, such as his theological discussions with Martha and Mary, her sister (John 20.11–40; Luke 10.38–42) and the Syrophoenician woman (Mark 7.24–30; Matt. 15.21–28). His frank encounter with a Samaritan woman of low status and dubious past broke many of the taboos of the period (John 4). In the New Testament the faith of many women is shown to be exemplary, and leading women such as Mary, the mother of Jesus, Mary, sister of Lazarus, and Mary Magdalene have privileged knowledge of the purposes of God in Christ (Matt. 28.9–10; Mark 14.3–9; Luke 1.32–35; John 2.1–11; 11.23–27; 20.18). Other New Testament documents also show a vision of the Church as a new society in which traditional social boundaries are overcome, and there is 'neither male nor female' (Gal. 3.28). Because of the centrality of the Bible in theological discourse, many Christian feminists have applied themselves to recovering or reinterpreting the biblical record and developing feminist hermeneutics (Dube 2001; Evans 1983; Fiorenza 1983; Kroeger and Kroeger 1992; Kwok 1995; Sawyer 2002; Tamez 1982; Trible 1984).

With regard to the treatment of women in the tradition, there is strong evidence that women were co-ministers in the earliest Church in a way that became unthinkable later on when Churches became institutions (Fiorenza 1983). Later Christian tradition generally excluded women from Church hierarchy and public ministry, and doctrines developed that tended to lay the blame for human sin on Eve and, despite the veneration of Mary, the mother of Jesus, minimize the contribution of women in salvation (Warner 1985). Despite this, many women have made outstanding contributions to the Church, Christian spirituality and even theology before the modern period. Some of them are recognized as saints and heroines, but others now honoured were until recently dismissed as heretics (Ruether 1998). The crucial turning point of the twentieth century was not women coming into leadership in Christian faith but 'the explicit recognition, in the context of the feminist movement, of the ways in which earlier theology had tended systematically to silence women and to lend ideological support to their oppression' (Muers 1997, p. 431) and of the impact of gender on all aspects of theology (Graham 1995). Since they have had a voice in the discipline of theology, feminist theologians have been reassessing theological tradition, challenging and even rejecting it, and developing it by drawing on new resources of women's experience, feminist theory and other traditions – both sacred and secular.

In this chapter we will begin with an overview showing how feminist theology is multicultural, and consider why several commentators have remarked that feminist theology emerging from the global South is significantly different in its approach and goals from that in the global North. As Ruether indicates in the quote above, this is due on the one hand to differing social and political contexts, and also on the other hand to different religio-cultural traditions that express what is feminine and set norms for gender relations. We will go on to look at selected Christian feminist theologies from Asia, and then highlight some of the challenges and advantages of tackling gender issues interculturally.

Feminist theology as multicultural

Chronologically, the first women to apply self-consciously to academic theology the feminist theory emerging from wider movements in Western societies for women's liberation and rights were Roman Catholics in the USA in the late 1960s. Some, like Mary Daly, renounced the faith altogether as irredeemably patriarchal and misogynist, on the grounds that 'if God is male, then the male is God' (Daly 1986, p. 19). Daly, influenced by the feminist philosophy of Simone de Beauvoir, advocated a feminist alternative to the Church. Daly's sisterhood was an 'anti-church' bound by a 'cosmic covenant' based on pre-Christian traditions (Daly 1986). Rosemary Radford Ruether, while similarly drawing on sources outside the Christian tradition, nevertheless found hope within it and continued to engage with Christian theology. She argued, however, that revolutionary reform of the language of theology and Christian liturgy was needed and, influenced by Latin American liberation theology, advocated the formation of 'feminist base communities' to reinvent the Church from within (Ruether 1983). Feminist theologians recognized a relationship between dualistic notions of male and female and other dualisms of spirit and matter, reason and emotion, soul and body. Rather than assent to the superiority of male-spirit-reason-soul, feminist theologians – drawing on Christian doctrines of the incarnation – instead sought to affirm the earthly life in the body, especially women's bodies, and also the earth itself, which is often thought of as 'Mother' (Muers 1997, pp. 436–7). Ruether, who is probably the leading feminist theologian of that first generation today, went on to develop 'ecofeminist theology', a theology of earth-healing and non-violence (Ruether 1975; 1994).

In the Roman Catholic Church women are not part of the hierarchy but are encouraged to join religious communities in which the emphasis is on practising spirituality rather than doing theology. In the 'third wave' of feminism this came to be regarded as a strength rather than a weakness, especially as with the rise of fundamentalism, 'religion' became even more associated with rigid doctrine and patriarchal oppression. In contrast to 'religion', spirituality allowed for a crossing of traditional boundaries between confessions and appeared accessible to those outside the hierarchy. Feminist theories on the different paths of development of women and men stimulated interest in women's spirituality (Conn 1986). The next generation of Roman Catholic theologians paid greater attention to gender relations rather than essentialist definitions of femininity, and raised theological questions about genders within the Trinity. Elizabeth A. Johnson has attempted to remain within orthodox Roman Catholic teaching and yet portray an alternative vision of God as 'She Who Is' by drawing on feminine images of God in the Bible (Johnson 1992). The work of Johnson and other women theologians, such as Anne Hunt (2005) and Catherine Mowry LaCugna (1991), on the Trinity is now widely recognized in Roman Catholic theology.

Developments among Protestants in the USA followed a similar pattern. For example, Letty Russell, drawing on the Civil Rights movement and Latin American liberation theology (Russell 1974, p. 21), also developed 'women-church'. And Sallie McFague pioneered new metaphors and models for talking about God, drawing on biblical and ecological sources (1993). In Europe, the influential German liberation theologian Dorothee Sölle's work explicitly addressed feminist issues in her 1984 book as part of her wider theological agenda against authoritarianism. European women particularly draw on a strong tradition of women's spirituality and literature in Western culture (for example Loades 2001; Grey 2001). Those with a political concern emphasize sisterhood and have been stimulated by their discovery of solidarity with women in the Majority World (King 1994; Graham 2007; Grey 2004).

The feminist theology emerging in the USA and Europe soon spread to other continents through Roman Catholic religious orders and through WCC organizations, especially the Ecumenical Association of Third World Theologians, which after 1983 organized consultations of women theologians. There it sparked other movements of feminist or women's theology. One of the first 'Southern' feminist theologians, the Indonesian Marianne Katoppo, who was a Presbyterian and a Marxist, found sources for women's empowerment in Mary the Mother of Jesus and also in the Asian goddess traditions (Katoppo 1979). Sun Ai Park, a Korean

Protestant, founded the influential journal of Asian women's theology, *In God's Image*, and organized the Asian Women's Resource Centre for culture and theology (www.awrc4ct.org), which continues to articulate Asian Women's theology. In the 1980s, Virginia Fabella and Mary John Mananzan, both Roman Catholics from the Philippines, pioneered a distinctive Asian women's spirituality. Against the background of the struggle for democracy there, their strongly Christocentric approach recognized the salvific value of suffering and women's capacity for love: 'passion and compassion' (Fabella 1988, pp. 109–11).

In the 1990s feminist theology was dominated by the movement of eco-feminism, and feminist theologians from the global South were at the forefront of Christian eco-feminism (Muers 1997, p. 437). Eco-feminism is particularly strong in India, where the lives of village women may be largely determined by the need to find water and fuel and other environmental questions. Against a background of high-profile campaigns by women against the destruction of forests and construction of dams, Aruna Gnanadason, who directed the women's work of the WCC, drew on the goddess traditions of India as well as the example of biblical women leaders (Gnanadason 1994). Gnanadason, and the WCC women's work, moved on in the early twenty-first century to address 'violence against women, which is seen as symptomatic of wider violence in society entrenched in social structures, and with women's potential for peacemaking, reconciliation and healing' (Gnanadason, Kayoro and McSpadden 1996).

Korean theologian Chung Hyun Kyung became the face of Asian feminist theology when, at the Canberra Assembly of the WCC in 1991, she illustrated her presentation 'Come, Holy Spirit, renew the whole creation' with a shamanistic exorcism (Chung 1991). Chung was both lauded by those who thought she was breaking new ground with indigenous women's theology and condemned by those who felt she had departed altogether from the Christian tradition (Kim 2004). She drew on the *Minjung* strand of Korean theology that was used to motivate the struggle for human and civil rights against military dictatorships in Korea, and at the same time criticized the first generation of *Minjung* theologians for excluding women (1990). On behalf of other African and Asian theologians, Chung articulated a shared spirituality of eco-feminism (1994). Chung and other Asian feminists are also concerned about the sexual exploitation of women. This includes the plight of the so-called 'comfort women' abused by the Japanese military during their occupation of Korea; the suffering caused by the dowry system in India; and sex tourism in South-East Asia (Kwok 2000, pp. 20–3; Chung 1990, pp. 39–47). Probably the most influential Asian feminist today is Kwok Pui-lan, an Anglican from Hong Kong and a specialist in post-colonial perspectives. However, Asian feminism, like Asia itself, is extremely diverse (Fabella 1988; Kang 2008, p. 205, n. 1; Kwok 2000, p. 36), and what reaches the West is only a small proportion of the whole.

The main vehicle of African feminist theology has been the 'Circle of Concerned African Women Theologians', inaugurated in 1989 by Ghanaian Methodist Mercy Amba Oduyoye for 'women who do not consider that African's men's theology should suffice for the entire faith community'. 'African women's theology' is 'African Christian Theology in the women-centred key'. The women concerned are all 'keen church women', lay and ordained, and their theologizing goes 'beyond the written word to liberative and transformative action' (Oduyoye 2001, p. 10). Oduyoye sees African women's theology as beginning with the storytelling tradition of Africa and the Bible (Oduyoye 2001, p. 11). Historical theology is less significant in it since this is largely foreign to African women's experience (Oduyoye 2001, p. 16). From their reading of the Bible, theologians such as Roman Catholic Teresa Okure from Nigeria have emphasized the equality of women and men both in their giftedness and in their responsibility for God's creative mission (Okure 1988; cf. Oduyoye 1994). The reflections of the Circle continue to combine African women's wisdom with biblical texts and current issues in new and imaginative ways (Dube 2001).

As in Korea (above), African women are less affected by modernization than men and therefore have a greater sense of continuity with African traditions (Kanyoro 2001, p. 112; Oduyoye 1994, p. 362). On the other hand, they are less inclined to romanticize the tradition because of its oppression of women (Ruether 2002, p. 15). They recognize that 'Culture is frequently a euphemism to protect actions that require analysis' (Oduyoye 2001, p. 13). From this standpoint they have taken issue with cultural traditions, such as female genital mutilation, and also with proverbs that denigrate women (Oduyoye 2001, pp. 14, 30–1). Oduyoye stresses the centrality of marriage, family life and child-bearing to African women's lives, and therefore to their theology, in which mothering and its associated qualities of 'nurturing', 'mentoring', 'life-enhancing' and 'community-building' are to the fore (Oduyoye 2001, pp. 37–8). Like African Traditional Religions, African women's theology is concerned with bringing wholeness, which is 'all that makes for fullness of life, and makes people celebrate life' (Oduyoye 2001, p. 34). And this wholeness is brought about by healing. The Circle, and especially Oduyoye herself, have understood salvation as 'primarily a cry for health and wholeness' necessitated by the brokenness of African life (Oduyoye 1986, p. 44). This salvation is not limited to the Church but encompasses wider society and the whole eco-system, which are bound up together in the African 'circle of life' (cf. Oduyoye 2001, pp. 34–5).

Other theologies are stimulants but not sources for African theologizing, which proceeds by making and elaborating statements of faith, using the critical perspective of liberation, rather than by analysis and argumentation (Oduyoye 2001, p. 11). The independence of African theologizing is a result of awareness that Christianity has not been an unmitigated blessing on Africa (Njoroge 2001). Indeed, Western Christianity may be seen as 'an assault on the African way of life launched by ethnocentric Europeans in collaboration with colonial administration and colonial violence' (Oduyoye 2001, p. 28). The cultural criticism of African women's theology therefore also addresses Western Christian culture, and has a powerful critique of the models of Church imported into Africa, calling on the Church to recognize the gifts of women and their commitment to the Church in the hope that it may become 'a living community of women and men relating to one another and to their Source Being' (Oduyoye 2002, p. 100).

Latin American feminist theologians have generally worked within the socio-economic discourse of Liberation Theology, which was pioneered on the continent, and were part of its diversification to include not only the economically poor but also those oppressed by colour, race and gender. Women found themselves the subjects of a double oppression by poverty and sexism (Bingemer 1994, p. 309). The cult of *machismo* or 'exaggerated masculinity' (Chant 2003, pp. 15–17) is partly explained by the behaviour of the *conquistadores*, whose plunder of the land was accompanied by the rape of Indian women, and whose 'spirit of the conquest' is still alive today (Esquivel 1990, p. 75). Christian feminists have been actively working to free women from male violence (for example, Caipora Women's Group 1993, pp. 21–3) and also to use traditional veneration of motherhood to subvert male power (Chant 2003, pp. 9–13). Within the Catholic tradition in Latin America, the post-Vatican II freedom to read the Bible led to a new appreciation of the Virgin Mary as 'God's face seen from a feminist perspective' (Gebara and Bingemer 1994, p. 280). Apart from the spiritualized tradition, the material poverty of the earthly Mary from which she was exalted struck home and identified her as not only 'Mother of God' but also 'Mother of the Poor'. Mary's song, the Magnificat (Luke 1.46–55), can thus be paralleled with Jesus' manifesto three chapters later (Luke 4.18–19); both proclaim God who blesses the poor and raises up the lowly, dealing harshly with the agents of oppression (Katoppo 1979, p. 23). In feminist liberation theology in Latin America, Mary was portrayed as a Latin mother, struggling with poverty and suffering the loss of her Son like the 'mothers of the disappeared' in the so-called 'dirty wars' of the 1970s (Arellano 1988, pp. 147–50). Protestants in Latin America also re-read the Bible with a hermeneutic of liberation that helped to free them from conservative readings (Tamez 1982; Chopp 1997, p. 419).

Feminist theologies have also emerged from the so-called 'Fourth World', minority ethnic groups in the West, especially in North America. Among the Hispanic community, expatriate Cuban Ada María Isasi-Díaz has developed *Mujerista* theology – a women's liberation theology from her context, drawing on Hispanic resources to encourage Latina women's self-esteem and moral agency (Isasi-Díaz 1996, p. 1). African American women rejected both the feminist theology of Ruether and others in the USA and also the black theology of James Cone and others, describing their approach instead as 'Womanist' (Townes 1993). Reflecting on the double experience of sexism and racism, the story of Hagar, the Black (Egyptian) wife who bore Abraham his son Ishmael and then was cast out in favour of Sarah and her son Isaac, and the experience and spirituality of Black Christian churches together formed the inspiration for the leading Womanist theologian Delores S. Williams' classic, *Sisters in the Wilderness* (1993).

This brief survey shows the variety of feminist responses to the differing conditions of women in different regions and of different ethnic groups (for a wide selection of readings, see Soskice and Lipton, 2003). However, within this variety several authors make a broad distinction between the feminist theology of North America and Europe and that of the Majority World, or between the feminism of the Third World, or colonized world, and the colonizers, or the West (Scott and Cavanaugh 2007; Kwok 2007; Muers 1997, p. 432). While there is a danger that this perceived division is simply a reflection of a Northern view of the rest of the world, which sees it as an undifferentiated bloc (cf. Graham 2007, p. 211; Kwok 2002, p. 25; Kang 2008, pp. 208–11), it is a view that also finds support among feminist theologians who see themselves as part of the Third World or colonized world, and who do not regard Northern feminist theology as addressing the issues affecting women's lives that are raised by this, or as using appropriate method for their situation (Kwok 2007). In part this distinction is due to a conscious reaction of feminist writers from the Majority World to the feminist theology of the North and West, but it is also a reflection of the different contexts in which women are doing theology. The difference in context can be described in two ways: first, the difference of socio-economic status between the global North and the global South; and second, the difference in cultural and religious background, which is most marked in Asian theologies – a difference between West and East.

In what follows we will discuss in two sections the differences between feminist theologies from the North and South, and from the West and East. These categories are not mutually exclusive because, as postcolonial theory shows, political and economic dominance was necessarily accompanied by a 'colonization of the mind' that was cultural and religious. However, they are useful here, as we will show. In order to do this we will narrow down the field to feminist theologians of Asia and will deal with only two aspects of Christian theology: Christology and pneumatology.

Feminist theologies from the South: Jesus who frees from oppression

From his wide knowledge of Third World theologies, John Parratt has observed that rather than being 'a revolutionary countermovement', feminist theology in the global South is 'concerned with women's role in the wholeness of a single humanity' (Parratt 1995, p. 51). There are a number of reasons for this. First, feminist theology in the global North emerged in a period and among a social class in which women had already achieved a large measure of autonomy and could earn their own living, live independently of male support, and without children if they so chose. In the South, however, women were more likely to be inextricably linked to men and to have dependants, and the behaviour of women is more tightly controlled. In such a context, antagonizing men has serious effects on women and children. The greater cohesion of Asian communities also militates against individualism and in favour of common good (Kang 2008, p. 209). Second, Northern women had already achieved a political voice while, as Kwok explains, in the South women were and are much more often marginal to national politics and women's movements operate more at a community level (Kwok 2007, p. 194). Furthermore, women who associated themselves with Western feminism were scorned and nationalistic discourse was turned against their aspirations. Women who campaigned for their rights were seen to be following a Western agenda and destabilizing traditionally family-orientated Asian societies (cf. Kwok 2002, p. 27). Third, in the global South, feminist theology in the North is seen to 'narrowly focus on gender inequality and on the freedom and liberation of women', whereas as Kwok Pui-lan explains, in the South, because of the history of colonization experienced by both women and men, 'feminist struggles are generally seen as part of the overall liberation of the whole people' (Kwok 2007, p. 195). In the South, feminist theology is not primarily a matter of women's personal and political freedom and self-defined identity, but is inseparable from the struggle for nationhood and the vision of a new, post-colonial society. In other words, feminist theology in the global South grew not within the discourse of women's rights but in the wider discourse of international development and human flourishing (Kwok 2007, p. 194; Kwok 2002, pp. 23–39). For this reason many Asian feminist theologians prefer to talk about 'Asian women's theology' (Kwok 2000, p. 9). In Asia, Katoppo argued that 'woman's liberation is also man's' (Katoppo 1979, pp. 9–24). She regarded women's liberation as the freedom of all from patriarchal society by the development of women's gifts – particularly through education, which is seen to bring benefits to men, children and the whole society. The 'Northern' feminist theologians of the 1970s and 1980s were most concerned not with social issues (which were being addressed by wider feminist movements) but with the Church, and how it could be re-formed in such a way that women could have freedom and be included within it (Ruether 2002, pp. 7–8; Graham 2007, p. 210). But in the Church, most Asian women faced greater obstacles to leadership than their white Northern counterparts. Therefore campaigns for education and the opportunity to exercise their gifts are more prominent in Asian feminism than calls for ordination.

Most feminist theology from Asia written for a Western audience begins by introducing the Asian context. Some writers major on the detrimental effects of capitalism or colonialism on women's situation (Gnanadason 1993; Kwok 2000, pp. 12–24). However, as Katoppo recognized, the societal structures against which feminists struggle in Asia, which they often label patriarchy, are due not only to external colonization but also have their roots in the religious cultures of the continent (Katoppo 1979, pp. 9–16; cf. Kwok 2000, pp. 47–50). Although it is generally unspoken, some form of *yin-yang* philosophy is often implied in the starting point for discussions of women's social status, for example in the title of a well-known introduction to Asian women's theology, *Struggle to be the Sun Again* (see Chung 1990, pp. 51–2). The concept of *yin-yang* is linked to Taoism, Confucianism and Buddhism, and therefore pervasive of East Asia, and the *yin-yang* symbol of a circle in two colours divided by a curved line with (or sometimes without) circles of the opposite colour in opposing halves is found widely in India as well. *Yin* and *yang* are the complementary forces that explain the whole of life. *Yin* is thought of as female and *yang* as male. As images of male and female they correspond closely to dualisms of masculine and feminine found in European societies; however, they are more far-reaching and probably more influential. They are used to explain all other polarities in the cosmos. *Yin*, female, includes the concepts of earth, dark, cold, moon, old, weak, passive, intuitive and absorbing; *yang*, male, includes their opposites of heaven, light, hot, sun, young, strong, active, rational and penetrating. Although *yin-yang* may be promoted as a means to social harmony, it is also used to sanction oppressive rule and male domination (see Park 1998, p. 156). Because *yang* appears higher than *yin*, it can be used to justify the higher social status of men, the authority of men over women, violence towards women and the separation of society into public and private, which prevents women's involvement in the wider society. *Yin-yang* analogies can be used to connect patriarchy with other oppressive systems in society, such as racism, classism, colonialism and cultural imperialism. Indeed, the connection between the oppression of women and the degradation of nature, which Northern feminists have worked hard to demonstrate (Ruether 1975, cf. Muers 1997, p. 437), is obvious in Asia. Asian feminist theologians commonly draw parallels between women's subjection to male domination and the colonization of their nations. Namsoon Kang, for example, sees Asian women's experience as of layers of colonization by the West, by Western feminists, by Asian males and by Asian religions (Kang 2008, pp. 217–20).

Asian feminist theology has proceeded largely by case studies of women's conditions and theological responses in different contexts. These have been gathered together in anthologies (for example, King 1994) and shaped into pan-Asian theologies in monographs and articles (Chung 1990; Kwok 2000; Orevillo-Montenegro 2006). They have been published in English and for an audience of educated Westerners for whom Asia is culturally uniform. This method is useful for political campaigning, and the pan-Asian gloss has a clear political purpose, but it also encourages generalization, homogenization, cultural essentialism and exclusion of those voices that do not fit the construction of Asian theology (Kang 2008, pp. 205–11). Feminist theologians have struggled to reconcile theologies that emerge from such diverse social contexts that they actually have little else in common except that they are by women (for example, Fabella 1988). There is some internal colonization going on as theologians of different nations present their own versions of Asian women's theology. More recently some Asian feminist theologians have called for greater engagement with feminist critical theory (Kang 2008, p. 207; Orevillo-Montenegro 2006, p. 200). From a theological point of view, much could also be gained from in-depth systematic reflection in different Asian contexts that could then be shared in a wider conversation (Kim 2007).

Nevertheless, it is possible to identify some themes that cut across Asian women's theologies articulated in English insofar as there is a shared Asian background. Considering Christology in the context of *yin-yang* thinking, Jesus Christ, who is both God and man, appears as the overcomer of all dualisms, uniting heaven and earth (Col. 1.20), body and soul (1 Thess. 5.23) and bringing about a reconciled society where there is no Jew nor Greek, slave nor free, male nor female (Gal. 3.28). He did this through his identification with humanity in his incarnation and passion. Although for some Western feminists Jesus' maleness is an insuperable obstacle and demands a feminist alternative to Christianity, most Asian feminist theologians seem to be able to go beyond Jesus' maleness to his humanity (Orevillo-Montenegro 2006, pp. 56–7) and see him as a fully liberated human being (Kwok 2000, pp. 82–6). Many of all the encounters of Jesus with women ring particularly true in Asian contexts. For example, in India the Samaritan woman at the well (John 4) is easily read as the meeting of a caste man with an outcaste or Dalit woman (Vandana 1989, p. 78); the healing of the woman with the issue of blood (Luke 8.43–8) shows how he overcame taboos about menstruation that are present in many Asian societies (Orevillo-Montenegro 2006, p. 70).

Orevillo-Montenegro pointedly remarks that it is the suffering Christ, rather than the 'white western European conqueror', who is the 'Jesus of Asian women' (Orevillo-Montenegro 2006, pp. 11, 200; Chung 1990, pp. 53–9). Jesus is 'lord' only in the sense that he is the liberator who frees 'from the false authority of the world over them and empowers them to claim true authority' (Chung 1990, pp. 57–8, 62–4). Jesus' lordship is 'the lordship of justice' (Park Soon Kyung quoted in Chung 1990, p. 59). Asian feminist theologians differ in their interpretation of the incarnation but the presence of Christ 'with us' is a recurrent theme (Chung 1990, pp. 59–61) and, especially in countries influenced by Buddhism, Jesus' suffering is a sign of the presence of a compassionate God (Kwok 2000, p. 81). Muriel Orevillo-Montenegro shows how in the Philippines women's experiences of suffering form the basis of feminist theology and are lived out in the processions commemorating the passion of Christ, and then vindicated in the resurrection (Orevillo-Montenegro 2006, pp. 125–39).

Having developed a picture of a fully human saviour, Asian theologians have then suggested feminine images of Jesus Christ to express the extent of that identification with women in struggle and pain. The image of Jesus as the compassionate mother who 'weeps with our pain' is found across Asia (Chung 1990, pp. 64–5; Orevillo-Montenegro 2006, pp. 104–7, 150–3; Kwok 2000, pp. 76–8; cf. Matt. 23.37; Luke 13.34; Matt. 14.34). Other feminine images focus on theology of salvation, on how Jesus Christ is liberating for women, the Woman Messiah (Orevillo-Montenegro 2006, pp. 107–11). In Korea, Chung Hyun Kyung and others have portrayed Jesus as a female shaman, solving problems and bringing about reconciliation in the spirit world (Chung 1990, p. 66). Indian theologians – Elizabeth Joy, Aruna Gnanadason and Gabriele Dietrich – have connected Jesus' shedding of blood with the menstrual blood of women that brings life (Chung 1990, pp. 66–71; Orevillo-Montenegro 2006, pp. 70–5). Across Asia, supported by biblical images of God as feminine (see Johnson 1992, pp. 76–103), various goddess traditions are used to describe Jesus Christ: the earth-mothers of the different tribes in the Philippines (Orevillo-Montenegro 2006, pp. 153–6); the popular Chinese Buddhist goddess of compassion, Kwan-In (Chung 1991), and the various forms taken by feminine power *Shakti* in Hinduism – Shiva, Saraswati, Durga or Kali (Gnanadason 1994; Vandana 1995; Katoppo 1979, pp. 72–3; Orevillo-Montenegro 2006, pp. 197–8). The biblical feminine motifs of the *Shekinah* glory of God and Sophia, holy wisdom, have been combined with these Asian ones of epiphanies and sages to describe Christ the Glory and the Wisdom of God (Orevillo-Montenegro 2006, pp. 76–82; 111; 177–83). In the Bible the glory and wisdom of God are evidenced in deeds of liberation, empowerment and life-giving (Orevillo-Montenegro 2006, p. 181; see Matt. 11.2–6; John 14.11; Luke 7.22).

Feminist theologies from the East: the life-giving Spirit

As well as the socio-economic and political contexts in which women find themselves, which may be reinforced by cultural traditions such as *yin-yang*, feminist theologians also find cultural resources on which to draw constructively. Goddess traditions (above) are one such. Furthermore, as Kwok Pui-lan explains:

> When Asian feminists talk about God, they do not begin with the abstract discussion of the doctrine of the Trinity, the debate on the existence

of God, or the affirmation of God as omnipotent . . . Rather they focus on God as the source of life and the creative, sustaining power of the universe. (Kwok 2000, p. 66)

Apart from the Semitic religions, Asian religions are 'cosmic in that they revere gods and goddesses, nature spirits, cosmic deities that dwell in the universe, and the spirits of the ancestors', although the major ones (especially Hinduism, Buddhism and Confucianism) also have metacosmic, or philosophical, dimensions (Orevillo-Montenegro 2006, p. 9). Since women are generally excluded from religious education, they practise cosmic religion: local religions and popular forms of the major religions. They inhabit the plural and unpredictable world of many spirits that are encountered in the natural world and human behaviour. For them God is Spirit, a greater power beyond all the others who gives life, gifts and power. In Christian theology the doctrine of the Holy Spirit (pneumatology) comes closest to this. To quote Chung Hyun Kyung: 'What matters [to Asian women] is not doctrinal orthodoxy . . . not Jesus, Sakyamumi, Mohammed, Confucius, Kwan In, or Ina, but rather the life force which empowers them to claim their humanity' (Chung 1990, p. 113). Furthermore, because of the connection between woman and earth, the Spirit of Life is construed as feminine and so related to the power of women.

Asian theologies, especially women's theology, are therefore a stimulus and resource for development of pneumatology – a much-neglected aspect of theology in the West (Kim 2007, p. 2). Asian feminists also have seized on the feminine pronouns used of the Spirit in the Old Testament and the feminine images with which the Spirit is associated, and led the development of feminist pneumatology (Vandana 1989; cf. Johnson 1992). In India and Indo-China, the feminine life-force is often referred to as *Shakti*. Vandana, formerly Provincial (leader) of the Society of the Sacred Heart (Roman Catholic) in India, has powerfully explored theology of the Holy Spirit in dialogue with Hindu images of *Shakti* to produce a uniquely Indian theology, which is also a statement of the power of the feminine (see Kim 2007, pp. 80–7). In *Waters of Fire* (1989), a commentary on John's Gospel, she traces the theme of water – a symbol of the Spirit (John 7.37–39) – throughout the Gospel: in the baptism narrative (John 1.31–33), at Cana in Galilee (John 2.1–11) and so on. For her, the image of water evokes a spirituality that is 'flowing', 'flexible', 'fiery' and above all 'feminine' (quoted in Kim 2007, p. 81). In *Shabda Shakti Sangam* (1995), she provocatively describes Christianity as a religion of the Spirit, emphasizing thereby its feminine aspects. Using the discourse of spirituality rather than religion, she demonstrates that she has brought together a wide coalition of Christians and Hindus in order to bring peace between religions. Although Vandana's allegiance is to Jesus Christ as the Supreme Guru (Vandana 1987), in her work Jesus Christ appears primarily as the source of the Spirit, which is beyond all the names and forms of different religions and is mediated through many different channels. In this way Vandana also gives priority to the feminine and to the womb from which all life comes, which she often refers to – combining Hindu and Catholic mysticism – as 'the cave of the heart'. Using the analogy of the River Ganges, source of her life and Mother of India, Vandana regards her theological task as travelling back upstream from the delta along the distributary that is the Christian religion, and then merging with all the other religious rivers to reach the common Source, Womb and Life of them all (Vandana 1995).

From East Asia, Chung Hyun Kyung's approach to theology is also essentially pneumatological, although whereas Vandana's thought tends to monism, Chung's is rather dualistic. Chung's work is set against the background of Korean Shamanism, which is despised in Korea as women's religion. She represents the struggle for women's liberation and empowerment as a cosmic struggle in which the Holy Spirit, 'the Spirit of our brother Jesus', mingles with the many spirits of nature and ancestors, and struggles to overcome the evil spirits of death and destruction (Chung 1991, p. 39). The pneumatological approach allows Asian women's theology to develop in a way that circumvents the categories and prerequisites of male-dominated traditional theology. Furthermore, it enables Asian women's theology to reach across religious boundaries through a common experience of life that is shared with other women. Christian women's experience differs from that of women of other faiths in that the example of Jesus Christ defines the characteristics of the Spirit and the vision of life, but in many ways it is continuous with the hopes and spirit of the whole of humanity. Theologically, it is understood that it is through, or because of, the sacrifice of Christ that the Spirit's power is channelled to impact the lives of women, men, families, the wider society and the whole creation (cf. Vandana 1989, pp. 76–92).

From a Southern feminist perspective, therefore, the liberation of women to fulfil their life-giving role is prior and integral to all other liberation. Healing gender relations is a crucial and inseparable part of achieving the wider reconciliation needed to restore the harmony God intends for creation, and any model of society that does not address the oppression of women and violence towards them is unacceptable and doomed to failure (cf. Katoppo 1979, p. 79).

Tackling gender issues interculturally

Feminist theology is multicultural in that it is found in diverse cultural forms, and also intercultural because of the way in which the experiences of women are inextricably bound up with one another across cultures – through patriarchy and the histories of slavery, colonialism and genocide (Kwok 2002, p. 28). Kwok argues for a relativizing of theological systems on grounds of cultural theory so that 'No theological system can claim to be universally valid because it is closer to the origin' (Kwok 2000, p. 35). Chronologically, the first women to call themselves 'feminist theologians' and construct 'feminist theologies' in a systematic way were Roman Catholics in the 1960s USA. However, as Kwok insists, this does not mean that they should be regarded as 'fore-mothers' on whose work everyone else builds. Kwok goes on to undermine the privileged place of North Atlantic feminism by pointing to the racist discourse of the early feminist movements, to their indebtedness to struggles for civil rights and nationhood, and to a tendency to universalize European women's experience in a colonialist way (Kwok 2002, pp. 24–8). Although such criticism is valid and necessary, it is not necessary for Asian theologians to criticize Northern and Western feminist theology in order to prove the worth of their own approach since it is well recognized today. In particular, Asian women theologians have challenged Western feminists to widen their theological concern to see issues of women's liberation as symptomatic of wider disharmony in gender relations that is inextricably linked to other problems of society and suffering in the universe. They suggest that the solution is not to overthrow tradition but to work with it and through it to bring about a transformation of attitudes and reconciliation between the genders.

Asian, African, European, Latin and North American and other different cultural forms of feminist theology enrich one another. Indeed, 'One of the strengths of feminist theology has been the promotion of global dialogues, on questions of global concern, among theologians from very different social and cultural contexts' (Muers 1997, p. 432). Many of the texts on feminist theology emanating from the global North referred to in this chapter reveal a very high level of South–North dialogue, which marks out feminist theology among theological disciplines in the North as being particularly intercultural.

Conclusion

Intercultural theology requires mutual respect between different theological communities. When this is achieved, doing theology interculturally has many advantages, as feminist theology demonstrates. First, it widens the possibilities for talking about God, stimulating new thought and action, offering new resources for theologizing. Second, theologizing interculturally casts new light on biblical material and reveals new dimensions of the meaning of key biblical and theological concepts such as God, spirit, incarnation and so on. Third, doing theology interculturally may shift theological interest to new sub-disciplines, as for example in the case of Asian interest in pneumatology. It may also suggest new theological frameworks and constructions as Christian theology encounters other religions and cultures. Fourth, it shows up what is culturally conditioned in theology against what may be considered universal. In particular it reveals the extent to which what is regarded as orthodoxy – such as the secondary place given to women – may not in fact reflect the biblical witness or the practice of the early Church but may rather be the result of European and other cultural conditioning. Fifth, in the case of feminist theology in the global North, we have seen how perspectives from the South have challenged its initial blindness to the socio-economic realities of most of the world. The Northern emphasis on Church politics, for example, is secondary in the Majority World to basic issues of women's health and literacy. And finally, the West–East dialogue highlights the importance of sensitivity to culture in theologizing. Globalizing forces are met with national and ethnic ones so that the cultural norms that define ethical and social questions in Europe and North America do not necessarily apply in other societies – or in minority ethnic groups in Western countries. Women theologians in Asia, Africa and Latin America have rightly insisted on their own agendas for theologizing, while also engaging in global conversation.

6

When Buddhist Women Go to Church: Reflections on the Nature of Ethical Mission

LOUISE NELSTROP

Introduction

This chapter sets out to explore the nature of ethical mission, a concern that has received fresh impetus from phenomenological discussions of alterity, which emphasize the need to respect otherness and recognize the human tendency to reduce other things and people to less than they are. In particular, this chapter considers Cosimo Zene's understanding of 'dialogue', in relation to which he posits that the beliefs and culture of others must always be prioritized over those of the missionary or anthropologist (Zene 2002). While Zene seems willing to accept that some social challenges can be ethical, he is far less certain about religious ones. This chapter aims to challenge this bias within Zene's thought. As well as offering some theoretical objections to Zene's understanding of ethical mission, it critiques Zene's approach on the basis of empirical data gathered through fieldwork. The chapter aims to show the value of 'practical theology' gained through anthropological study as a way of nuancing our understanding of mission and the contemporary theories that surround it.

The fieldwork was carried out with slum-dwelling women in Bangkok. These women articulated benefits from their involvement with PIME's (*Pontifical Institutum pro Missionibus Exteris*)[1] missionary activities of a psychological/spiritual nature, expressed in terms of Thai psychological notions of well-being. PIME's approach to mission, however, differs significantly from that advocated by Zene, falling into a category that he deems less than ethical. The women's responses form a practical critique

---

[1] The Pontifical Institute for Foreign Missionaries.

of Zene's method of privileging alterity in an absolute sense, raising questions about whether his theory itself constitutes either a valid or truly ethical approach to mission.

Mission and alterity

The field of missiology has witnessed a growing awareness of the need for contextualization. The early twentieth century saw the issue move to the heart of missiological strategies.[2] Recent phenomenological thinking has intensified this impetus, bringing recognition that traditional notions of contextualization, such as 'inculturation', are perhaps an insufficient response to otherness. Missiologists within the Protestant traditions, such as Bevans and Schroeder, argue that a more holistic worldview must now underpin mission, positing that God is already at work within all cultures (Bevans and Shroeder 2004, especially p. 396).[3]

They hold that missionaries should therefore see themselves as assistants in God's work rather than as those who introduce Christ to a culture where he was hitherto absent. Within the Roman Catholic tradition, inspired by what he sees as the 'crisis' within both anthropology and missiology brought about by phenomenological discussions of alterity, Cosimo Zene offers a re-evaluation of the notion of 'dialogue' that underpins Vatican II. Drawing on Hans-Georg Gadamar and Emmanuel Lévinas, both philosophers within the phenomenological tradition, Zene offers an interpretation of Vatican II that he believes allows it to be understood as an extension of phenomenological and postmodern concerns with otherness. He uses this as a platform for a definition of 'ethical mission' – one that preserves the alterity of the other and in particular empowers those on the margins of society. As the missionary activities that are considered here are those of a Roman Catholic missionary society, I will reflect particularly on Zene's model. The discussion of this paper, however, has wider implications for current considerations of mission and contextualization in terms of what it means to conduct 'ethical mission'.

---

2 For an early discussion, see Kraemer 1938, especially p. 408. For more recent considerations, see Lee 2008, pp. 148–56. For various discussions of contextualization in relation to Islam, see http://www.indigitech.net/index.php?option=com_content&task=view&id=27&Itemid=45.

3 Bevans and Shroeder are indebted to earlier missiologists like Lesslie Newbigin and David Bosch. See, for example, Bosch 1995 and Newbigin 1963.

Cosimo Zene's Notion of 'Dialogue'

Concerned to address the issues of alterity raised by postmodern reassessments of missiology, Cosimo Zene turns to Vatican II to reflect on the nature of Church that it professes. It is clear from Vatican II documents, such as *Ad Gentes*, that the Roman Catholic Church sees itself as fundamentally missional:

> The pilgrim Church is missionary by her very nature, since it is from the mission of the Son and the mission of the Holy Spirit that she draws her origin, in accordance with the decree of God the Father.[4]

Yet Zene is keen to stress that this does not mean that Vatican II paints a picture of modern Roman Catholic missiology that is a simplistic theology of Christianization. Within the various Vatican II encyclicals and documents, Zene finds much of promise for those seeking to subscribe to a vision of mission that makes room for other cultures and beliefs. He notes that the encyclical *Redemptoris Missio* and instructions from the Pontifical Council for Interreligious Dialogue, such as *Dialogue and Proclamation*, contain multiple definitions of 'conversion', which suggests a complex account of what evangelization means. These are further complicated by the establishment of the Pontifical Council for Interreligious Dialogue itself (established immediately after Vatican II), which holds that dialogue and the proclamation of the gospel are 'interrelated components' (Zene 2002, p. 9).

Zene draws particular attention to the discussions of 'dialogue' that he finds in Vatican II declarations such as *Nostra Aetate*, which expressly states that Roman Catholics are called into 'dialogue' with other religions, whose beliefs are to be respected, along with many of the socio-cultural values they underpin:

> The Church, therefore, urges her sons to enter with prudence and charity into discussion and collaboration with members of other religions. Let Christians, while witnessing to their own faith and way of life, acknowledge, preserve and encourage the spiritual and moral truths found among non-Christians, also their social life and culture.[5]

---

4 Vatican II decree *Ad Gentes Divinitus* (1965) referring to the dogmatic constitution on the Church, *Lumen Gentium* (1964), in Flannery 1996.

5 Vatican II declaration on the relation of the Church to non-Christian religions, *Nostra Aetate* (1965), in Flannery 1996, p. 739.

He notes that this stress on 'dialogue' is coupled with an emerging sense of the need for what is termed 'inculturation' (see Shorter 1994, pp. 3–16, especially p. 10 n. 12). Traditionally, inculturation has been understood as a means of contextualizing the message of the gospel while altering the cultural dynamic so that it comes to reflect the principle of the gospel. As Aylward Shorter explains, inculturation is:

> The incarnation of Christian life and of the Christian message in a particular cultural context, in such a way that this experience not only finds expression through elements proper to the culture in question (this alone would be no more than a superficial adaptation) but becomes a principle that animates, directs and unifies the culture, transforming it and remaking it so as to bring about a 'new creation'. (citing Fr Pedro Arrup in Shorter 1994, p. 11)

However, Zene suggests that the notion of 'dialogue' in Vatican II can be understood from a more postmodern perspective than this – one which better counters the 'crisis' that he sees within missiology and anthropology that has been brought about by 'a Western metaphysics which represents the epitome of the absorption of the Other by the Same' (Zene 2002, p. 419).

Zene turns to Simon Critchley, who makes use of the philosophy of Emmanuel Lévinas in an attempt to alter the power dynamics within contemporary understanding of history (Critchley 1999). Critchley sets out to write an 'ethical history' in which the victims are given voice (see Zene 2002, p. 420). Zene attempts to replicate this approach in missiology, also drawing on Lévinas, to create an 'ethical mission' that constitutes practice in which 'victims' (by which he means the poor and disempowered) do not have their 'difference' nullified. Key to this, for Zene, is an understanding of 'dialogue' with Levinasian roots:

> It is not by advocating the end of mission activity or the end of anthropology that the Western Self will cease exercising its power over the Other. On the contrary, the alternative to the recurrent mood of negativity is to promote a different approach to both mission and anthropology. Even the solution of renouncing 'the talismanic properties of Otherness', is only partial and in need of a more radical discourse and for this reason I have suggested following a Levinasian reading of alterity whereby the Same becomes a responsible and ethical self subjected to the Other. (Zene 2002, p. 419)

As the above quotation suggests, Zene's understanding of dialogue is one in which both missionaries and anthropologists must come to other cultures with a sense of responsibility that allows them to subject themselves to the other. Within his philosophical discussions, Lévinas stresses the need to see each individual as a face, as someone who speaks, before whom we assume a sense of guilt. We are forced by the face of this other to empty ourselves out in an attempt to grasp fully the other's alterity. Zene draws particular attention to Lévinas's metaphor of substitution, in which the self realizes that it must always come ready to be taught rather than to teach (see Lévinas 1981). Thus Zene quotes Gadamer and recommends the merging of horizons to which Gadamar assents:

> To reach an understanding in a dialogue is not merely a matter of putting oneself forward and successfully asserting one's own point of view, but being transformed into a communion in which we do not remain what we were. (Gadamer 2004, p. 341)

Zene posits that true Roman Catholic dialogue must be defined by such an understanding of alterity, which always approaches other human beings in a manner that does not reduce them to something other than they are.

To get a better sense of what this means in practice, Zene discusses five types of mission initiative, with reference to previous missionary activities among a Dalit population, 'the Rishi', in Bangladesh, with whom Zene has had particular contact.[6]

> 1) Some want as many Rishi as possible to be converted as soon as possible; 2) For others, the conversion, Christian formation and social uplift of the Rishi must proceed at the same pace; 3) others again, who represent a majority of the missionaries committed to the Rishi, would postpone conversion for an indeterminate period of time, concentrating first on the human and social uplift of the group (possibly integrated with the work of other missionaries); 4) in 1991, one missionary started to re-visit the old Rishi villages contacted in the past by the missionaries, with the purpose of establishing a relationship not based on Rishi material gain; 5) a minority of missionaries do not consider it necessary (and even feel it may be detrimental) for the Rishi to convert to Christianity since it would alienate them from their group, creating a 'caste within a caste', as well as from their fellow countrymen, since

---

6 Dalits have formerly been referred to as 'untouchables'.

once converted they belong to a Church which tends to consider itself, practically, if not ideologically, as foreign. (Zene 2002, p. 19)

In this respect, while Zene praises the Xavians for their 'witness as mere presence' approach to mission, he seems highly distrustful of the motivations behind their baptism of ten catechumens in 2000 (Zene 2002, p. 380.) For Zene, this constitutes a 'monologue of thinking' (Gadamer 2004, p. 363) rather than the dialogical approach to mission that he derives from Lévinas. It is only the fifth type of missionary, who see conversion as unnecessary (and possibly harmful), that practise 'dialogue' as Zene defines it, since such mission in no way attempts to absorb the host culture into the foreign ideas of Christianity, thereby 'creating a "caste within a caste"'.

Theoretical objections to Zene's approach

Paul Tremlett argues that Zene's approach is, however, objectionable on two counts. From a missiological perspective, Tremlett maintains that it is likely to lead to a form of Christianity that is so synchronized with and dominated by the receiving culture as to be unrecognizable to Christian practitioners (Tremlett 2006, pp. 481–3). On these grounds he questions whether it constitutes a valid missiological strategy. However, more troubling to Tremlett is that despite Zene's claims to overcome the problem through his adoption of a Levinasian phenomenological model, Zene's model still seems to fall foul of Habermas' criticisms of Gadamer – namely that it gives no recourse to critical reflection and so is actually itself open to accusations of being unethical.

Zene's reliance on Lévinas' metaphor of substitution, in which one is encouraged to empty oneself out in one's entirety in order to understand the other, seems to lie at the heart of this problem. Not only is Gadamer's notion of epitome or bracketing generally held to be impracticable, Tremlett argues that the merging of horizons that underpins it, and to which Zene for the most part appears to subscribe, can lead to unethical practice. Tremlett stresses that both missionaries and anthropologists are often faced with issues of sanitary and medical ignorance that he believes it is unethical to ignore (Tremlett 2007). In such cases Tremlett does not believe that the views of the receiving culture should necessarily be privileged over those of the anthropologist or missionary.

Yet while opposed to religious conversion, Zene seems somewhat conflicted regarding this latter point. He warns against being 'mesmerized by the talismanic properties of Otherness' (Zene 2002, p. 419) and praises one Father Antonio Marietti, who although immersing himself in the culture, retained a distance that allowed him to pass judgements on aspects of the culture that were undesirable, in particular the caste system. As Zene writes:

> The secret to Marietti's success lay, however, in his early decision to adopt 'a simple Indian mode of living', which permitted him to be close to his people and to become 'native' . . . To become 'native' for Marietti did not, however, imply accepting caste distinctions among the Christians as proposed by other missionaries, for he had a great affection for the Rishi. As a consequence, the Rishi recognized him as 'the Father'. (Zene 2002, p. 111)

Here it appears to be Fr Antonio Marietti's very rejection of an integral aspect of culture, which he found unacceptable from a Christian perspective, that caused him to be held in high esteem by those to whom he ministered. On the one hand Zene seems willing to accept that such challenges to social structures can be ethical, yet on the other he paints changes of a religious nature as non-beneficial and unethical. Such inconsistency naturally raises questions about Zene's view of religion and spirituality. The bias that it betrays against religion and spirituality is one that is challenged by the fieldwork that I carried out in Thailand into the work of PIME.

The *Pontificium Institutum pro Missionibus Exteris* (PIME) in Bangkok

PIME is a Roman Catholic society of secular priests and lay people who have dedicated their lives to missionary activities.[7] They have been working in Thailand since 1972, and at the time of the study had 12 priests serving around the country and one brother operating a rehabilitation centre for disabled children and young adults in Phrae, Northern Thailand.[8] The activities of PIME in Thailand are focused in two main areas:

---

7 PIME was officially recognized as a missionary organization in 1926, after the merging of two groups established independently in Milan and Rome in the late nineteenth century (see http://www.pimeusa.org/).

8 Interview with head of PIME in the region. This number differed from the information on the official website, which stated that there are 14 PIME priests operating in Thailand at the time. Although an independent missionary organization, as a Roman Catholic society, PIME priests are subject to the local area bishop.

work among hill-tribe peoples in the North of Thailand, and ministries in and around various Bangkok slums. Both of these foci were established through the activities of one priest, Father Adriano, originally sent to Thailand some 27 years previously to explore the possibilities of inter-religious dialogue after Vatican II. As such this makes the work of PIME a particularly apt model for reflecting on Zene's interpretation of mission as advocated by Vatican II. The data presented here is part of an empiri-cal study of PIME's missionary work in two Bangkok slums, Tuk Daeng and Wat Chonglomb.

The fieldwork was carried out over a relatively short period – seven weeks between September and November 2006. However, I was already familiar with some of the PIME priests and their work with orphan slum children from volunteer work at their orphanage in Pakkred in 2005.[9] Thus after an initial week of orientation, visiting various PIME proj-ects across Thailand and interviewing the head of PIME in the region, I began my observation work – living in two different slum communi-ties, Wat Chonglom and Tuk Daeng, with the women who form the main focus of this study. I also spent time living in the orphanage in Pakkred.

During the study I conducted 18 in-depth semi-structured interviews with women associated with PIME, most of whom had HIV.[10] Many of the women were engaged in various kinds of employment by PIME – helping raise children in the slums or caring for people who had various diseases, including AIDS. Others had or were being assisted by PIME in terms of health or finance. Most of the women had, at some point, at-tended catechism classes led by PIME in Pakkred, and many attended small informal Roman Catholic masses held in the various slum commu-nities, a number of which I also attended. The purpose of the interviews was to gain a sense of the role that the Christian religion played in the lives of these women, especially as most of them professed to be Bud-dhist. The interviews attempted to tease out whether the spiritual aspect of PIME's work could be differentiated from the obvious economic and social advantages of being associated with PIME.

For the most part, a hermeneutic phenomenological methodology was employed. This was supplemented by a rigorous thematic analysis of the

---

9 I was resident in Thailand in 2005, working as a lecturer in the Department of Religious Studies at Mahidol University, Bangkok.

10 All interviews were conducted in Thai, except in one instance where the participant chose to speak in English. All interviews were taped and sections tran-scribed by a native Thai speaker. I would like to thank Yuttaphum Sabthangsam and Robin Jingit for their assistance with the transcription and translation.

interviews following Burnard 1991 (pp. 461–6). Table 1 illustrates the three key themes and related subthemes derived from this analysis, all of which point to a complex interplay between social, economic and religious concerns in the lives of these women.

High-order themes	Low-order themes
I Faith, Religion and Culture	i Culture vs Shock ii Buddhism vs Christianity iii Money vs Belief
II New Life	i Work ii Health iii *Jai yen/sabaay jai*
III Expectations	i The Good Christian Worker ii Rivalry

Table: Themes arising from data analysis

Why Buddhist women attended church

Contextualization

The PIME priests working in Thailand stated that they fundamentally viewed mission as an attempt 'to show the face of God' to others. This idea encapsulated an understanding of the gospel as a message of liberation and empowerment, echoing Luke's Gospel, in which Jesus reads a passage from Isaiah 61.1–2 with the implication he came to 'preach good news to the poor . . . proclaim freedom for the prisoners . . . recovery of sight for the blind [and] to release the oppressed' (Luke 4.18, NIV). Knowing that this inevitably entailed working with those on the margins of society, the priests were clear that their aim was holistic personal liberation, not governed by any ulterior desires to see conversions. As one priest commented:

> The pope told that you cannot use the needy people just to make them Christian. Your love has to be pure, *boorisoot* pure, I mean, and very open, just because you need to show the face of God. If they decide to convert, not because you push them, no no. If they decide to convert, it's because the grace of God works in them.

The priests made it clear that had their motives been otherwise, the Thai people with whom PIME worked would not have wanted to be associated with them.

The women interviewed for this study certainly felt that PIME made every effort to be culturally sensitive. They praised Father Adriano, for example, for his excellent command of Thai, and the polite manner in which he addressed them. They complimented him by describing him as Thai. Some of the women also described him teaching them a *vipassana* meditation technique (although they did not identify it as such or as Buddhist) as a way of helping them to control their emotions. As one woman explained:

> The Father came to teach [breathing meditation], loving as we breath. Breath in – love. Breath in – anytime you think of it – love. I was, as they say 'hate is stupid, anger is madness!'.[11] As I got to know prayer and meditation, listening to lessons on prayer, it taught me about something they call 'lightening a heavy load!'[12] meaning taking my hot temper from 100% down to 10%.

The priests described other instances relating to their work among hill-tribe groups where it was clear that they placed great value on traditional culture. One priest reported how he had encouraged many of the traditional festivals and sacrifices among converts, even blessing dead chickens that were brought to church.

Invading the space of the other

This said the priests were unashamed to challenge the various Thai cultures in which they worked. They stressed that where culture is contrary to the underlying message of the Christian gospel, it is only right that it should be challenged. As one priest stated:

> Sometimes faith can show you what is going wrong in your culture – this is what I believe. Faith is very important because receiving faith, something immediately is going to be changed in your life and in your culture. So there are many things wrong in this culture and there are many things wrong in my culture . . . in front of Jesus, the gospel, you always find that there are many things you must change.

---

11 A Thai Buddhist expression meaning that hate makes you like a stupid person, anger makes you like a crazy person.

12 Meaning that big problems become small problems.

In their work in the North, the Priests related particular instances where they felt it necessary to challenge culture. One priest recounted how the Akha people have a tradition of killing twins at birth because it is thought to bring great impurity and danger to the family and village as a whole. The priests stressed that they had supported a couple who, as tradition dictates, were exiled from their village after deciding to keep their twins.[13] They also suggested taking a baby to hospital that was black and blue with bruises, having been beaten with sticks in an attempt to remove the demons that were thought to be causing its sickness. In terms of their work in Bangkok, the women interviewed for this study talked about three main ways in which they felt that PIME challenges their culture: PIME's responses to 1) hierarchy, 2) Thai 'gossip culture' and 3) racism.

The PIME priests were said to be no respecters of hierarchy, a central concept in Thai society. The women expressed amazement that they could have such direct contact with priests, suggesting it would be harder to have close contact with a Buddhist Abbot. Christianity was described as shocking in this respect – although given the low status of these women they did not consider this disruption of their religious expectations to be negative. A particularly touching story was recounted by an elderly woman in her sixties who had converted. She described a scene in which a priest had enacted Jesus washing the 12 disciples' feet (although she did not identify it as such). It was an image that had remained with her for over ten years. She had been amazed to see an important figure acting like this towards children:

> The Father came to the [the church at] Rama the 6th [bridge] and washed the 12 disciples, feet. Oh! It was so overwhelming! Oh! Thai people don't have this kind of tradition, except that children have to wash the feet of their elders. The adult washed the children's feet, wiped them dry and kissed the 12 children. And I said to myself, What? I've

---

13 Deborah E. Tooker notes that many expensive sacrifices have to be made after the birth of twins, and that some Akha, who cannot afford to make them, decide to 'convert' to Christianity (Tooker 1992, pp. 799–819). It is not clear what the case was in the situation discussed by the priests. What was clear was that the priests in no sense supported this practice, commenting that their challenge to certain aspects of Akha traditional belief and practice had brought them into conflict with NGOs who seek Akha preservation, a fact that seemed to be confirmed in conversations at the inauguration of a new building that I attended in the North, where both PIME priests and representatives of such an organization were present – although neither group supported the practice of killing twins.

never felt so strange or seen anything like this. I was a Buddhist then and I was more than 50. And I thought, What! How come the Father can do this? The foreigner is good.

Such actions of inversion were things that the women found very difficult to understand. They likewise struggled with the Christian conception of forgiveness, even after years of catechumenate. In this respect the women acknowledged that PIME challenges what they described as the Thai 'gossip culture', in which just one mistake can cost you your reputation. The priests were said to represent the opposite – always (the woman suggested perhaps too often) ready to give someone another chance. Some of the confusion expressed here can possibly be accounted for by the perceived disadvantage that such forgiveness might have. They expressed disbelief that on being repeatedly told about the misdemeanours of certain workers, the priests ignored this 'gossip' rather than giving the job to the hopeful informant. Nonetheless, on the whole this challenge was also viewed as positive.

Less positive were their feelings about PIME's employment in Bangkok of people from minority ethnic groups (often from the North of Thailand). Many resented this (and the resentment was felt by those workers from hill-tribe communities that I interviewed). Not only are these people out-siders in terms of the slum community, but more importantly from hill-tribe communities and thus considered second-class citizens. The women accused many, with a few notable exceptions, of working for PIME solely for fiscal reasons, and without (Christian) compassion.[14] Those with HIV suggested that many of these workers lacked education about HIV and AIDS, which made them unable to carry out their jobs for fear of con-tracting the disease. One woman commented that the priest in charge didn't really know what these workers were like. She stressed that her motive in telling me this was to protect the priest's reputation:

So, Father says, Thai people, Thai people aren't open-minded. And they are prejudiced against hill-tribe people. But when it comes to this point, I don't have this problem. I work right here, so I know . . . Be-cause Father says that hill-tribe people don't lie, but Thais are great liars. But maybe the Father doesn't really know that when they leave the mountain they change a lot.

This woman had had her employment with PIME discontinued on the grounds of unsuitability. Her resentment is therefore understandable.

---

14 *gamlang jai*, which translates literally as 'encouragement'.

Yet other women also expressed similar sentiments. Unlike PIME's challenge to hierarchy and gossip, which had potential benefits for the women in terms of elevated status and job security, PIME's challenge to racial prejudice meant that outsiders gained jobs that the women would like to have had or to have kept within the community. This, more than the fact that PIME's approach to mission challenged aspects of Thai culture or introduced Christianity into their lives, seemed to be what they found most unpalatable. Yet at the same time the women stressed that by challenging them in this way, PIME had made them more open-minded, *birtjai*, which they begrudgingly acknowledged as a good thing.

New Life

Despite such reservations, however, the overall effect of PIME's work was considered highly positive, resulting in what the women called 'New Life'. The women talked about this idea in relation to three types of change that had occurred through their involvement with PIME: 1) new work opportunities, and changes relating to both 2) health and 3) emotions and belief.

Many of the women now worked for PIME in some capacity. This work obviously brought added income and, as such, had changed their lives (in this connection several women drew my attention to pieces of furniture in their homes). Even those who did not work directly for PIME had been assisted in finding a legal trade through which to sustain themselves and their children – for example, some now painted batik, others made the paper flowers that are burnt at Buddhist funerals. Such changes in employment brought a renewed sense of self-esteem. One woman spoke of the new sense of dignity that involvement with PIME had given her. Like many of the women, she recounted how she had ended up sleeping on a footbridge with her children after her husband deserted her. She spoke of the intense pain she had experienced when her marriage had broken down, and how her relations had found her deranged and wandering the streets. Like her, many of the women talked of abusing drugs and alcohol. Even those with more stable marriages described previously having severe alcohol or drug-related problems, which had left them despairing of their lives. One elderly woman recounted:

I was drinking alcohol, and I wanted to throw myself off a bridge and commit suicide. I often had thoughts like this. But I went to stay with the Father – I studied catechism.

However, a combination of being given responsibility and studying the catechism had brought about dramatic changes.

The women recounted many moving personal stories about the ways in which the work of PIME had resulted in positive life changes. One woman was asked to be the cook in a slum orphanage, despite being an alcoholic. She refused on numerous occasions, suggesting the idea was ridiculous. However, she found herself helping out when the housemother fell sick. Feeling unable to be drunk around the little children, she slowly realized that when she was helping these children (and not intoxicated), she was happy. Although having had more than eight abortions and feeling that she had been a very bad mother to her own children (both she and her husband were in and out of jail and always drunk), the trust placed in her by PIME turned her life around. She gave up alcohol and amphetamines and has, for the last ten years, raised children for PIME – with her husband now working as the orphanage handyman.

Another woman spoke of initially being very suspicious of PIME. Abandoned by her husband, she had feared that the priests wanted to take her children away. However, after months of refusing work, she and her whole family moved into the orphan house, where she became a housemother. She spoke about how, despite having HIV, she had now gained a new sense of self-worth – one that meant that when her husband asked to try again, after years of being with another woman, she was able to decline because she now had a 'new life', despite the fact that his leaving had broken her.

Most of the women clearly stated that the benefits derived from involvement with PIME were not only fiscal but also emotional/spiritual. Some of these benefits had been gained directly from studying the catechism, where in catechism classes they had been taught about love – of God and family (and also a kind of *vipassana* meditation technique). In one particular moving account, a woman employed to care for people with HIV talked about how this led her to the realization that she still struggles with the lack of love she encountered as a child, which makes her crave love despite being married and a mother of two children:

> And the Father asked what is your objective in coming and what do you need. Most people, lots of people would say, 'Well Father, I need money, I need that, I need this.' As for me I answered that I didn't need anything. But what I needed was love . . . I need, I need love, and if you ask me why I need love, I need love from the Father because if I go back to my childhood, in that time when I was little, I should have played like a child. But in that time I had to do every kind of work and even

though I was a child I had to battle with myself to be mature in everything, because my mum was always sick. I had to battle in everything,
like my body was a child's, but my mind was an adult's. And when we
come back to the present, my body is old but my mind is like a child's,
and I need love. Even if I am with my children, it's like this. I flashback
and think about myself. I want to look for love any way I can. But if
you ask yourself, it's hard to get.

Although her claims to need nothing but love are perhaps somewhat
exaggerated, it is clear that through attending catechism classes she
had come to realize that many of her own negative actions, which had
caused numerous marital problems, stemmed from her constantly crav-
ing love.

The women described the overall effect of catechism as a greater
awareness of their emotional states. The women realized that they were
often emotionally out of control. Through these classes, however, they
reported almost without exception having become calmer and more able
to engage in normal relationships. Most of the women talked about how
they had moved from having a highly volatile personality to being *jai
yen*, a characteristic highly prized within Thai culture. It is the ability
to remain calm in the face of difficulties. For one of the women, this
had saved her marriage (although initially she had been very sceptical
about the ability of a Roman Catholic priest to give marriage advice!).
Thus while the women admitted that there was no question that money
was unimportant, their involvement with PIME had led to additional
emotional benefits that sprang directly from the spiritual dimension of
PIME's work.

The PIME priests were very sensitive to the need to offer psychological and emotional support to those with whom they worked. At the time
of the research they had two volunteer trainee psychologists from Italy
working in one of the orphan houses for older boys, helping them work
through issues of abandonment. One of the foreign PIME workers also
stressed that she teaches child-rearing skills to the housemothers who
raise the orphan children. Since many of the housemothers had experienced deprived childhoods, they had no positive role models on which
to draw. This worker taught them positive, albeit foreign, childcare patterns, deeming these to be better than those from the women's own childhoods, even if they were not indigenous. Such notions of intercultural
interchange was said to bring positive benefits to both foreign workers
and Thais. The priests stressed that many foreign volunteers went away
healed from emotional hurts through their work. The sense of overall

benefit expressed by the women seems to confirm this. Most described the sum total of their interactions with PIME as *sabay jai*, a sense of peace, contentment and general well-being highly valued within Thai society.

Religious belief

In terms of their religious beliefs, it was apparent from the interviews that the women had a predominantly externalized appreciation of Buddhism, with little knowledge of its teachings and philosophy. They expressed little internalized belief, and none talked about internal benefits, either emotional or spiritual, that can be gained from taking part in rituals associated with Thai Theravada Buddhism. When asked about Buddhism, the women stressed the need to offer money and food to monks as part of merit-making. Most of them saw Buddhism as a religion that only caters for the rich elite and cared little for poor people. In contrast, their interactions with PIME had led them to believe that Christianity was a religion that cared for the poor, the sick and the dying:[15]

> It's good – Christianity is good. Helping, helping such as helping people with AIDS, or other diseases. The Father helped as much as he could – poor children, orphans, and people near death. It's like these are people who were going to fall off the edge of a precipice and someone pulls them up.

Yet the relationship between faith, religion and culture in the lives of these women was complicated by the perceived relationship between being Buddhist and being Thai. Although a minority of women had converted (mostly older women in their sixties or beyond), and one woman stated that in practice she had no religion because she had never gone to the temple even before her involvement with PIME, for most of the women, being Buddhist was an integral part of being Thai. To convert meant abandoning one's nationality. As one woman put it:

> I'm still probably my old religion, that is Buddhist, because I'm Thai. But if you ask, in our hearts, we can't have many religions. I believe in Christianity, but I can't take the step and follow it fully because on the one hand, I'm still Thai. So I believe in our religion.

---

15 For many of them, the priests in PIME had quite literally saved their lives, taking them to the hospital and getting them into the free government scheme that provides medication for HIV.

During the interviews, several women expressed a desire to convert; most, however, reported that the priests had told them they were not ready. Others spoke of a belief in God alongside a faith in Buddhism, such as the woman quoted above, and in some of the houses pictures of Jesus were evident alongside Buddhist and 'animist' religious artefacts. Since the women viewed me a possible connection to PIME, in some of the interviews the women tried to impress upon me their need for more money. Some of their claimed allegiance to Christianity therefore needs to be viewed in this light. Certainly the interplay between culture, religion and faith was intensified by the issue of money. This, however, does not necessarily lessen the emotional/spiritual benefits that the women expressed in relation to catechism classes.

The fact that the priests had not allowed many of the women to convert is testimony to their sensitivity to these complex issues, in relation to which they stressed that each person must make up their own mind, and that Thai people make decisions of this nature only after careful personal consideration – another reason for insisting on extended catechumenate. The priests were rather critical of other Christian groups who came, made converts, and left, causing both divisions within society and leaving people with very little knowledge of their new faith. This said, they were certainly not against conversion – conversion was allowed so long as the person concerned had arrived at a point of decision on the basis of their own careful consideration.

Conclusion: alterity vs invading the space of the other

Cosimo Zene's understanding of dialogue is not without its positive merits. Stressing the need to come to others expecting to be taught rather than to teach instils an awareness of the likelihood that, in encountering another culture, one is much more likely to learn than have something to give. As such, it counters a certain Western arrogance that has historically viewed other cultures as primitive and in need of civilizing. Yet for all this, Zene's notion of 'dialogue' appears remarkably monological since it does not allow those who come to another culture to have a voice, certainly where religious issues are concerned. Although allowing for some cultural exchange on social issues, Zene's understanding of 'dialogue' appears to have no room for positive notions of 'invasion' of a spiritual or religious kind. In this respect Zene seems guilty of an overly static notion of culture – one that in turn skews his understanding of 'ethical mission'.

Approaching missiology and ecclesiology from a postmodern perspective, Kathryn Tanner has convincingly shown that cultures are neither as homogenous nor as static as is sometimes supposed. The stability that appears within culture is only a 'temporary precipitate' (Tanner 1997, p. 51), part of a continuous process of change. When looked at in more detail, culture is not a static monolith that can be applied to people. Instead, people themselves create culture through social interactions with one another. It is for this reason that, when we engage in practical theology of an anthropological nature, we find contradictions just as likely to provoke change as ideas brought in from outside:

> What makes the modern notion of culture wrong is not the bare claim that culture is an ordering principle. What is wrong is the *way* culture is talked about as an ordering principle: the idea that culture is an already constituted force for social order simply waiting to be imposed upon or transmitted externally to human beings to passively internalize or mechanically reproduce it. (Tanner 1997, p. 50)

Tanner stresses that an overly static and isolationist reading of culture can perpetuate unethical practice, despite attempting to do the opposite, since it fails to notice power structures that support inequality. She argues that if missionaries are to work ethically, they must not forget that cultures need to be seen as part of a wider global context in which power dynamics are always at play (Tanner 1997, p. 54):

> However well-intentioned, the separate-but-equal view of self-contained cultures expresses tolerance by ignoring the political realities of inequality . . . [O]ccluded thereby are the actual unequal political and economic relations between them . . . (Tanner 1997, p. 55)

Zene does not initially appear guilty of such a 'separate-but-equal' mentality, since his use of the Levinasian metaphor of substitution leads him to emphasize a merging of horizons. However, it is a merging in which one party is always privileged in order to overcome the power dynamics that are, as he points out, necessarily loaded in favour of the Western missionary or anthropologist. In suggesting this, Zene seeks to overcome a type of colonial arrogance that fails to acknowledge the merits inherent within other cultures:

> If anthropology has the power to discuss and unmask the power of other institutions, this can be done by making concrete choices and

placing the Other in a privileged position whereby the discipline cannot escape responsibility, while judging the power of other. Aware of its own power, anthropology has also become aware of its weaknesses and limitations, so that no dogmas can be imposed in the name of 'truths' to be defended. (Zene 2002, p. 425)

While an important sentiment, which perhaps still needs acknowledging within both missiology and anthropology, in attempting to turn Lévinas' philosophical account of ethics into a practical ethics, Zene solidifies what Kathryn Bevis has highlighted is a fundamentally *metaphorical* discussion of ethics (Bevis 2007). Zene concretizes these metaphors out of a desire to allow 'concrete choices' based on ethical responsibility. However, Derrida, on whom he also draws, points out that while choices must be made, it is not possible to have certitude regarding the choices that one makes in any absolute sense if one wishes to retain the post-structuralist approach to truth that Zene appears to advocate (see Derrida 1995). The process of ethical decision-making must be one of ongoing learning, in the face of uncertainty, in which it is not possible always to privilege one party over another. To do so creates a centre where a post-structuralist account would not find one – and as such abandons a truly postmodern view of culture for a more static one (Tremlett 2006, p. 483). In doing so, Zene's approach to mission and anthropology becomes ethically questionable.

The empirical data from the study of PIME brings such cultural rigidity into question, especially where religion is concerned. Here intercultural exchange has led to benefits that are expressed in terms of key notions of Thai psychological well-being – open-mindedness, calmness and peacefulness. It matters little that these were brought about through instruction in practices and beliefs alien to the culture. There is of course a danger that cultural change will occur, yet this is an ever-present 'danger', whether or not external ideas are introduced into supposed homogenous cultures, as Tanner point out.

In their missionary strategies, PIME priests and workers sought to be culturally sensitive. They demonstrated a great love and respect for the various Thai cultures and peoples with whom they found themselves interacting. Yet they were unafraid to challenge aspects of culture that they felt were unethical and/or conflicted with the message of the gospel – which for them is a holistic message of liberation. The interviews with slum-dwelling Buddhist women suggest that this is a view of empowerment that has efficacy from a Thai psychological perspective, and as such I would like to suggest that it constitutes *an* ethical approach to Christian mission that challenges Zene's definition of 'dialogue'.

7

Context and Catholicity:
An Anglican–American Dilemma?

MARTYN PERCY

Introduction

What an interesting year 2008 turned out to be. The world witnessed an election for the US presidency, in which Barack Obama won a pretty handsome majority in senate and congress, and also won the popular vote by some margin. And just a few months before, the world's media was also invited to be both spectator and speculator on a Lambeth Conference for Anglicans, which passed off more or less peacefully, even managing to avoid the consequences of various ecclesial manoeuvres in the American Episcopal Church from overly distorting the agenda. But what is the connection between these two events? Quite simply, I want to suggest that some of the current crises in Anglican identity are partly rooted in some of the un-surfaced cultural and contextual assumptions that shape American life.

That said, this brief essay is not intended to be a rant. It is, rather, an invitation to begin critically exploring the relationship between catholicity and enculturation, and sketch some of the dilemmas facing global Anglican polity. I should say at the outset that the choice of the word 'dilemmas' is itself deliberate: I do not say 'problems'. A problem is something that can be solved. Dilemmas are, however, arenas where issues and values can only be balanced. And I believe that part of the crisis facing Anglican polity at present is rooted in the inability to distinguish between problems and dilemmas. But I am ahead of myself already, so let me begin at the beginning.

One event, two people and several issues

With the inauguration of President Obama now many moons ago, it may seem a little strange to some observers looking back on the event that quite a bit of the focus was on Rick Warren, the pastor of Saddleback megachurch in southern California. Obama had chosen Warren to give the invocation on 20 January – conferring the kind of status on a pastor that would normally be reserved for the likes of Billy Graham. The other noteworthy person present at the inauguration was the Bishop of New Hampshire, Gene Robinson, who led the prayers. Robinson was elected bishop in 2003, and as a divorcee and gay man, has seen his elevation to the episcopacy become a focal point for the divisions in global Anglican polity. To some he represents the ascendancy of imperialistic Episcopalian liberalism. To others he is a prophetic forerunner – a champion for gay rights who is challenging the innate homophobia of a Church that is resisting both modernity and equality.

In choosing both Warren and Robinson to participate in the inauguration, Obama appeared to have selected two Christian leaders to represent the right and the left, and in so doing achieved some creditable political and religious balance. Here, perhaps, was the wisdom of Solomon in action? Yet I want to suggest that both Robinson and Warren have much more in common than might appear to be the case, and that this arguably highlights a problem in the relationship between catholicity and context. So let me say more, and begin with Warren.

It was Warren who hosted the first debate between Obama and McCain that kick-started the presidential race. Warren is a well-known exponent of conservative Christian values on all the cornerstone issues that currently unite and divide evangelicals: gay rights, abortion and so forth. So selection of Warren to give the invocation is not without controversy. But what exactly was a black northern liberal doing inviting a white southern conservative to preach? Cue the predictable banshee cries and wailings of protest from the political left.

The choice of Warren, however, represented a more interesting conundrum in contemporary American life. Warren's books, such as *The Purpose-Driven Church* (1995) have sold hundreds of millions. The sentiments express that unique American recipe: the subtle and seductive fusion of religion and pragmatism; of manna and mammon. The ambiguity of this fusion is printed on every dollar bill: in God we trust. So techniques in marketing and any kind of general organizational theory are imported into belief and practice, so that the potential of faith is maximized in its service of the consumer. Cue abundance: happiness and self-improvement is within the grasp of any faithful believer.[1]

---

1 See, for example, Thomas Lynch and his critique of American culture – Lynch 1998, p. 25.

In the USA, user-friendly forms of Christianity are a dime a dozen. The common DNA that unites them all is the promotion of religion as a panacea: something that will solve problems and improve the lives of individuals. It is a rather functional, pragmatic attitude to faith. And when it ceases to work, one simply discards it and moves on.[2] There is bound to be something better in the spiritual marketplace for the restless consumer; something more 'me', a faith that is even more effective and affective than the last. This is, after all, a faith-land where Jesus might be Lord, but the customer is actually king. (And by the way, like any other customer, always right.)

However, the kind of Christianity espoused by Warren expresses both the problem and the opportunity that the Obama presidency faces. For with the collapse of confidence in capitalism, the dawning realization that growth cannot be indefinitely expediential and that not everyone can be a winner, comes the haunting sense that some deeper values may have to come to the fore in shaping the America of the next few decades.

To be frank, the pursuit of happiness and self-improvement, and accompanied by a thick spiritual veneer, will not easily survive the ravages of a new Great Depression. Or for that matter the new emerging world order. Something more substantial will be needed for the long road ahead. A collective vision for discipleship will be required that is rooted in challenging American values as much as affirming them. Locating a vocation that will serve others, and not just be about sustaining one's self, will be a priority.

What, then, of Robinson's role in the inauguration? As the Bishop of New Hampshire he is the first openly gay man to be called by an Anglican diocese to such a position. Despite the fact that Robinson was chosen by a two-thirds majority of the local electors, his elevation to the episcopate has caused a storm of international debate and disagreement, even threatening the unity and identity of the Anglican Communion. Even by Anglican standards, it could be comfortably described as almost off the barometer scale.

Given that Robinson would be rendered culpable by some for creating the recent inclement ecclesiastical weather that has dogged so much of Anglican polity, even the title of his book seems open to the charge of hubris. Can it really be appropriate to imply that there is any calm place

---

2 For an illuminating discussion and critique, see Ehrenreich 2009. Ehrenreich suggests that the positive thinking has, among other things, powerfully infected religious belief and practice, turning demanding discipleship into forms of consumer-focused spirituality that meets individuals at their point of need.

left in which to reflect on the nature of the gospel and the Church amid such heated exchanges on sexuality and biblical authority? Yet in his recent book, *In the Eye of the Storm* (2008), we find a temperate, measured lucid and composed writer – a rather touching irenic memoir, in fact, from a man who despite being at the centre of such controversy, and held responsible by many for the potential dismemberment of the Anglican Communion, is nonetheless keeping his cool.

Indeed, Robinson's book should be understood as a kind of quintessentially Anglican polemic: the very embodiment of fervent detachment – a delicate fusion of biblical, personal, ethical, theological and reflective material. And the substance of the text ranges far and wide, covering a familiar litany of topics that are near and dear to the hearts of your average North American Episcopalian. Chapters concentrate on sexuality and justice; faith and life; diversity and exclusion; politics and inclusion; and end with communion and identity. This familiar terrain is, however, addressed in a manner simultaneously moderate and ardent, capturing something of the heart of Anglican polity (at least in style) – as well as neatly expressing its current dilemma (in substance). Here is a cradle Anglican expressing his mind and heart; baring his soul for the world to read.

However, the book cannot escape the production and reception of its underlying context. Anglicanism has never considered itself to be a sect or denomination originating in the sixteenth century. It considers itself to be both catholic and reformed, and with no special doctrines of its own. Yet there is something about the style of Anglicanism – its cadence and timbre – that gives it a distinctive feel. While one can never generalize – there are, after all, several kinds of Anglican identity – there is nonetheless a unifying mood in the polity that rejoices in the tension between clarity and ambiguity, decisions and deferral, to say nothing of word and sacrament or protestant and catholic.

Caught between extremes, critics of Anglican polity have often ruminated that Anglicanism cannot escape its Laodicean destiny. So neither too hot nor too cold – just warm. In other words, the classic *via media*: tepid – and proud. And because Anglicanism is born of England, just like its climate, the polity often struggles to cope with extremities. Anglicanism is mostly a temperate ecclesial polity: cloudy, with occasional sunny spells and the odd shower – but no extremes, please.

Temperature, then, is an important key to understanding the very context from which Robinson's book has emerged, as well as its content. For his work has materialized out of the new ecclesiastical climatology witnessed at the beginning of the twenty-first century, which just like the rest of the planet now finds itself exposed to extremities. Normal and temperate weather configurations seem to have given way to immoderate and excessive patterns of behaviour that are driving a new agenda. The sense of 'furious religion' has returned. Cool, calm religion – that beloved export of Europe for so many centuries – is giving way to hot and sultry expressions of faith that despise moderation and temperateness. And Anglicans of all hues are caught up in the new extremes of spiritual weather. Ecclesiastical global warming has arrived.

So while *In the Eye of the Storm* offers us a telling apologia for calmness and centred-ness, in which Robinson acknowledges the weather around him, he inevitably abrogates any real responsibility for the conditions that have drawn so many into the subsequent hurricane of controversy. In many ways, he is probably right to be so coy. The turbulence that regularly erupts in Anglican polity has been around for many centuries and has only recently found expression in the new debates on gender, politics, Scripture and ecclesial order. Sexuality was never going to be any different; the storm merely points to the endemic weakness, and strength, embedded in Anglican diversity.

But what *In the Eye of the Storm* cannot help Anglicans with is how precisely to face and resolve the divisive dilemmas that seem to threaten the very future of the Communion. Some churches, of course, thrive on intensity and heat; it is a sign of vibrant life and feisty faith. But others who are of a more temperate hue find this disturbing: heated exchanges, anger and passions seem to dismay more than they console. Anglicanism, then, as a *via media* expression of faith, finds the soul of its polity profoundly troubled by excess. For it strains to embody what one distinguished Anglican has described as 'passionate coolness'.

'Passionate coolness' is a typically Anglican phrase: framing ecclesial identity within an apparent paradox. So I suppose one could say that what currently afflicts Anglicanism is not this or that issue – but the heat and intensity that often accompany the debates, because Anglicans are used to temperate, cool disputations. What Anglicans have in the sexuality debate is hot passions mixing with cool reserve: heated exchanges suddenly being expressed in a traditionally temperate climate. And when heat meets coolness, a storm can brew. Robinson is in there of course – and right at the centre too.

But this book is, as I say, a model of mild yet ardent temperate Anglican polity. And ultimately, that is the only grounded future where Anglicans will truly be able to face one another with their manifest differences. So perhaps this is where some of the hope lies for the Anglican Communion, and indeed for the wider world. For surely now, and in the immediate future, what societies need are robust models of breadth that can genuinely live with difference and diversity, and offer a passionately moderate polity that can act as a counterbalance to religious extremism and narrow forms of exclusion that vilify and divide.

Context and catholicity

Given these opening remarks, I am aware of the risk of relegating a hurricane to the status of a storm in a teacup. Robinson's appointment is a serious matter for Anglican polity, to be sure. And confidence in the resilience of Anglicanism – as a robust and discrete culture that can ride out some aggressive and intemperate weathering – is only part of the reality that Anglicans face. There is no question that the danger of schism is serious. Wars, as wise folk know, can be started at any time of one's choosing; but the author cannot choose the time and manner of the ending. So it is little wonder that the early Church Fathers, when faced with a choice of living with heresy or schism, always chose the former. Doctrine and practice can be corrected over time, but schisms are seldom mended; ecclesial fractures do not have a record of healing well.

That said, Anglicans could now look back at the most recent Lambeth Conference with some degree of satisfaction. In general the verdict seems to be that for the most part it passed off peaceably. Of course, much ink was spilled in the run-up to the Conference, writing off Anglicanism, attacking the leadership of the Archbishop of Canterbury or pointing to the gathering forces of conservatism in movements such as GAFCON (Global Anglican Futures Conference) and FOCA (Fellowship of Confessing Anglicans). The media reporting prior to the conference was mostly gloomy and doom-laden – as helpful as a phalanx of Job's comforters staffing the telephones at your local branch of the Samaritans.

But Anglicans hardly need the media to provide the dubious comforts of depressive consolation, for they are very good at squabbling among themselves. Mired in a culture of blaming and mutual castigation, Anglicans all but seem to have lost the knack of cultivating and practising the virtues of tolerance and patience amid their differences and diversity. Moreover, the last few decades have seen unleashed an unholy and viral trinity of individualism, impatience and intolerance. This has rapidly spread to very different quarters of the Anglican Communion, yet with unsurprisingly similar results. So now each part of the worldwide Church, whether liberal or conservative, white or black, can claim to be true and right while expressing their individuality, irritation and annoyance with all those they disagree with.

I suspect the only antidote to this plague of rashness is an old Anglican remedy: the recovery and infusion of those qualities that are embedded in the Gospels and in deeper forms of ecclesial polity, namely ones that are formed out of patience, forbearance, catholicity, moderation – and a genuine love for the reticulate blend of diversity and unity that forms so much of the richness of Anglican life. But in the woof and weave of the Church these virtues have been lost – or rather mislaid – in a miscibility of debates marked by increasing levels of tension and stress.

There is support for this kind of polity. For example, in Kenneth Locke's recent book, *The Church in Anglican Theology* (2009), we find a subtle and careful exploration of the ambiguities that help form Anglican identity. Although be pays due and patient attention to some of the inherent weaknesses in this type of complex ecclesial formation, he is also clear about the depths and riches that make up Anglican life. Chapters cover authority, episcopacy and ecumenism – with some excellent comparative reflections drawing on Lutheran, Roman Catholic and Orthodox sources. The chapter on Anglican ecclesial authority is as illuminating as it is sobering. Locke recognizes that rich and dense ecclesial communities are also complex; so it is not so easy to be simple and clear, as some may hope (see Williams 2004).

Yet if this sounds like too much of a tangle for some, it is interesting to note that when Jesus reaches for metaphors that describe the Kingdom of God (and, by implication, the possibility and potential of churches), he often uses untidy images. 'I am the vine, you are the branches' (John 15.5, NIV) comes to mind. No stately cedar tree of Lebanon here; or even an English oak. Jesus chooses a sprawling, knotted plant that requires patience and careful husbandry. And one that is hardly pretty to look at either. (But the fruit and what it produces, interestingly, is another matter for taste and looks.) In another short parable he compares the kingdom of heaven to a mustard seed – one of the smallest seeds that can grow into 'the greatest of all shrubs, and puts forth large branches' (Mark 4.30–32, NRSV). The image is ironic and possibly even satirical. One has every right to expect the kingdom of God to be compared to the tallest and strongest of trees. But Jesus likens the Church to something that sprouts up quite quickly from almost nothing and then develops into an ungainly sprawling shrub that can barely hold up a bird's nest.

So what exactly is the problem? If Anglicans could settle for a little less clarity and simplicity, and embrace complexity and catholicity, would all be well? Yes and no. Part of the problem for Anglicans, at the moment, lies in our inability to discern the underlying issues that are causing tensions, and in squabbling about the presenting issues. Or put another way:

dealing with symptoms not causes. Sexuality is a classic example of the dilemma Anglican polity faces at present, and I want to suggest that finding a new conciliation and peace in the Communion will rest with discovering and addressing some of the deeper cultural pulses causing similar kinds of problems for other denominations, institutions and societies.

There are some encouraging signs that some Anglican commentators and scholars have also perceived this, and Bill Sachs' *Homosexuality and the Crisis of Anglicanism* (2009) is one such. True, many Anglicans could be forgiven for the almost audible inward groan that emanates at the mere mention of homosexuality and Anglicanism in the same sentence. Surely, haven't Anglicans had quite enough of the issue? Worn out by the divisive debates and debacles, is it not time for the Anglican Communion to move on and perhaps tackle something a little less contentious – such as mission and ministry, or justice and peace? The answer to these questions is, of course, 'yes'. But that should take nothing away from Bill Sachs' remarkable, indeed peerless book, which surveys the terrain of one of the knottier problems to have arisen in Anglican polity for many a year. His thesis will repay careful reading, and is well worth the time one might invest to ponder how a crisis such as this assumed the proportions it did, and where any hope for the future of the Church might lie.

There cannot be many Anglicans who do not hold an opinion on the subject in question. But as Sachs points out, eloquently, Anglicans across the globe, whether liberal or conservative, traditional or progressive, are often caught between their biblical, doctrinal, ecclesial and legalistic frameworks on the one hand, and their experiential, contextual and pastoral concerns on the other. Indeed, one of the great strengths of his book is the lucid articulation of emerging contextual theologies and the ways in which they compete with hitherto unarticulated but assumed notions of catholicity, homogeneity and more complex forms of global belonging. The local, indeed, is both one of the strengths of Anglican identity, but also a potential source of weakness when attempting to speak and act on a global scale. Sachs articulates this potentially problematic dynamic beautifully and clearly, and without recourse to party-based sniping. There is no siding with liberal or conservative slants. Sachs knows too well that the Anglican Communion and its somewhat patchwork polity is far more complex than it seems. Anglicans all agree on what the Bible says; we are just spending quite a bit of time – and acrimoniously, on occasions – figuring out what it means and where, why and when to apply texts in the twenty-first century.

Sachs' first chapter sets the scene – the defining moments of the debates, as it were, which brought an issue that was bubbling below the skin of

Anglican polity and identity right to the surface. As Sachs suggests, even with regard to the elevation of Gene Robinson and the proposed elevation of Jeffrey John to the episcopate, the ensuing divisions in the Church were in fact already emerging. Tensions on sexuality existed long before 2003, caused significant difficulties at the Lambeth Conference of 1998 and had already coloured and clouded the archiepiscopacy of George Carey.

Sachs, as a contextual theologian, then locates these difficulties and disagreements in the wider milieu of ecclesial polity. Tensions, for example, have always existed in the contention for the shaping of early Christian unity (chapter 2). Ideals and realities can also be conflictual, as are the concentrations of power (in the centre or on the periphery, and between local and catholic) in the formation of a global polity (chapters 3, 4 and 5). Sachs contends that the key to understanding the debate is the realization that indigenous Anglicanism is both the foundation of its global polity as well as its nemesis. Drawing on writers such as Michael Sandel and John Tomasi towards the end of his thesis (see Sandel 2009 and Tomasi 2001), Sachs shows that the kind of activism that promotes rights – vindication through political processes – rather than seeking tangible social and communal harmony as a whole, and for the greater good of all, is bound to be deficient for a Church, where there are higher goals to reach for (see Sen 2009).

Sachs is in no doubt that there are difficult days ahead for the Anglican Communion. One way of resolving its future would be to plot a more assertive course; to chart a pathway, in effect, that would be directive and hierarchical. This would have its champions, to be sure. Another way forward would be to capitulate to despair, or simply to 'walk apart' – in effect, to cave in to endemic consumerist individualism. But there is another way, and Sachs carefully expounds this in his conclusion.

Taking respectful issue with Ephraim Radner's and Philip Turner's recent *The Fate of the Communion* (2006), Sachs suggests that unity will need to continue to be progressed through careful listening and speaking, and recognition of the blend between interdependence, intradependence, independence and dependence. All Anglicans dwell within this framework, and have to work through the consequences of practising 'contextual reliance on the authority of Spirit without the balance of a wider collegiality' (Sachs 2009, p. 247). This is an issue for Sydney as much as it is for New Hampshire.

Sachs believes that the future of the Communion lies in recognition of multiple contexts that partially form ecclesial polity, even though these same realities may need challenging and addressing from time to time.

Many Americans, for example, operate quite happily and unconsciously within a 'spiritual marketplace', leading to an individualist and consumerist mindset that picks a tradition or combination of traditions that suits lives at particular points in time. The result is that the local congregation tends to express and interpret the wider tradition for individuals, but at the expense of the broader and deeper adherence to a given denomination. Local congregational life, therefore, and for the purposes of constructing meaning, value and concepts of wider belonging and catholicity, is now far more dominant than it used to be.

That said, the 'Communion' of the future must entail a readiness to be in fellowship with one another, but without this necessarily meaning 'agreement' on all things or ceding authority to one another. As Sachs points out, 'no position on homosexuality could embody the whole of (the) Anglican tradition' (p. 249). I am sure this is right. However, the argument for the future of Anglican polity does not necessarily hinge on dissenting from this kind of view. It might rest, ironically, on accepting that some positions (among traditionalists, progressives, conservatives and liberals), while being faithful expressions of a localized contextual theology, are nonetheless not easily able to commune fully within a body seeking to rediscover its catholicity.

I suspect, then, and following Sachs, that the roots of current crises in Anglican polity lie not with sexuality (at least in the long term) but rather with some of the deeper cultural drivers that shape American life. These largely un-surfaced assumptions are exported the world over through Americanized versions of capitalism and democracy: the complete right to choose and self-determine; the intrinsic goodness of (almost unlimited) consumerism; the basic rightness of rights that lead to happiness and the pursuit of individual freedom and purpose, thereby subordinating a broader catholicity and sociality; and finally, that the ends justify the means.

Americans might be surprised at this short list. They may complain, with some justice, that these are by no means found and held exclusively on their continent, and they would be right to do so. Yet I think what is at issue here is this particular concentration of un-surfaced assumptions in American culture, which can be found in the marketplace, public sphere and in the media. Take, for example, the majority of American television programmes and series that concentrate on crime, justice and police work. Almost all of them uphold the rightness of the law; so justice is served. Yet many will also express something beyond this, namely that when justice is seen to fail or fall short, then the righteous are to take the law into their own hands. The law, in other words, is contingent, not absolute. While this is clearly a generalization, 'the ends justify the means' would serve as an adequate subtitle for many episodes of most American police, legal or crime dramas.

Small wonder then that whenever the American sense of liberal ideal- ism in Church polity is challenged by another power, Americans tend to react in a way that is true to their theological and cultural instincts. Are there not choices for all? Did this course of action not seem right to us at the time? Have we not done the right thing in moving forward now? Why then, should we be stopped? Local democracy becomes an apotheosis. It is the Boston Tea Party all over again. Don't argue and debate – it is time- consuming. Take control of your life: act now.

Were proof needed of this, I need only recall chairing a seminar some years ago in the USA. We had taken as our topic the fall-out from the Gene Robinson affair, and were exploring Anglican patterns of mediation and, in particular, the eirenic polity advocated by Richard Hooker. But this was too much for some. In the plenary that followed, one questioner exploded: 'We voted for this! What can be wrong with that? They voted for the creeds at Nicea. It's just the same!' Except it isn't. One group of voters in New Hampshire is not on a par with an ecumenical council that drew together the entire Christian world as it was then known.

Read like this, the cultural and contextual difficulties currently plagu- ing Anglican polity need some unmasking.[3] Sexuality is clearly an im- portant issue. But it is also an unnecessary distraction – exactly not the issue that the Church and the wider Communion should be focusing on. Yet that Anglicans have become so hopelessly and helplessly distracted in recent years is hardly surprising, for it is also part of the wider cultural milieu and malaise. The playwright David Hare has characterized the last decade as a decade of distraction. Instead of looking at the issues and situations that truly need examination, many Christians have looked away and focused on other matters, allowing ourselves to be distracted by simple pursuits rather than wrestling with complexity (Hare 2009, pp. 5–7). Thus when 2,948 people from 91 nations die in the Twin Tow- ers of New York, the response is to invade Iraq – pursuing the wrong suspect for the crime. Afghanistan is also invaded. But most of the 9/11 hijackers, it turns out, were from Saudi Arabia.

---

3 For a useful discussion of American culture and ecclesial polity, see Podmore 2005. Podmore explores how decisions are taken in the Church; the roles of syn- ods, bishops and primates; how the Archbishop of Canterbury's ministry should develop; what does being 'in communion' and 'out of communion' mean; and how significant are diocesan boundaries in an age of globalization?

In the Church, with much angst and anxiety about declining church attendance, the response is interestingly not to reinforce the front line of mission (parish and established sector ministry) but rather to pour millions of pounds and resources into specious missiological schema that go under the nomenclature of 'fresh expressions' or 'emerging church'. Which, ironically, simply turn out to be ways of manoeuvring faithful Christians into lighter forms of spiritual organization that do not carry heavy institutional responsibilities or broader-based ministerial burdens. The Christian consumer entering the new world of 'fresh expressions' or 'emerging church' can enjoy all the fruits of bespoke spiritual engagement and stimulation, but with almost none of the tariffs incurred through belonging to an ordinary parish church.

As the oft-quoted saying goes, 'If you don't want to know the result, look away now'. Alas, many Christians do. Unwilling to do their sums and calculate the cost of weaning a new generation of Christian consumers on light, carefully targeted spirituality, the Churches simply end up losing some of their brightest and best potential leaders to projects that are essentially a form of distraction, people who otherwise could bring much-needed energy and effort into helping shape the broader institution. Distraction is endemic: fed by consumerism, choice and the need to keep people engaged, fulfilled and happy, it is rife in the churches – to the left and right, among conservatives and liberals, traditionalists and progressives. It is a tough time to be an ordinary church member; but happy the person who has found their cultural and contextual home in a new 'fresh expressions' or form of 'emerging church'.

This may seem harsh. Yet I want to return to the suggestion that a good deal of the presenting issues that seem to be destabilizing Anglicans (and other denominations) at present are in fact symptomatic rather than underlying and causal. To be sure, many of the attempts to return polity to its truer or truest state are full of sincerely held beliefs and worthy goals. But the common denominator is the lack of deeper ecclesial comprehension here, resulting in a real failure to read the cultural and contextual forces that are shaping polity at deep and profound levels. The consequence of this is that the Churches tend to miss the moment.

Christianity does indeed face dangers in the developed world. But they are not, I think, secularization or industrialization. Plenty of people will turn aside from such things to embrace faith and meaning if that is all society can offer. The real threat comes from both within and without. Within, it is the uncritical absorption of individualist, consumerist assumptions that corrode catholicity and bonds of belonging. This moves the Church, effortlessly, from being an established institution or body that faithfully replicates and transmits trustworthy and historic values, to being a series of attenuated organizations that have more short-term and utilitarian goals, including competing with each other for numbers, truth and vindication.

The threat from without is one of comprehension. Christianity is intrinsically 'foreign' in any context. Every believer is a citizen of somewhere, but also of heaven. We are in the world, but not of it. Yet the foreign-ness of Christianity in the modern world has now begun to assume a new identity: alien. Whereas foreigners may speak other languages, learn yours and otherwise mingle, aliens are unwelcome, treated with suspicion and often repelled. Seen as invasive and intrusive, they are frozen out rather than welcomed in.

To some extent, 'fresh expressions' or 'emerging church' movements have tried to stem this tide. But all too often, and in so doing, many have sold the pass, culturally. By becoming too relevant they have lost the necessary otherness religion brings to society. Fearful of being alien, the foreigner has gone native. In the same way, liberals have sometimes been guilty of treading the same path. Many conservatives, on the other hand, have disengaged, and while succeeding in protecting their own identity, have only made an enclave for themselves from which to make occasional and specious forays into the wider body politic. Each time this happens, the foreigners take one more step down the road to becoming aliens.

So what is to be done? The risk of un-policed and uncritical enculturation has always been absorption – into one's self and into the society one is supposed to be transforming. And there is every sign at present that on issues of sexuality – secondary and symptomatic – the Anglican Communion, like all Churches, needs to engage in two simple tasks. First, there is the challenge to figure out the constraints and opportunities afforded by balancing local contexts with catholicity. Second, to discern the potential for a higher vision of cultural transformation, that theology and mission might rightly seek.

Theodore Roszak, in *The Making of a Counter Culture* (2000), suggests that the agenda before those who seek to transform society is not centred on organizing, managing or repairing reality. It is, rather, about asking 'How shall we live?' 'The primary aim of counter culture is to proclaim a new heaven and a new earth . . . so marvellous, so wonderful, that the claims of technical expertise must of necessity withdraw to a subordinate and marginal status . . .' (Roszak 2000, p. 13).

In a similar vein, T. S. Eliot's vision for a Christian culture is not one where right has triumphed over left, liberals have achieved ascendancy over conservatives or traditionalists and progressives have battled to a creditable stalemate. It is, rather: '[A] society in which the natural end of man – virtue and well-being in community – is acknowledged for all, and the supernatural end – beatitude – for those who have the eyes to see it' (Eliot 1939, p. 42).

If Anglicans could find the grace and humility to conduct their debates with this kind of higher vision in mind, we might be able to see that the present difficulties and differences are also our opportunity. For if we can find a way forward to live with diversity, and yet in unity, we shall have held up to the world such an example of polity that the wider public sphere and body politic might itself seek the renewal of its mind and heart, as surely as Anglicans earnestly seek this for themselves.

Conclusion

The Anglican Communion, then, might take some comfort from the present problems it is experiencing. It may need to get beyond them too, and see that the presenting, besetting issues are not as serious as the stubborn and underlying cultural trends that have given them such force and identity.

The Church, meanwhile, might take some comfort from the lips of Jesus. Like the mustard seed, the Church can continue to be an untidy sprawling shrub. Like a vine, it can be knotted and gnarled. Neither plant is much to look at. But Jesus knew what he was doing when he compared his kingdom to these two plants. He was saying something quite profound about the nature of the Church: it will be rambling, extensive and just a tad jumbled. And that's the point. Jesus seems to understand that it often isn't easy to find your place in neat and tidy systems. And maybe you'll feel alienated and displaced for a while. But in a messy and slightly disorderly Church, and in an unordered and rather rumpled institution, all may find a home.

At the same time, and to mix our metaphors for a moment, Jesus did not feed the storm. In one Gospel he apparently slept through the maelstrom, only stilling it when roused by his disciples. But calm it he did. So despite the current storms that bedevil the worldwide Anglican Communion, I predict that the outlook is ultimately calm, and the long-term forecast remains moderate. Indeed, this is the best hope for religion in the modern world. And I daresay we might discover, when we look back in, say, a century, that Bishop Robinson's role in the eye of this particular storm will have emerged as something more complex and ambiguous than many currently suppose.

The irony of the present debacle is that it reminds us of how significant current cultural and contextual bearings can be for theological and ecclesial disputes. Americans are in love with choices, and this is the one American Anglicans now face. Whether on the one hand to go with a catholicity that will be experienced by many as constraining or on the other to capitulate to the endemic context of consumerism, which is sometimes at the expense of a broader catholicity. Or put another way, the local against the global.

At this point Americans will doubtless remind themselves of their sacred duty – to uphold democracy and not give in to intimidating third parties; so no climb-downs. Yet the track record of American foreign policy does not paint such a neat picture. As many small nation states have found to their cost, in Central and South America and in the Caribbean, democracy is fine – just so long as the right choice for Uncle Sam is made. That said, not all controversy, dis-ease, debate and difficulty is bad. Anglicanism is inherently 'open' and provisional, and as Bruce Reed's work reminds us: 'Biologically, (ecclesial) life is not maintenance or restoration of equilibrium, but is essentially the maintenance of dis-equilibrium, as the doctrine of open systems reveals. Reaching equilibrium means death and decay' (Reed 1978, p. 147).

So to return to the inauguration with Warren and Robinson present, Obama is on stronger ground than many of his predecessors. His choice of these two ecclesial paragons, on one level, reaches out to both the right from the left, and implicitly calls for a pause in traditional liberal–conservative hostilities. It challenges the old cold-war impasses of democrat versus republican or traditionalist versus progressive. The old ways of trench-war debating will not suffice for the twenty-first century. Obama's campaign was framed on calling his country to higher and deeper principles. But what might these be rooted in?

Obama's strength lies not in the bewitching power of the new but rather in the renewal of the old. His campaign and much of what he stands for is rooted in the original vision of the founding fathers of America: that freedom is an inalienable right – but only worth something if all can enjoy it; and that out of diversity comes a genuine and collective strength. From the outset, America was birthed not in one dominant ideology but rather a whole farrago of Christian expressions that forged a nation rooted in diversity, and still later was to become a more complex alloy of competing and complementary faiths.

So perhaps it now falls to Obama to inaugurate a new kind of presidency, in which religion plays a different role. This will undoubtedly be one that displaces the old hegemonies and rivalries that have characterized the country in the post-war era, and promises to establish new kinds of conversation that are generative and constructive for the common good. For a country that normally likes to keep religion and the state well apart, Obama's vision for the nation is already turning out to be one of profoundly deep Christian visualization and realization.

It is still far too early to say if President Obama will be ushering in a new age for American politics and religious rapprochement – or for the culture that chose him. And Anglicans cannot yet know the true causes of their present difficulties. But in time the malevolent forces that have brought such instability into Anglican polity will be unmasked. And I suspect we shall see that sexuality and gender are mere symptoms of disease and not causes. Indeed, we may be surprised at the root and branch problem: perhaps it will be the assumptions we make about choice, individualism and the nature of institutions – all of which have eroded our sense of catholicity and moral responsibility for the parts of Christ's body we seldom see or know. We cannot tell. But what can be said with some certainty is that the consumer age we have grown up with is now passing, as all ages must. In God we trust.

8

Intercultural Theology, Walter J. Hollenweger and African Pentecostalism

ALLAN ANDERSON

Introduction

Observers of African Christianity have to reckon with the amazing growth of Pentecostalism in the sub-Sahara. The Pew Forum's *Spirit and Power: A 10-Country Survey of Pentecostals*, conducted in 2006, estimated that in all the countries surveyed, Pentecostalism constituted a very significant percentage of Christianity. In six of the countries Pentecostals and Charismatics were over 60 per cent of all Protestants. As far as Africa was concerned, over half of the population of Kenya and a third of that of South Africa were defined as 'Pentecostal'.[1] These figures, though speculative, indicate the strength of African Pentecostalism today, but they beg the question whether such a widely inclusive definition is justified (see Anderson 2009, pp. 13–29). New independent Pentecostal Churches have mushroomed in Africa since about 1975 and are prominent in African cities. These more Western-orientated Pentecostal Churches are actively growing throughout Africa, particularly in Zimbabwe, Zambia, South Africa, Kenya, Nigeria and Ghana. On the African continent, Pentecostalism is now one of the most prominent forms of Christianity, which has profoundly affected older mission churches that have become 'Pentecostalized' as a result.

One of the most dramatic examples of the new form of Pentecostalism is to be found in southern Nigeria. Not only do the largest 'mainline' Churches like the Anglicans, Methodists and Roman Catholics have a prominent charismatic form of their tradition, but what have become large and successful Pentecostal denominations presided over by religious

---

1 http://pewforum.org/surveys/pentecostal/ accessed 3 August 2007.

entrepreneurs have sprung up overnight. In the south-west, on the road between Lagos and Ibadan, is the sprawling headquarters of the Redeemed Christian Church of God called 'Redemption City', where vast crowds estimated at over a million attend the monthly 'Holy Ghost service' presided over by their leader, Enock A. Adeboye ('Daddy G. O.') in an open-walled and constantly expanding auditorium. One of the largest enclosed church buildings in the world, seating 50,000 persons, is found at another impressive campus outside Lagos called 'Grace Land', headquarters of the Living World Outreach (better known as 'Winner's Chapel') founded by David Oyedepo ('Bishop Oyedepo II'). There, a Christian university and private school offering tuition for all ages adorn this multifaceted complex that unashamedly espouses a prosperity gospel in sync with older African religious beliefs that prosperity is a sign of the favour of God. From West Africa the new Pentecostalism spread rapidly eastwards and southwards throughout Africa's cities in the 1990s. Holding services that are usually emotional, enthusiastic and loud (especially as most make use of electronic musical instruments), this has become a major expression of Christianity in Africa, emerging all over the continent. In Ghana the Church of Pentecost is now the largest religious organization in the country with over a million members. The streets of Accra, Lagos and other African cities are peppered with signboards and slogans demonstrating the pervasive influence of Pentecostalism in popular African urban societies (Anderson 2004, pp. 159–62). These new forms of Pentecostalism have imbibed globalization and often use English, Western electronic music, printed and internet resources and expository preaching as their main avenues of expression. They represent a young and modernizing society in Africa's cities. They make widespread use of the mass media, and the setting up of new networks that often incorporate the word 'international' in their title, frequent conferences with international speakers that reinforce transnationalism and the growth of churches that provide total environments for members and international connections are all features of this multidimensional Pentecostalism, which promotes this global meta-culture constantly. There are much older forms of Pentecostalism in Africa that have interacted more with African popular religion in the rural areas, but these forms are no longer seen as paradigmatic of African Pentecostalism (Gifford 1998, p. 33).

This chapter discusses the significance of Pentecostalism in Africa and the contribution of Walter J. Hollenweger to Pentecostal studies. It gives particular attention to the family resemblances of the older African independent 'Spirit' churches with Pentecostalism, and the ways that these have opened the way for the study of intercultural theology. It discusses a debate in Southern African studies on the understanding of 'African Pentecostalism' and considers what it is about Pentecostalism that resonates with African cultures. How this contributes to our understanding of intercultural theology is illustrated by adapting Hollenweger's list of the characteristics of Pentecostalism.

Hollenweger's legacy in Birmingham

Walter J. Hollenweger (b. 1927) was a Swiss member of the *Pfingstmission*, who after attending a Bible school in England in 1948–9 became a Pentecostal pastor, resigning from his church in 1958. Between 1955 and 1966 he studied at Basel and Zürich University for a doctorate and became a minister in the Swiss Reformed Church in 1962. His groundbreaking doctoral thesis on Pentecostalism completed by 1966 was a ten-volume epic. Before coming to Birmingham in 1970 as Professor of Mission, he served for two years as Secretary for Evangelism in the Division of World Mission and Evangelism of the World Council of Churches in Geneva (Price 2002, pp. 5–15). His background in Pentecostalism, combined with academic learning and ecumenical involvement, gave him understanding of and admiration for Pentecostalism but also brought him into conflict with the movement. His earliest volumes on Pentecostalism, *The Pentecostals* (first published in German in 1969), was written when little academic reflection on this movement had been carried out anywhere (Hollenweger 1972). There were hardly any academic books and no academic journals on the subject, no academic associations and no graduate students. For Pentecostal studies Hollenweger's work was monumental and pioneering. When the rest of the Christian world considered Pentecostalism a quaint, misguided fundamentalist sect (at best), and academia was interested only in its most exotic and so-called 'syncretistic' fringes, Hollenweger raised important questions and made observations that made the study of this movement the growing and creative activity it is today. Although we have moved beyond Hollenweger in many respects, and some of his work now appears anachronistic, no one should study Pentecostalism without reference to him. We cannot overestimate his enormous achievements. He almost singlehandedly created a subdiscipline within theological studies that made my job in Birmingham possible in 1995; and today there are at least five dedicated centres for the study of Pentecostalism in European universities. Of course, Hollenweger's interests were much wider than global Pentecostalism alone, but his background as a former Pentecostal and his work on this subject set the tone for several publications thereafter in various parts of the world. This was especially the case with the 16 University of Birmingham PhD students who studied Pentecostalism under his supervision and were forced to reckon with his emphases on both intercultural and ecumenical theology.[2] There were 31 other PhD studies completed under Hollenweger in Birmingham – an impressive total of 47 in less than two decades (he retired in 1989).[3] His students of Pentecostalism, however, were directly affected by his intercultural approach, and they in turn influenced his approach to Pentecostalism.

What was distinctive about Hollenweger's work in Birmingham? From my perspective the answer to this question was not only that he pioneered the academic study of global Pentecostalism but also that he set it within the context and parameters of his 'intercultural theology'. For him, Pentecostalism was the prime example of intercultural theology in practice. He repeatedly stated that theology is more than a written text – in Pentecostalism it comes to life in the practices, liturgies, prayers, dances and testimonies. In the first edition of *The Pentecostals* he did not develop the strong emphasis on the 'Black oral root' of Pentecostalism that was to characterize his later work. Most of his research on Pentecostalism in Africa was conducted in South Africa but depended mostly on secondary literature. He wrote a chapter on the beginnings of the white-led Apostolic Faith Mission and the Assemblies of God, one on Nicholas Bhengu (an Assemblies of God African leader), one on the Latter Rain Assemblies (a communitarian white group) and then, most significantly, a fourth chapter entitled 'uMoya – the Spirit in the Independent African churches', drawing extensively from the earlier works of Sundkler and Barrett (Hollenweger 1972, pp. 149–75). Unlike these scholars, Hollenweger made the connection with Pentecostalism by declaring that these Churches were 'independent African Pentecostal churches'. Instead of the strident criticism of these Churches as 'syncretistic' that was common among European observers at the time, Hollenweger saw the need for common understanding and dialogue (Hollenweger 1972, pp. 149, 166). It was his observations linking African Zionism with Pentecostalism

---

2 Bittlinger, 1977; Nelson 1981; Raj 1983 published as Raj 1986; Hocken 1984; Massey 1987; Laan 1987; Yoo 1988; Martin 1987; P. van der Laan 1988; Faupel 1989; MacRobert 1989; Colletti 1990; Gaxiola-Gaxiola 1990; Gill 1990 published as Gaxiola-Gaxiola 1994; Saracco 1990; Gerloff 1991 published as Gerloff 1992.

3 All Hollenweger's research students are listed by Cornelis van der Laan in Jongeneel 1992, pp. 359–66.

that aroused my own interest as a research masters student in theology at the University of South Africa 20 years ago, resulting in three slim books and a doctoral thesis.[4] Surprisingly, not a single one of Hollenweger's students had studied Pentecostalism in Africa, and it was only in the 1990s that such studies began in Birmingham, producing eight PhDs on African Pentecostalism in the past eight years: four on Ghana, three on Nigeria and one on Kenya.[5]

Hollenweger's second major tome on Pentecostalism updated and developed his earlier ideas with reference to more recent academic literature. As far as Africa is concerned, there is another chapter on South Africa and one on Kimbanguism in the Congo, where he gives attention to the catholicity of the movement and makes an excursus into African theology (Hollenweger 1997, pp. 41–80). The questions raised by African theology and Kimbanguism alike point to 'questions central to Africa (*and* Europe), although it is debatable whether they have yet found adequate answers', he wrote (Hollenweger 1997, p. 77). In the South African chapter he describes the struggle against racism in the Apostolic Faith Mission and refers to my work in *Moya* on what he terms 'a Black Pentecostal Pneumatology'. His discussion focuses on socio-political aspects, but he also acknowledges the historical and theological continuum between Pentecostalism and African religions on the one hand, and between the different kinds of Pentecostalism in Africa on the other (Hollenweger 1997, pp. 41–53). But by this time he had a full-blown thesis on the importance of Pentecostalism to intercultural theology. The relationship between Christianity and culture, and by implication the relationship between Christian faith and other faiths, is a much debated topic, but one seldom discussed in Pentecostal theological thinking. Nevertheless, the global expansion of Pentecostalism in the twentieth century can be attributed at least in part to cultural factors, and its encounter with other faiths cannot be avoided.

Hollenweger sees the 'oral structures' of the origins of Pentecostalism, like Christianity itself, as the reason for its initial growth, and not in any 'particular Pentecostal doctrine'. His list of characteristics of these oral structures is now well known: an oral liturgy, a narrative theology and witness, a reconciliatory and participant community, the inclusion of visions and dreams in worship, and understanding the relationship between body and mind revealed in healing by prayer and liturgical dance. These

4 Anderson 1991; Anderson 1992a; Anderson 1992b; Anderson 1993.
5 Asamoah-Gyadu 2000; Jehu-Appiah 2001; Onyinah 2002; Clarke 2003; Padwick 2003; Burgess 2004; Park 2005; Olaniyi 2007.

132

features, he observes, are also predominantly African cultural features, evident in the leadership at the Azusa Street revival (1906–9) of the African American preacher William Seymour, whose 'spirituality lay in his past'. Seymour's Pentecostal experience meant more than speaking in tongues, and included loving in the face of hateful racism. For Hollenweger, Seymour was the founder of Pentecostalism and represents the 'reconciling Pentecostal experience' and 'a congregation where everybody is a potential contributor to the liturgy'. Seymour's Pentecostalism is 'the oral missionary movement, with spiritual power to overcome racism and chauvinism'. Hollenweger demonstrates the pervading influence of the Azusa Street revival, both upon early Pentecostalism and upon later forms of the movement, especially in the Third World, where the majority of Pentecostal adherents now live. He makes the connection between Pentecostalism and African religions and culture, and points out that Pentecostalism is not a predominantly Western movement but both fundamentally and dominantly a Third World phenomenon (Hollenweger 1997, p. 23).

Harvey Cox's book on global Pentecostalism, *Fire from Heaven* (1996), reflected the identification of African Independent Churches (AICs) with Pentecostalism, but without referring to Hollenweger. Cox wrote a chapter on Africa to support his main thesis that Pentecostalism was a resurgence of 'primal spirituality'. Beginning with a description of an African Apostolic Church gathering in Zimbabwe, he wrote that the more than 5,000 independent churches all bore 'the familiar marks of Pentecostal spirituality, plus many distinctive qualities of their own' (Cox 1996, p. 245). They were 'the African expression of the worldwide Pentecostal movement', he stated. He qualifies them as 'Pentecostal' first because of their style as 'phenomenologically Pentecostal . . . exhibiting all the features of pentecostal spirituality we have found from Boston to Seoul to Rio de Janeiro'. Second, they are Pentecostal because of their origins and the influence of 'the high-impact spread of the American Pentecostal movement' (Cox 1996, p. 246). Cox describes the Pentecostal style of the African independent churches as follows:

> People dance and clap and testify. The preachers rely more on stories than sermons to carry the message. The worship incorporates dreams, healing, trances, and a high degree of lay participation. The churches also assimilate a wide variety of indigenous religious practices – in this case, African ones – into the fabric of Christian prayer and praise, so much so that like Pentecostal churches elsewhere they are often accused of 'syncretism' . . . The result is a thoroughly 'Africanized' version of Christianity. (Cox 1996, p. 247)

Philip Jenkins writes that 'Africa has now for over a century been engaged in a continuous encounter with Pentecostal fires, and the independent churches have been the most obvious products of that highly creative process' (Jenkins 2002, p. 51). I have suggested that the term 'Pentecostal' in Africa refers to Churches that, in common with Pentecostalism worldwide, emphasize the working of the Spirit in the Church, particularly with ecstatic phenomena like prophecy and speaking in tongues, healing and exorcism. These phenomena are widespread in Africa across a great variety of Christian Churches (see Anderson 2000, pp. 34–7; Turner 1979, p. 97). Using the term 'Pentecostal' to refer to AICs is controversial, especially for other Pentecostals. Most AICs do not refer to themselves as 'Pentecostal' and those that do tend not to refer to other AICs by this term. But there are phenomenological, theological, liturgical and historical reasons for arguing that many AICs are 'Pentecostal', as Hollenweger and others have done. Because of the rapid expansion of newer forms of Pentecostalism, these AICs might no longer be as representative of African Pentecostalism as Hollenweger and Cox imply, but they are certainly an important expression of it. Several thousand AICs throughout the sub-Sahara go by different names. In Southern Africa, the majority are known as 'Zionists' after the Chicago healing movement of John Alexander Dowie that began in South Africa in 1902, and 'Apostolics' after the Pentecostal movement that arrived as the Apostolic Faith Mission in 1908. In most parts of Africa they are called 'Churches of the Spirit', and in south-western Nigeria 'Aladura' ('owners of prayer') Churches. In some African countries like South Africa and Kenya, these Churches form the majority of Christians, an extremely important component of world Christianity. The 'Churches of the Spirit' in Africa have much in common with Pentecostals. They practise gifts of the Spirit, especially healing and prophecy, and they also speak in tongues. Because of their 'Spirit' manifestations and pneumatic emphases and experiences, most earlier studies of these Churches misunderstood or generalized about them, and branded them 'syncretistic', 'post-Christian' and 'messianic'. Understanding the pneumatology of these movements in the context of African religions is important, as part of the problem that Western observers had with the 'churches of the Spirit' was that they were often seen as accommodating the pre-Christian past, and linked with traditional divination, ancestor rituals and the like. More recent studies have shown this to be an erroneous view (Anderson 2001). In similar fashion, early Pentecostals in the West were often tarred with the same brush by their fiercest critics, especially by fundamentalists who branded them as 'devil inspired' (Anderson 2004, p. 62).

Pentecostalism has fundamentally altered the character of African Christianity as a whole. The Spirit Churches, however, differ from Western Pentecostals in several ways; and the passing of time has accentuated these differences. There are external differences like the use of healing symbols including blessed water and oil, other symbolic ritual objects representing power and protection, forms of government and patterns of leadership through bishops and prophets, the use of some African cultural practices and the wearing of distinctive church apparel. But they also differ in their approach to African religions and culture, in liturgy, in healing practices and in their unique contribution to Christianity in a broader African context. This distinct and innovative approach often differs sharply from those Pentecostals more heavily influenced by Western Pentecostalism, and this creates a certain amount of tension (Anderson 2000, pp. 27–8). Interestingly, in recent years some of the newer independent Pentecostal Churches have moved closer to AICs in liturgical practices like the use of 'anointing oil' and the practices of appointing 'bishops' and 'prophets'. Pentecostal AICs are found throughout Africa, and are often Churches that emphasize healing through prophets (Anderson 2001, pp. 69–190). The variety and creativity in African Christianity in general and African Pentecostalism in particular is remarkable (Anderson 2004, pp. 103–22). Most observers of African Christianity, however, will admit that the AICs have been in the forefront of the contextualization of Christianity in Africa for over a century. The 'Pentecostalization' of African Christianity in the twentieth century can be called an 'African Reformation' that has fundamentally altered the character of Christianity, including that of the older churches (Cox 1996, p. 246; Anderson 2001, pp. 4–5). No observer of African Christianity can afford to ignore this important phenomenon.

The Southern African debate on 'African Pentecostalism'

Although I only met Hollenweger for the first time in 1996 in Birmingham, I had already been influenced by his research in my own studies of African Independency. But as is often the case, my early research was more profoundly influenced by my doctoral supervisor, Marthinus L. Daneel at the University of South Africa in the 1980s. He represents a different perspective from Hollenweger on the significance for intercultural theology of what he calls the African 'Spirit-type' Churches, particularly because of his many years of fieldwork in Zimbabwe, his country of birth. His grassroots approach to research and theology in Africa resonated

ALLAN ANDERSON

with my own experience of being raised by missionary parents in Zimbabwe and 23 years as a minister among African Pentecostals in Southern Africa. From Daneel I learned several important lessons: to appreciate the riches in African religious and cultural heritages and the need to be sensitive to these in theologizing in Africa. I also learned to value the AIC movement and the potential resources of this for intercultural theology. 'African' religions are not homogeneous, nor are 'African independent churches' identical in their approaches to African religions and cultures. It is not correct to assume that an African 'religion' or 'worldview' exists with common features throughout the continent that are different from so-called 'primal' religions existing elsewhere. Nevertheless, AICs had selectively combined Western forms of Christianity with African ones in such diverse ways that they became living laboratories of what African Christianity might look like if left to itself. Their creative expressions of Christianity were immersed in the cultural and religious thought-patterns of Africa, and in this way they became expressions of intercultural theology. That the great majority of these Churches exhibited 'Pentecostal' characteristics was highly significant.

Notwithstanding Daneel's 'western-ness' (Daneel 1974, p. 311), his approach to questions like the so-called 'syncretism' and 'heathenism' of AICs is sympathetic, but he does not share my enthusiasm for pointing out the resonances between Pentecostalism and African Churches of the Spirit (Daneel 2007, pp. 13–19). This may be partly because he has often had to defend the 'Christian' nature of the AICs in Zimbabwe against those many Western critics who see them as 'heretical' or 'post-Christian'. He is often intent to prove that they follow 'historical' (especially Reformed) Christianity in their fundamental beliefs. His passionate defence of 'Spirit-type' Churches and his penetrating criticisms of those misinterpretations common since Sundkler's ground-breaking *Bantu Prophets in South Africa* (1961), coming as they so often did from misunderstandings of African cosmology, were to influence my own writing (Daneel 1974, p. 347; Anderson 1991, p. 59; Anderson 1993, p. 113). But Daneel's thick descriptions of life in Zionist and Apostolic churches in Zimbabwe in the considerably detailed volumes of his writings are pregnant with Pentecostal images with which I am familiar. I share his scepticism of the crass nature and showmanship of those newer forms of Pentecostalism that think that spirituality is measured by material possessions, success and physical health. During my four years' field research in Soshanguve, Gauteng, in the early 1990s, at least in this South African context, the liturgical, phenomenological and theological parallels observed between the Churches of the Spirit and those Western Pentecostals that I was more acquainted with struck me. I also noticed that there were distinct historical connections, particularly with South Africa's largest 'classical' Pentecostal Church, the Apostolic Faith Mission, founded in 1908, and the Zionist and Apostolic Churches founded thereafter. 'Spirit-type' churches cannot by any stretch of the imagination be regarded as an importation of American Pentecostalism; the creative innovations and adaptations Daneel describes so eloquently are derived from their particular African cultural and religious contexts. Describing these Churches as 'Pentecostal' is not an attempt to gather them into an arbitrary Western category but to indicate phenomenological and liturgical family resemblances (Anderson 2000, pp. 30–7). I have attempted to point out some of the differences between AICs in South Africa and those in Zimbabwe, with particular reference to the Zion Christian Church (Anderson 2003, pp. 103–19).

Prominent South African theologian and my one-time colleague at the University of South Africa, Tinyiko Maluleke, points to the possibility of a continuous rather than a discontinuous relationship between the so-called 'mission Churches' and AICs. He suggests that 'growing sections (for example worship) of traditional Black churches . . . are becoming "AIC" and "Pentecostal" in both theology and praxis' (Maluleke 1996, p. 41). There is indeed much to confirm this 'Pentecostalization' throughout Africa. There is also the danger that scholars may romanticize the AIC movement and unconsciously see it as statically related to the past without acknowledging the considerable historical, phenomenological and theological continuities between AICs and 'mission Churches', the continuities with other forms of Pentecostalism and their modernizing processes. There are also questions about whether 'discontinuity' necessarily means 'syncretism' in a negative sense or whether this discontinuity should rather be seen as an indication of a developing intercultural theology – and therefore a positive development. Although African Pentecostals seldom have an elaborate theology such as is found in most of northern Christianity, they have a distinct and considerable contribution to make to intercultural theology. The AICs in particular have inculturated theology in an intense and far-reaching way. Daneel considers that the main significance of AICs lies in their 'spontaneous indigenization of Christianity, uninhibited by direct [w]estern control' and in their unique erection of 'bridgeheads between the Christian gospel and traditional thought forms' (Daneel 1989, p. 54). Although AICs have little formalized theology, they have what Hastings terms a 'praxis and a spirituality in which a theology is profoundly implicit' (Hastings 1979, p. 54). The faith and life of AICs *are* in a real sense intercultural theology. Questions about what is 'legitimate'

Christianity and what is not are often questions about who has the power to decide.

In a 1996 article on 'AIC Contributions to the World Church', the Nairobi-based Organization of African Instituted Churches stated, 'We may not all be articulate in written theology, but we express faith in our liturgy, worship, and structures' (quoted in Ositelu 1998, p. 70). Theology is a human response to God's Word. The African Pentecostal pastors, bishops or prophets who lay hands on the sick and lead their congregations in rituals of worship are enacting an intercultural theology. Members of these churches have responded to God's Word to them in particular ways. Their interpretation of the working of the Spirit as emphasized in the daily life and practices of their churches is real theology. If, as Justin Ukpong observes, the main goal of African theology is to make Christianity 'attain African expression' and be 'relevant to and expressive of the way [Africans] live and think' (Ukpong 1984, p. 520), then the creative and practical ways in which AICs have done that are an intercultural theology. Probably more than any other form of Christianity in Africa, the 'Spirit' AICs have given an African character to a universal faith. Theology as a human response to God's Word must be intercultural, contextual and expressive of everyday life, or be in danger of becoming inconsequential. African Pentecostals have made creative adaptations to their Christian faith that amount to a comprehensive intercultural theology. In their organizational liberation from colonial ecclesiastical structures, AICs have also achieved a liturgical transformation and have been able to re-evaluate African culture and religion. Daneel speaks of the 'religiocultural liberation' of AICs being a true 'liberation theology' also (Daneel 1989, p. 59). AICs take seriously both their particular African worldview and their own Christian response to it; and in representing an interface between the two perspectives, they demonstrate an intercultural theology. AICs have what Daneel has described as 'enacted theology', which is 'a vitally significant component of a developing African Christian theology' (Daneel 2007, p. 312). The continuing dialogue between Pentecostals and popular culture and religion helps clarify the issues involved in intercultural theology in Africa.

The research of AIC scholars in South Africa has been scrutinized by Maluleke (Maluleke 1993, p. 186; 1994, p. 61; 1996, p. 34). Two particular observations have relevance to this discussion. The first has to do with methodology and the claims of 'insiderness', 'participant observation' and 'empiricism' as validating AIC research without a lucid theoretical framework. Daneel's most abiding legacy may lie in the theme that forms a thread behind all his research: the process of contextualization that he calls 'adaptation and transformation', a theological process that involves the interface of Christianity with African culture. The prophetic healing practices are therefore the outer layer of this deeper causative factor which he states 'largely contributes to the attraction of the Independent Churches for rural Africans . . . herein lies the secret of the unique appeal' (Daneel 1974, p. 309). It is important to note at this juncture that a fine distinction can be made between 'intercultural' and 'contextual' theologies. I think that intercultural theology has more to do with an examination of the relationship between the different intercultural and interreligious elements that constitute all theology – hence Hollenweger's insistence that all forms of Christianity are 'syncretistic' (Hollenweger 1997, p. 132). On the other hand, contextual theology has more to do with those theologies that have developed in response to a wide variety of different social and political contexts. Maluleke asks whether the African traditional/rural worldview is the 'only searchlight through which the complex forest of AIC praxis can and must be examined' (Maluleke 1993, p. 191). Furthermore, in so-called 'empirical' case studies, AICs are seen through the eyes of the author of the study who is 'analysing, sifting and prescribing' (Maluleke 1994, p. 61). Indeed, without the inevitable subjectivity of empirical research, no human knowledge is possible. But Maluleke thinks that the claim by some observers that their research lets AICs 'speak for themselves' is idealistic and misleading. He suggests that the voices of these researchers 'are actually drowning the sources' and that 'the sources can speak for themselves only before we lay our hands, eyes and minds on them!' (Maluleke 1996, p. 41).

A second and equally justifiable criticism Maluleke levelled was the negative theological evaluation given to African religions, particularly from the perspective of those African Pentecostals I examined who had rejected most forms of these religious practices, like ancestor veneration and consulting traditional healers. Daneel too may have placed any 'mixing' of AIC beliefs and traditional ones in what for him is a negative category of 'syncretism'. He often emphasizes the discontinuity and distance between Christian faith and African religion, particularly with regard to ancestors. His conservative Reformed theological background is sometimes the grid through which he views these departures from so-called 'orthodoxy'. For example, AIC prophets are viewed from the perspective of the 'Reformed sense of the Word of God being preached . . . and in the Old Testament sense of revelations and divine communications being transmitted' (Daneel 1988, p. 25). There is another possibility that in the New Testament, particularly in the Acts of the Apostles, these two perspectives are combined and find expression in AICs – this would also be the view of some other Pentecostals. In any case, as Hollenweger has observed, syncretism is not necessarily a negative concept. There needs to be what he calls a 'theologically responsible syncretism' in the adaptation of Christianity to African culture – that is, there needs to be a responsible intercultural theology (Hollenweger 1997, p. 132). Students of African Pentecostalism must also ask whether what is done is studying the Churches for their own worth, or as an exotic backdrop from which to view ourselves and our own 'mission' failures (Maluleke 1996, p. 23). There may be nothing wrong in such an approach as long as it is admitted. A related admission is that of advantage: for whose primary benefit are AIC studies conducted; for those being researched or for the researcher him/herself? These studies, like most academic studies, do not fundamentally empower the communities being studied, although they may facilitate mutual understanding and co-operation. In contrast, Daneel's work illustrates the benefit his philanthropic concerns have been to the grassroots communities he has lived and worked among, particularly in his environmental activities in tree-planting and theological education programmes (Daneel 1998; 1999).

The intercultural theology of African Pentecostalism

The study of Pentecostalism in Africa leads to further understanding of the relationship between Christianity and culture. This is not only the case in the study of the AIC component of it, for Pentecostalism has more recently responded to the cultures of urban, modern Africa in creative ways that have been the subject of current scholarship. Harvey Cox based his assessment of AICs on the phenomena that Hollenweger has described as the 'oral structures' characterizing Pentecostalism worldwide; but in doing so he may have looked for similarities without also recognizing essential differences. Because these features are central to what Hollenweger thought of as intercultural theology, I will discuss and modify them with reference to African Pentecostalism as a whole.

Oral liturgy

Because large parts of rural Africa remain pre-literate or functionally illiterate societies, and because Africans are more sensitive to non-verbal signals and forms of communication than Westerners are, Pentecostalism with its emphasis on a non-literary and spontaneous liturgy is more attractive to many Africans. Hollenweger elaborates on these oral structures in Pentecostal music and liturgy, pointing out that spontaneity and enthusiasm, rather than leading to an absence of liturgy, produce flexible oral liturgies memorized by the Pentecostal congregation. The most important element of these liturgies is the active participation of every member, elaborated below (Hollenweger 1997, pp. 269–71). Pentecostal liturgy has also social and revolutionary implications, in that it empowers marginalized people. It takes as acceptable what ordinary people have in the worship of God and thus overcomes 'the *real* barriers of race, social status, and education' (Hollenweger 1997, pp. 274–5).

Narrative theology and witness

Preaching is an important part of Pentecostal liturgy, and the most successful preachers are usually those who can tell a story and use illustration, narrative and humour to make a point. Theology in its formal, traditional way, such as is found in more conservative forms of Christianity, does not attract people in the same way. Theology as it is prayed, sung, danced and narrated in the Pentecostal congregation is often preferable in African societies. The experience of the Spirit's presence is seen as a normal part of daily life and is brought to bear upon all situations. God's salvation is seen in different manifestations of God's abiding presence through the Spirit in everyday life, seen by Pentecostal believers as divine revelations that assure them that 'God is there' to help in every area of human need. The narrative most used by Pentecostal women in Africa is that of the personal testimony telling of divine intervention in what are often situations of extreme hardship and male domination. African women predominate in Pentecostalism, and the testimony empowers them with an acceptable opportunity to participate in and profoundly influence the theology and witness of the congregation.

Reconciliatory and participant community

One of the strongest appeals of Pentecostalism is its ability to accept and empower all people who embrace its way of life, without regard to gender, social status or education. Everyone is made to feel at home and has the opportunity to contribute meaningfully to the community. The church service is one place where maximum participation is encouraged, but this is extended into the involvement of people in church activities throughout the week. The experience of the power of the Spirit is for Pentecostals a unifying factor in a global society still deeply divided, and can be the catalyst for the emergence of a new society where there is justice for all and hope for a desperately violent world. Pentecostal Churches see themselves as God's people, called out from the world around them with a distinct mission. They have a sense of identity as a separated community whose primary purpose is to promote their cause to those outside. 'Church' for them is the most important activity in life, and Christianity is brought to bear upon every situation. Unlike older forms of Christianity, Pentecostalism is not as dependent on foreign specialists and trained clergy and the transmission of Western Christian liturgy and leadership. For migrant African Pentecostals in Europe for example, their churches have practical functions – whether obtaining a visa to remain in the country, receiving employment, dealing with racism and rejection, finding financial help, advice regarding marriage and family affairs, or healing from sickness and other afflictions seen as the attack of Satan. In short, the church is a caring, therapeutic community and at once a refuge from the storms and difficulties of a new life and an advice centre for every possible eventuality. Many European Churches, influenced by their individualistic and secular society, have largely lost this sense of therapeutic community and belongingness that is so much a central characteristic of African Pentecostal Christianity.

Visions and dreams

In Africa, visions and dreams are an important part of divine revelation, and this is especially the case in Pentecostalism and especially among AICs. Through visions and dreams, people are called to special tasks and to ministry, warned of impending dangers and given various revelations by the Spirit. African Pentecostals justify this aspect of their practice by reference to the Bible, where visions and dreams are seen as a normal means of divine revelation. 'Words of knowledge' and 'words of wisdom' in Pentecostalism worldwide often involve seeing visions and revealing God's purpose for individuals and communities. Among many AICs the prophet is the main channel and interpreter of these divine communications in a role not unlike that of the traditional healer.

Healing by prayer

Healing by prayer has always been one of the most important features of Pentecostalism in Africa, and one of the main reasons for its wide appeal. Healing, exorcism and other manifestations of the Spirit illustrate what Daneel calls 'the relativity, if not futility, of our neat western theories when confronted, in practice, with the belief systems and stark pastoral realities of Africa' (Daneel 2007, p. 312). Healing and deliverance from evil are essential parts of the life of African Pentecostals because these problems affect the whole church community. African experience is the crucible in which an intercultural theology is made. In the healing and exorcism rites of AICs in particular, liberation from the terrors and insecurities inherent in African experiences of evil powers in society is achieved. The phenomenon of growing Pentecostal Churches indicates that there are unresolved questions facing the Church, such as the place of both healing and material provision in regions where there is desperate need, and the holistic dimension of 'salvation now'. Many African Pentecostals see financial success and prosperity as evidence of the blessing of God and the reward for faith in difficult financial circumstances. However, this 'prosperity' is also seen as the means for advancing the work of God and for the ability to give generously to the needy. Tragically, it is also in the area of financial giving that Pentecostal members are most open to exploitation and manipulation by unscrupulous leaders. The 'here-and-now' problems being addressed by these Churches are problems that still challenge the Church as a whole (Anderson 2001, pp. 175–86).

Liturgical music and dance

African societies have always had a penchant for celebratory music and dance. Participation in almost every kind of Pentecostal community is characterized by participating in a joyful celebration of praise and dance. Africans are well known for their rhythmic music and dance that is usually accompanied by strong and vibrant percussion. Many AICs make frequent use of drums accompanied by dance as a central part of their liturgy in keeping with African religious and cultural practices. Usually African Pentecostal dance is not choreographed (like the so-called 'creative dance' in Western Charismatic churches is), and it expresses the desire of participants to celebrate their freedom in Christ. For Pentecostal Christians in Africa, Christian worship is a joyful experience to be entered into with the whole person. This free, exuberant Christianity is not merely because it is a cultural trait of Africans to be enthusiastic, rhythmic and noisy – a European football match will demonstrate that Europeans can have the same enthusiasm. A new emphasis on the role of the Spirit in the worship, work and witness of the Church is one of the main reasons for this enthusiasm. Although most noticeable in Africa, the antiphonal, boisterous singing, simultaneous and spontaneous prayer, and rhythmic music and dance are found throughout global Pentecostalism, emphasizing the freedom, equality, community and dignity of each person in the sight of God. With its offer of the power of the Spirit to all regardless of education, language, race, class or gender, Pentecostalism has been a religious movement that has subverted conventions of the time.

Conclusion

Harvey Cox reversed his well-known position on secularization and wrote of Pentecostalism as a manifestation of the 'unanticipated reappearance of primal spirituality in our time' that would reshape religion in the twenty-first century (Cox 1996, p. 83). Despite the forces of globalization, Pentecostalism developed its own characteristics and identities in Africa during the twentieth century while establishing transnational connections and international networks. This chapter has sought to show some ways in which Pentecostalism has interacted with African cultures, and has suggested that this points towards a better understanding of how intercultural theology works in practice. Admittedly, the contribution of African Pentecostalism to intercultural theology has yet to be explored fully. African culture is not a static phenomenon, and in today's world there are global forces changing the nature of this African movement in all its variety. The extent to which globalization and migration in the late twentieth century have affected the shape of this very significant African religious player is something that requires careful analysis. The shapes of the Pentecostalism that have emerged as a result of the globalization process, how these both resemble and differ from the older networks of denominational Pentecostalism and AICs, and the extent to which Pentecostalism has permeated and affected the beliefs, values and practices of other Christians have yet to be analysed fully. Only when these investigations have taken place will we be better able to understand the external forces that forge the religious identities of people in contemporary Africa, and the increasingly important role of Pentecostalism as an expression of intercultural theology.

9

'Practical Christianity and Public Faith': Nigerian Pentecostal Contributions to Intercultural Theology

RICHARD BURGESS

Introduction

The relationship between gospel and culture is at the centre of contemporary theological reflection, and is closely linked to the evolving relationship between the global and local, a defining feature of post- or late modernity. Gradually, a new understanding of contextual theology is emerging, which allows for diversity and hybridity in theological and liturgical expression. Robert Schreiter (1997, pp. 127–8) refers to this as a new 'wholeness', a 'renewed and expanded concept of catholicity', which may serve as a theological response to the challenge of globalization and will involve an ability to hold disparate theologies together in tension as contributing to the whole. He calls for a stronger sense of intercultural exchange and communication.

Frans Wijsen (2001, pp. 221–3) refers to intercultural theology as a new perspective and a new method in theology. It is comparative in the sense that it encourages the investigation of similarities and differences between the great varieties of theological expressions. It is critical and creative in that it provides opportunities for mutual enrichment and critical interrogation. According to Wijsen (2001, pp. 221–2), there are several reasons behind the emergence of an intercultural perspective. The first is the shift in Christianity's global centre of gravity southwards and the emergence of new models of Church and local theologies. Theologians from the global South (Asia, Africa, Latin America and the Pacific Rim) are now questioning the presumption of European theology to be a universal theology. The second is that the predominance of European theology is being challenged from within its own context by secular philosophies and by ethnic minority Churches. The last is the awareness of the Roman Catholic Church, following Vatican II, that it had become a World Church.

Nigeria is particularly important in this respect. As Africa's most populous nation, it is the location of one of the most vibrant Christian communities in world Christianity. This is largely due to the popularity of its Pentecostal constituency and the penetration of Pentecostal spirituality into the mainline churches, including the large Roman Catholic and Anglican communities. The emergence of Nigerian-initiated Churches in Europe, such as Kingsway International Christian Centre (KICC) and the Redeemed Christian Church of God (RCCG),[1] provides new opportunities for intercultural exchange. This chapter explores the possible contributions Nigerian Pentecostalism can make to the global theological dialogue.

Post-colonial attempts to develop African theology have followed two broad routes. The first – African Christian theology – is concerned with cultural identity and liberation from European cultural domination. Early African writers, mostly Western-trained, sought to explore the continuities between Christianity and Africa's primal religious heritage. The second approach – Liberation Theology – is concerned with socio-political and economic injustices, and concentrates on liberation from class domination and neo-colonialism through social change and praxis (Young 1993, pp. 13–33; Bediako 1996). Increasingly, scholars are paying attention to 'ordinary theologies',[2] those emerging from the experiences of local African Christian communities as they seek to live out their faith. As such, African Pentecostalism is now recognized as an important source for theological reflection.

John Parratt (1995, p. 207) has suggested that African theology throughout the Continent finds common ground in three basic elements: the Bible and Christian tradition; African culture and religion; and the contemporary socio-political context. Paul Gifford (1998, p. 333) has taken issue with this, insisting that Africa's new Pentecostal Churches largely ignore Christian tradition, demonize African religion and culture, and dismiss the contemporary socio-political situation as theologically irrelevant. In this chapter I will argue that Nigerian Pentecostalism appeals to popular religious sensibilities precisely because it resonates with the pragmatic orientation of indigenous spirituality and provides alternative means of engaging with socio-political realities.

---

1 The London-based KICC is the largest single congregation in Western Europe, and the RCCG is one of the fastest-growing Pentecostal denominations in the UK, with close to 400 branches.

2 Jeff Astley (2002, p. 56) defines 'ordinary theology' as 'the theology and theologizing of Christians who have received little or no theological education of a scholarly, academic or systematic kind'.

Nigerian Pentecostal hermeneutics and the influence of worldviews

I begin by examining Nigerian Pentecostal hermeneutics and epistemology. This is important because Nigerian Pentecostals claim to derive their theology directly from the Bible. In his book *Engaging with Contemporary Culture*, Martyn Percy discusses the influence of worldviews on theological reflection. Drawing upon the congregational studies of James Hopewell (1987), Percy (2005, p. 107) suggests that people's attitude to faith is preconditioned by their worldview, which acts as a filter for the processing of information and the acquisition of knowledge. For Hopewell, 'world views reflect and give a focus to group experience, providing a map within which words and actions make sense' (1987, p. 85). In his posthumously published book *Congregation* (1987), he developed a fourfold scheme or 'world-view test' that enables researchers to position congregations and individuals according to their theological outlook. First, the Canonic genre tends to regard the Bible as the authoritative Word and will of God 'by which one identifies one's essential life' (1987, p. 69). Second, the Gnostic genre relies more on an intuitive processing of the world. Third, the Charismatic genre requires 'reliance upon evidence of a transcendent spirit personally encountered, where supernatural irregularities are regularly witnessed' (1987, p. 69). Finally, the Empiric genre relies more on personal experience and empirical evidence. According the Percy (2005, p. 106), conservative Evangelicals generally fall within the Canonic category, Pentecostals/Charismatics within the Charismatic genre, while more 'liberal-minded' religious adherents are heavily Empiric in orientation.

On first sight, Nigerian Pentecostals with their emphasis on obedient submission to the Bible as the authoritative Word of God and their commitment to the Reformation tradition of *sola scriptura*, would seem to fit the Canonic genre. However, the situation is more complex than this. The role of experience and reliance on the transcendent Spirit in Nigerian Pentecostal hermeneutics, as described below, also suggests parallels with the experientialism characteristic of theological liberalism and Hopewell's Empiric genre, as well as the Charismatic genre associated with Pentecostal expressions of Christianity. The Canonic tendencies of Nigerian Pentecostals tend to make them intolerant of alternative readings of Scripture by those outside their particular constituencies, and accept without question the interpretations of their leaders. This militates against dialogue not only with other Nigerian Pentecostals but also with non-Nigerians and non-Pentecostals. Their commitment to the Bible as the 'pre-eminent African text' (Maxwell 2002, p. 13) also discourages dialogue with non-Christian religious traditions, and especially Islam. In this sense, it runs counter to Hollenweger's model of intercultural theology, which is driven by ecumenical and multicultural concerns. In answer to the question, 'Who interprets Scripture correctly?' Hollenweger (1997, p. 325) insists that 'no one person interprets Scripture correctly on his own. It is only in conflict, debate, and agreement with the whole people of God, and also with non-Christian readers that we can get a glimpse of what Scripture means.' In Bible studies I have attended in Nigeria and the UK, while there is scope for dialogue between members, the opinion of the General Overseer or local pastor is rarely challenged publicly, presumably in recognition of their status and their role as power brokers. This may be connected to the idea that the actual words of the Spirit-anointed leader are loaded with spiritual power. Gifford (2008, pp. 206, 218) refers to this as a performative or declarative use of the Bible, whereby the preacher, through the use of his words, is able to 'effect what the words say', thus elevating his or her position to an entirely new level. By rejecting the particular meaning attached to the preacher's words, Pentecostals risk forfeiting the practical benefits associated with them. Thus the leader's interpretation is accepted not on the basis of intellectual argumentation but on the empowering and transformative potential of the words themselves.

The problem arises when leaders use the Bible to control or exploit, rather than liberate, their members. One example is the selective (mis)use of biblical texts by some Nigerian prosperity teachers to extract money from their members for personal enrichment. One of the values of intercultural theology is its capacity to expose the misuse of power and provide space for ordinary people to challenge dominant ideologies. Emmanuel Lartey (2007, p. 277) refers to this as the principle of 'authentic participation', 'which affirms the right of all to participate in discussion and examination of an issue on their own terms, realizing that there are strengths and weaknesses in every approach'.

According to Hollenweger (1986, p. 29), an intercultural approach to theology operates on the basis that Scripture is the point of contact between Western and non-Western theologies. However, what becomes evident, as Hollenweger points out (1997, p. 307), is that people come to very different conclusions on the meaning of Scripture. Usually this is because they employ different hermeneutical methods and approach the Bible from different social and cultural contexts. Here, as I have suggested, the issue of worldview comes into play. Nigerian Pentecostals, like their counterparts elsewhere on the continent (Gifford 1998, p. 333),

tend to handle the Bible in an uncritical way by neglecting its historical context. This is partly because they wish to make it relevant to their
contemporary situation. But it is also because they are reluctant to divest
the Bible of its supernatural character, which resonates with their own
worldview. Thus Nigerian Pentecostal theology presents a challenge to
the more abstract and rationalistic post-Enlightenment theologies from
the global North, which are based on Western philosophical assumptions
and tend to regard the 'enchanted' worldview of the Bible as pre-modern
and pre-scientific. They may also be regarded as post-colonial in the sense
that they reject Western theological methods as colonial constructs claiming universal application (Sugirtharajah 1995, pp. 460–1).

Like Liberation Theology, Nigerian Pentecostals seek to understand
local contexts in the light of Scripture, but they do so by retaining a literal-
ist approach to biblical hermeneutics that is dependent upon the Spirit.
They look for correspondences between their own life situations and the
Bible, and expect biblical texts to have practical relevance and problem-
solving potential. Thus they could be said to follow more contemporary
reading strategies, which stress the role of the receiving communities. In
this sense, as Philip Jenkins (2006, p. 41) has pointed out, they have much
in common with postmodern theories of reading, where the location of
meaning resides in the interaction between the text and reader(s) rather
than in the text itself or in the intention of the author.

Nigerian Pentecostals also have a fondness for narrative texts and find
particular affinities between the biblical world and their own. This leads
to a preference for the Old Testament and the narrative portions of the
New Testament.[3] Their pragmatic hermeneutical approach sometimes
leads to allegorical readings of biblical narratives. Without abandoning
a commitment to biblical literalism, they find multiple layers of meaning
in the text, which satisfy African Pentecostal aspirations for a practical
and experiential form of Christianity. They also expect the Word of God
to have life-changing potential through the ministry of the Spirit. For instance, a Nigerian Pentecostal Church Bible study states: 'God's word has
intrinsic power – that is, it carries its power within itself . . . It therefore
carries the power of God and fulfils the purpose of God' (All Christians
Fellowship Mission 2001, p. 32). This is what Pentecostal theologian
Steven Land (1993, p. 100) refers to as the fusion of Spirit and Word in
Pentecostal spirituality. The Spirit who inspired the Scriptures makes the
Word alive and powerful today by transforming those who encounter it.

---

3 For example, the sermon texts at RCCG's monthly Holy Ghost services during 2001 were largely taken from OT narratives; see Adeboye 2002.

Yet this pragmatic approach to the Bible can lead to what the Ghana-ian theologian Kwabena Asamoah-Gyadu (2006, p. 215) refers to as a selective hermeneutical method, where the tendency is to wrench bibli-cal texts out of context to support predetermined arguments. Asamoah-Gyadu suggests that this 'proof-texting' approach can result in 'truncated, if not erroneous, views on theological issues'. It is especially apparent in the way Nigerian Pentecostals construct their theologies of deliver-ance and prosperity, as we shall see later. Ogbu Kalu (2008, pp. 266–7) calls it 'bumper sticker' hermeneutics or 'experiential literalism', where '[p]ersonal and corporate experiences are woven into the hermeneutical task', fusing the horizons of the past and present with a 'pragmatic her-meneutical leap'.

Gospel and culture

While the intention of Nigerian Pentecostals is to be biblical, their the-ology is also shaped by local concerns and contexts. This is in keeping with Hollenweger's observation that all theology is culturally conditioned (1986, p. 29). An intercultural approach seeks to understand the role of culture in the production of local theologies. Lartey (2007, p. 277) refers to this as the principle of contextuality, which 'asserts that every piece of behaviour and every belief must be considered in the framework within which it takes place'. According to Lartey, intercultural theology takes culture's influence on belief and behaviour seriously, 'without it being seen as determining them, nor as the sole factor to be explored in exam-ining them'. However, as Volker Küster (2001b, p. 4) points out, culture and religion are dialectically related in such as way as to 'reciprocally in-terpenetrate each other'. Nigerian Pentecostalism is not only conditioned by culture, it also challenges elements of culture deemed incompatible with the Bible. In this sense it corresponds to Stephen Bevans' 'counter-cultural' model of contextual theology, which insists that for the gospel to take root in a particular context, its 'liberating and healing power' must challenge and purify that context (Bevans 2007, pp. 117–18). The relationship between gospel and culture is well summed up by Schreiter (2003, p. 30): 'Theology is not subservient to culture; indeed one of its most important functions is to critique the cultures in which it finds itself. Yet theology is always connected with culture in one way or another.'

Despite a tendency to demonize traditional culture and to present themselves as modern individuals, Nigerian Pentecostals interpret Chris-tianity through the lens of existing religious categories and especially the traditional search for spiritual power, a pervasive theme in Nigerian societies such as the Yoruba and Igbo (Okorocha 1987, pp. 206, 278; Peel 2000, pp. 216–17). For the Yoruba, the quest for power (*agbara*) to enhance life is the hermeneutical key to understanding their attraction to all religion, including Pentecostalism.[4] There are two aspects of the traditional religious belief and ritual system that have translated successfully into Nigerian Pentecostal culture and form the basis for other elements of theology and practice. The first is the belief in a plurality of lesser spirits, corresponding to Robin Horton's lower tier in his theory of African conversion (Horton 1971).[5] One of the key elements of Yoruba traditional spirituality, for example, is the belief that an invisible world (*orun*) of benevolent and malevolent powers is constantly interacting with the visible material world (*aye*). Because of the activity of these powers, and their potential manipulation by human agents, this world is a dangerous and precarious place (Ray 1993, p. 270). The second is a belief in the efficacy of prayer (*adura*). Yoruba religious rituals, such as prayer, divination and sacrifice, are intended to attract benevolent powers and repel malevolent ones. Thus Yoruba religion is highly pragmatic, and worship is expected to bring tangible benefits in terms of the 'good things' of this life: children, prosperity, health and longevity.

While they reject the traditional system of divination and sacrifice, Nigerian Pentecostals have retained the belief in the influence of lesser spiritual entities over the material world and the efficacy of prayer as the key ritual for influencing the powers. John Peel (2000, pp. 314–15), in his exploration of the encounter between Christianity and Yoruba culture, refers to the way Nigeria's new Pentecostals regard these 'hidden forces' as potential hazards, impeding personal progress and preventing individuals from achieving their destinies. For Peel, the advantage they have over the older African initiated churches is that they can address these needs in terms of theologies that have international currency within the global Pentecostal constituency, and in ways that are thoroughly modern.

Deliverance theology, with its focus on liberation from the influence of evil spirits, is perhaps the best example of this. Because of its popularity, especially in the global South, and its incongruence with Western

---

4 For a discussion of the Yoruba concept of spiritual power, see Harris 2006, pp. 55–62.

5 Horton argues that prior to their exposure to an expanding world, the focus of African religion was on a lower tier of lesser spirits rather than an upper tier occupied by a Supreme Being.

models of modernization and secularization, it has generated considerable scholarly discussion (Hunt 1998; Walker 1993; Gifford 1998, 2004; Asamoah-Gyadu 2006). While African deliverance theology resonates with traditional piety, it is elaborated in forms that are consistent with global Pentecostal culture. This is evident from Gifford's work on Ghana's new Pentecostal churches. Gifford (2004, p. 89) shows the close similarities between Christian deliverance and Ghana's pre-Christian religion, where more attention is paid to the lesser deities than to the Supreme Being. However, the way it is expressed is influenced by Western deliverance specialists, whose books are readily available across Africa. Deliverance theology is also modern in its orientation. While it is viewed in negative terms as the removal of the effects of past religious and social associations, it is orientated towards the present and the future in ways that seem to resonate with modernity's notion of the autonomy of the self and its call to make a break with the past (Meyer 1998). Nigerian Pentecostals promote deliverance as a means of severing ties with social and religious pasts, thus removing obstacles to personal progress and enabling the construction of new religious identities. Yet the goal is primarily ethical rather than social, and the result is not so much increased autonomy and individuality but a new commitment to Christ and a new set of communal relationships. From an initial focus on holiness and healing, deliverance theology in Nigeria has been extended to include economic circumstances, geographical localities, people groups and socio-political structures, as we shall see later.

A prime example of this is Mountain of Fire and Miracles (MFM), currently one of the largest Pentecostal Churches in Nigeria with over 300 branches nationally, and with congregations in Europe and North America.[6] MFM's founder, Daniel Kolawole Olukoya, is a former scientist with a PhD from the University of Reading in the UK. Significantly, these academic credentials are vaunted by MFM, perhaps to commend its deliverance methodology to a sceptical Western audience. MFM describes itself as a 'do-it-yourself Gospel Ministry' and promotes 'violent prayer' as the solution to 'stubborn problems' (Olukoya 1999a). According to Olukoya (1999a, p. 9), '[t]he only language the devil understands is the language of violence and resounding defeat', and he exhorts his followers to 'fight until every foe is vanquished and Christ is Lord indeed'. Because of its emphasis on protecting and delivering people from

---

6 MFM's headquarters, located along the Lagos-Ibadan Expressway, claims to be one of the largest single congregations in Africa, with an attendance of over 200,000 at a single meeting.

the activities of malicious spirits, Afe Adogame (2005, p. 3) suggests that it should be classified under the rubric of the 'security gospel' rather than the 'prosperity gospel' movement. The titles of MFM publications, such as *Dealing with Local Satanic Technology*, *Overcoming Witchcraft*, *Power against Marine Spirits*, and *Dealing with the Evil Powers of your Father's House*, reflect the Church's preoccupation with deliverance from witchcraft and evil spirits, as well as past associations with 'occult' powers and traditional religious culture. MFM literature is filled with anecdotal evidence and contains an elaborate liturgy of prayers designed to liberate Christians from demonic powers and remove obstacles to individual progress and prosperity.[7] For churches such as MFM deliverance is usually focused on individual problems, for example sickness, poverty, unemployment, marital distress and, in the case of migrant churches in Britain, immigration and visa issues, reflecting the pragmatic nature of Nigerian Pentecostal theology.

The appeal of deliverance theology is obvious in a hostile economic environment like Nigeria, where access to medical facilities and to state funds is severely restricted. Its popularity also stems from its close affinity to biblical cosmology. Unlike many Westerners, Nigerian Pentecostals are reluctant to divest the Bible of its supernatural character and are particularly drawn to the Gospels and Acts, where healing and exorcism occur on a regular basis. Books on deliverance are filled with biblical references, often interpreted in imaginative ways to make a point or buttress an argument. Some contain elaborate demonic typologies based on extrabiblical material of unknown provenance. The focus of deliverance is on problems that beset African Christians in particular. Yet MFM believes that Western Christians are not immune to the effects of these malevolent powers, and it is keen to promote its deliverance methodology outside the African continent. According to Olukoya (1999c, p. 44), witchcraft is a global phenomenon that manifests itself in diverse ways in different localities. Europe's and Britain's liberal migration policy and multicultural society are sometimes blamed for allowing alien spirits from outside to gain entry, resulting in ungodly behaviour such as homosexuality, gun crime and terrorism. Thus deliverance theology is promoted by MFM as essential if Christianity's decline in the West is to be reversed. In the UK,

---

7 One example is Olukoya's book *Prayer Rain* (1999b), described on its front cover as the 'most powerful and practical Prayer manual ever written'. It contains over 500 pages of prayers, targeting such problems as hidden curses, evil blood covenants, marine witchcraft, poverty, marital lateness and marital distress, sickness, and destiny killers.

where it has grown to over 40 branches in eight years, MFM holds regular deliverance programmes aimed at releasing people from the influence of satanic powers. However, these meetings appeal mainly to African migrants.

While other Nigerian Pentecostal Churches may not place as much emphasis on deliverance as MFM, the modern concern for progress, new beginnings and the transformation of the self is a strong current that runs through Nigerian Pentecostalism, both at home and in the diaspora. This is reflected in the following extract from a church newsletter:

> The month of 'New Beginning' is a prophetic month for us in the Gateway Family . . . For this New Beginning, I stand to tell you that your past is not a prerequisite. Nothing you have done or have not done is strong enough to limit the extent of God's love. Do not let your past successes or failures be a stumbling block to what God is about to do. That is why in Isaiah 43 vs. 17 – 19, He says: 'Forget the former things; do not dwell on the past. See I am doing a new thing . . . ' Be ready as we step into our month of great starts. God asked me to tell you that in this month all your past errors will be wiped out.[8]

Another example is the following excerpt from a book entitled *A New Beginning* by Pastor Enoch Adeboye, General Overseer of the Redeemed Christian Church of God:

> When God decides to put an end to the past and begins a future, He can do it in such a way that it will be difficult for you even to remember what had happened in the past . . . He is the Controller of the past, present, and future. That is why the Bible says in 2 Corinthians 5:17 that if any man be in Christ he is a new creature, old things are passed away, behold, all things are become new . . . Let this day be a new beginning for you – a new beginning of joy; a new beginning of victory; a new beginning of prosperity. Ask Him to do a new thing in your life today. (Adeboye 1999, p. 92)

The related ideas of 'making anew' and the transformation of the self seem to resonate with sociologist Anthony Giddens' concept of the reflexive self, characteristic of late modern or post-traditional societies.

---

8 Pastor Eddie Iduoze, Gateway Ministries, *Newsletter*, vol. 2, issue 8, August 2008. Gateway Ministries was originally a church plant from Trinity Chapel, a RCCG parish in London, but now has independent status.

Giddens (1991, p. 5) suggests that, in contrast to traditional societies where identities are inherited and fixed, late modern subjects are increasingly free to reinvent themselves and revise their biographical narratives. 'In today's world, we have unprecedented opportunities to make ourselves and to create our own identities . . . The modern world forces us to find ourselves. Through our capacity as self-conscious, self-aware human beings, we constantly create and recreate our identities' (Giddens 2001, p. 30). Yet as the above example illustrates, the transformation of the self in Nigerian Pentecostal discourse is always related to the individual's experience of God's power and authority, and invariably linked to ethical renewal. It is God, through his Spirit, who removes the hindrances of the past through forgiveness of sins and deliverance from demonic influences, and enables believers to construct new identities for themselves.

Constructing local identities

Rather than consciously try to adapt Christianity to African culture by incorporating elements of traditional religion, as many African theologians have tried to do, Nigerian Pentecostals find other avenues for building local identities. One is a historical approach that emphasizes African contributions to biblical, Christian and secular history, and identifies various historical and cultural processes responsible for the continent's current social ills. Significantly, while they are critical of Western imperialism and its effects on African societies, Nigeria's new Pentecostals are generally grateful to Western missionaries for introducing the gospel. The main causes of Nigeria's present predicament in Pentecostal discourse are its traditional cultural patterns rather than global forces. As Ruth Marshall-Fratani (1998) notes, Pentecostal critique of Nigeria's present social, political and cultural forms 'focuses not on external interventions such as colonialism, or capitalism, but rather . . . on the *practices* of local agents', and specifically their personal rejection of Christ, which 'opens up the space in which the failure of the nation is manifested'.

Matthew Ashimolowo, Nigerian Pentecostal pastor of the largest single congregation in Western Europe, adopts this approach in a recent book, entitled *What is Wrong with Being Black?* (2007). Ashimolowo begins by emphasizing the role of Africans and African societies in biblical and secular history. While he condemns European imperialists for plundering the rich natural resources of the African continent, for racism and for creating a culture of dependency, he insists that many of Africa's social ills are cultural in origin and include persistent idolatry, witchcraft, superstition, distorted family values, tribalism, poor governance and an inferiority complex. Here his approach is similar to the Ghanaian Pentecostal, Mensa Otabil, so admired by Paul Gifford (2004, pp. 113–39). Like Otabil, Ashimolowo focuses on the minds of Africans and the need to confront prevailing cultural trends. His solution to the African dilemma and the alleviation of poverty is the transformation of African minds and hearts through studying the Bible and recognizing the rich contributions that Africans have made to world civilization.

A second way that Nigerian Pentecostals reinforce African identities is through the promotion of success-orientated theologies, which link faith and prayer with the expectation of material prosperity and success. For RCCG's Enoch Adeboye, poverty is a curse that brings untold physical and psychological hardships in its wake. In his book, *Heaven on the Move*, he refers to the lame man found begging for alms at the gate of the Jerusalem Temple (Acts 2):

> The lame man was lonely in his poverty until heaven passed by. Nobody is a friend of a poor man . . . The loneliness, rejection and disregard that poverty brings are a serious problem. From the day heaven moved upon him, his loneliness was removed . . . Everybody likes to associate with a success story. (Adeboye 2007, pp. 16–8)

Similar sentiments are expressed in a MFM publication entitled *Poverty Must Die*:

> Poverty is a force of destruction and it is an instrument of evil. Good things cannot stay where poverty prevails. Indeed, poverty attracts sickness, death, uncertainty, worry, fear and other agents of destruction into people's lives. Poverty must die for you to live a fulfilling life. (Oyewole and Ebofin 2000, pp. 6–8)

The tendency for Western scholars to regard prosperity teaching as a distortion of the Christian gospel has discouraged dialogue with Africa's prosperity churches.[9] This is counterproductive, especially as the latter are growing at the expense of the mainline Churches. Generalizations are sometimes made that fail to take into account the varied expressions

---

9 For critical analyses of prosperity theology, see McConnell 1990; Smail, Walker and Wright 1994; Perriman (ed.) 2003.

of prosperity theology and the different meanings attached to it. How can intercultural theology resolve this apparent impasse? An intercultural approach celebrates diversity and seeks to understand local theologies within their particular contexts in order to facilitate intercultural exchange. In the case of Nigerian prosperity teaching, existing religious preoccupations, local socio-economic context and global forces all came into play. To use an agricultural metaphor, there needed to be a fertile soil, a favourable climate and access to a ready supply of seed. Nigerian societies, such as the Yoruba and Igbo, traditionally associate the deities with prosperity. Related to this is an emphasis on achievement, progress and prestige, where status and moral standing in the community are associated with symbols of success acquired through religious power and the redistribution of wealth for the benefit of others. Thus there are close affinities between traditional religious aspirations and prosperity teaching, with its emphasis on material acquisition through faith, and this facilitated its assimilation into Nigerian soil. As Kalu (2008, p. 259) notes, one of the reasons for the popularity of the prosperity message was its resonance with African indigenous concepts of salvation, abundant life and goals of worship.

Two other conditions contributed to this process: a suitable socio-economic climate and access to a ready supply of seed, in this case the message itself. Matthews Ojo (1996, p. 106) states that in Nigeria, prosperity and success as religious ideas were 'indigenously developed as a response to the socio-economic changes of the 1980s'. Contrary to Gifford (1990), who stresses the American origins of prosperity teaching in Africa, Ojo (2006, p. 208) insists that Nigerian Charismatics read their Bibles for themselves and appropriated its message to suit local contexts, suffering from economic decline caused by corrupt political regimes and IMF-inspired Structural Adjustment Programmes. However, global flows through media and transnational exchanges of ministry were crucial in shaping Nigerian prosperity theology. While it resonated with traditional piety and satisfied local religious demands, it was expressed in standard American form (Burgess 2008, pp. 235–56). Perhaps the most obvious example of this is the principle of 'seed faith', lifted directly from American Word of Faith teaching, which encourages Christians to expect financial returns from their giving (see Roberts 1970).

Prosperity teaching has been criticized for discouraging Christians from productive economic activity (Gifford 2004, pp. 155–8). Yet in Nigerian Pentecostal discourse, hard work, self-discipline and financial responsibility are often promoted alongside faith as necessary conditions for success and material prosperity. For example, a sermon preached by RCCG's

Enoch Adeboye states: 'When you ask God to prosper you, what He will do is that He will give you work to do that will bring in money' (Adeboye 2002, p. 74). Nigerian-initiated churches in the UK, such as the RCCG, organize seminars on business management, investment, job skills and debt management. Church members are generally hard-working, self-disciplined and often highly skilled, and it is these qualities combined with an expectant faith in God's providential control that enable them to compete successfully in the job market. Thus prosperity teaching can be a motivation to economic mobility through work as well as faith. It encourages good stewardship of material resources and the attainment of job-related skills, as well as dependence on providential provision. Ogbu Kalu (2008, p. 262) believes that, when presented in this form, Nigerian prosperity theology resonates with the traditional focus on divine and human agency in poverty alleviation.

Critics of African prosperity teaching also tend to regard it as incompatible with active socio-political engagement because of its capacity to provide a moral justification for individual accumulation and its tendency to divert attention from the structural causes of poverty (Smith 2001, p. 602; Gifford 1990, pp. 373, 382; Marshall 1993, pp. 229–30). However, a closer examination reveals that there are differences between individual churches and denominations in terms of social orientation. Some churches, while adhering to a doctrine of prosperity, are redistributing their wealth into social welfare initiatives in the wider society. There is often a strong sense of obligation within these churches to work for the common good, which is sometimes missed in studies of this nature. For example, the leaders of Jesus House, the RCCG's flagship congregation in London, believe that it has been divinely blessed to be a blessing to others by providing financial assistance to less-privileged believers and alleviating poverty in the wider society, thus echoing God's promise to Abraham that he will be a blessing to all the peoples of the earth (Gen. 12).[10]

Another criticism often levelled against Africa's new Pentecostal churches is that by focusing on prosperity and success they lack a viable theology of suffering (Gifford 2004, p. 50; Asamoah-Gyadu 2006, pp. 218, 232). While not as prominent as prosperity, suffering is certainly an element in Nigerian Pentecostal theology. However, it is normally regarded as a temporary phase to be overcome through faith and prayer. One example of this is found in a magazine article, written by Agu Irukwu, Nigerian pastor of RCCG Jesus House in London, shortly after he had

---

10 See Jesus House, *Going the Extra Mile: 2007 in Review*, 2008, p. 14.

suffered the loss of his wife from cancer. Here Old Testament examples are used to illustrate the temporary nature of suffering:

> According to the word of God (John 16:33), we accept that there will be trouble in this life, but Jesus assures us ultimately of victory. In the Bible, Job had a new beginning after an encounter with God, and God spoke a word that caused him to receive a double portion of everything he had lost during the previous series of calamities. Joseph stepped into new beginnings after the ordeals of the pit and the prison. David stepped into a new beginning in the aftermath of the storms of war and persecution.[11]

Again we see the emphasis on new beginnings, referred to earlier, which encourages those suffering from adverse circumstances to have hope for a better future. This is a familiar theme in Nigerian Pentecostal theology and helps to explain its popularity, especially in contexts where suffering of various kinds is an endemic condition for many, and where enjoyment of the 'good life' is the expected outcome of religious observance.

Nigerian Pentecostals attach a variety of meanings to the experience of suffering. Sometimes it is regarded as an enemy to be overcome by faith, especially if it is believed to be satanic in origin. In this case, problems such as sickness, barrenness, poverty and failure are believed to be caused by human or spiritual agents of Satan, who are then counteracted by means of aggressive spiritual warfare. Here we see elements of continuity with traditional religious cultures, such as the Yoruba and Igbo, where affliction is often blamed on the activities of malicious agents, such as witches or evil spirits, and various preventative and purificatory rites are performed to immunize potential victims against their attacks (Peel 2000, p. 166; Awolalu 1979, pp. 69–74; Ikenga Metuh 1981, pp. 116, 97, 101; Okorocha 1987, p. 131). Suffering is also linked to divine chastisement, though this is less common in Nigerian Pentecostal texts. Yet even here the focus is on the positive outcome of suffering in terms of moral transformation, and its temporary nature. The cross features prominently in Nigerian Pentecostal discourse, but as a symbol of victory over the forces of evil rather than a model of suffering for emulative action.

Some Nigerian Pentecostal pastors have rightly been criticized for using prosperity teaching for personal enrichment at the expense of their churches' impoverished members. Yet most Churches in the global North would agree that the pursuit of prosperity and success is a desirable

---

11 Agu Irukwu, 'In The Crucible with Pastor Agu: A New Beginning', *Outflow*, September 2007, p. 5.

goal, even though they may prefer to achieve this through secular means, through hard work and wise investment. What Nigerian Pentecostals have done is to develop a theology in keeping with their holistic understanding of salvation, which combines secular and sacred means to achieve these ends.

Nigerian Pentecostals and civic engagement

As I have suggested, intercultural theology allows for a multiperspectival examination of particular issues and enables previously silenced voices to challenge dominant ideologies and worldviews (Lartey 2007). One area where the influence of worldview is felt most keenly is the realm of politics. The shifting role of religion in politics has been at the centre of debates on global Pentecostalism, partly stimulated by developments in the global south (Ellis and ter Haar 2004; Gifford 1998; Kalu 2008; Marshall 2009; Meyer 2004; Robbins 2004). Western Enlightenment thinking, which relegated religion to the private sphere, resulted in a separation of political and religious realms in many former colonies. However, increasingly African religious movements are reoccupying public space in ways that challenge Western models of modernization and secularization. Stephen Ellis and Gerrie ter Haar (2004, p. 10) suggest that 'Africa and its diasporas are playing a key role in the realignments of religion and politics that seem set to become a major challenge to everyone in the years ahead.' In Nigeria, religion has re-emerged as a potent political force and a dominant feature of national political culture. This is largely due to the strong presence of resurgent Islam and Pentecostal revivalism which according to Paul Freston (2001, p. 182) has made Nigeria 'globally unique in terms of evangelical politics'.

Historically, Pentecostals have a reputation for having an 'otherworldly' spirituality that eschews socio-political engagement in favour of getting people 'saved' before the return of Christ (Dempster 1993, p. 59; Miller and Yamamori 2007, p. 213; Petersen 1996, p. 229). However, a more nuanced assessment shows a diversity of Pentecostal political postures, ranging from the apolitical to the more politically engaged. In the case of Africa, and Nigeria in particular, a historical perspective is important, which takes account of changing religious, socio-economic and political contexts. Nigeria's turbulent post-independence history has witnessed a civil war, eight military coups, seven military regimes and three civilian governments. The geopolitical landscape has been complicated by inter-ethnic and interreligious rivalry, with different ethnic and religious factions competing for control. This history provides the backdrop for the shifting political orientation of Nigeria's Pentecostal constituency.

In its early period of the 1970s, the Pentecostal revival in Nigeria adopted an apolitical stance due to its location on the margins of society, its focus on eschatological salvation and its radical holiness ethic, which generated a perception of politics as a dirty business tainted by its associations with traditional religion and 'occult' forces, and linked to corruption and violence (Marshall 1995; Ojo 2006; Burgess 2008). The advent of prosperity teaching in the mid-1980s compounded the tendency for many Pentecostals to adopt a conservative non-critical stance. However, more recently there has been a shift towards a theology of political engagement, initially precipitated by a concern to protect their interests in a hostile environment characterized by Islamic hegemony (Ojo 2006, p. 183). The rapid growth of the movement, the emergence of a middle-class constituency and the onset of democratization and liberalization in the late 1990s have opened up space for new civil society structures and enabled Pentecostals to become significant players in the political arena. Contrary to Gifford's assertion that much of Africa's Christianity (that is, the Pentecostal sector) dismisses the contemporary political situation as theologically irrelevant (Gifford 1998, p. 333), many Nigerian Pentecostals are very conscious of it. While they lack a formalized political theology, it is implicit in their discourse and praxis. Theirs is an enacted theology that emerges through action as well as reflection. But rather than pursue a path of civil disobedience, contemporary Pentecostals have developed other strategies of political engagement.

One of the contributions of contemporary Nigerian Pentecostalism to intercultural theology is its focus on social and cultural transformation. This is exemplified by Tony Rapu, senior pastor of the Lagos-based This Present House.[12] Rapu is one of the more innovative and radical Pentecostal voices to come out of Africa. His weekly column, 'Voice of One', an incisive social commentary, is featured in the Sunday edition of Nigeria's national *THISDAY* newspaper, and members of his church regularly visit the most deprived areas of Lagos to distribute food and provide medical care, counselling and prayer for the poor and destitute. Rapu's holistic soteriology moves beyond the individualistic orientation of so many contemporary Pentecostals to include societal and national redemption. 'God is interested in saving us; He is also interested in saving creation, in

---

12 Formerly a pastor of the most dynamic Redeemed Christian Church of God congregation in Lagos, Rapu fell out with the Church over its increasing emphasis on miracles and prosperity to the detriment of its holiness ethic.

redeeming the structures and systems of human society which bear the scars of the fall of man' (Rapu 2006b). Responding to the chaotic disorder of Nigerian society brought about by a 'tragic over-dependence on government', he charts out what he believes is the Holy Spirit's new agenda for the Church 'as an agent of change' that will 'transform social, economic and political reality'. 'The order of Moses that brought the Church into its present position out of Egypt will have to give way to the order of Joshua that will take the Church into the next level of relevance in issues of politics, economics and governance.' This will involve 'a new post-Pentecostal, non-denominational order of ministers', who will model 'the alternative government of the Kingdom of God' and mobilize their members to address 'the real life human crises afflicting the land' through divinely directed and empowered social ministries (Rapu 2007). Rapu calls for Christians to confront 'the ungodly principles' operating in the social, economic and political structures and replace them with systems built on 'truth, integrity and righteousness' (Rapu 2006b).

> It is as competent Christians carrying the power of God begin to assume a position of responsibility for every sector of society and begin to discover the Divine blueprint for recovery and restoration on these fronts that change will begin. We can reverse the decay in governance, politics, society, the economy, business, law, health, education, the family etc. It is our mandate and calling. It is to this end that the Church must discard our church-building mentality, roll up our sleeves and get involved in the restorative processes for National Transformation (Rapu 2006a).

Rapu's use of the exodus motif and the biblical metaphor of the Kingdom of God suggest similarities with Liberation Theology. However, his political agenda is quite different. He does not seek to engender change through violent revolution, as some expressions of Liberation Theology have advocated, but by raising a new generation of leaders who will run for political office and seek employment in the public sector. As Ruth Marshall (2009, p. 204) points out, this entails the projection into the public space of a highly political agenda, but one that is dependent upon the conversion of individuals rather than 'a revolution to create a new institutional order, found a new constitution, or elaborate new laws'. Donald Miller and Tetsunao Yamamori (2007, p. 215) refer to it as a 'trickle-up' model of social change, where 'people with strong moral values move into positions of authority', bringing about gradual change in the institutions they lead.

Another way that Nigerian Pentecostalism differs from advocates of Liberation Theology is the importance it attaches to spiritual warfare prayer as a means of socio-political engagement (Kalu 2008). In Nigerian Pentecostal discourse, politics is presented in terms of spiritual causality, as a religious contest between good and evil, reflecting the dominance of supernatural ideas in African political culture (Ellis and ter Haar 2004, p. 7). Paul Gifford (2004, p. 161) refers to this as an 'enchanted' approach to politics, whereby demons are held responsible for adverse political circumstances, and their spiritual power must be broken through prayer warfare. Nigerian Pentecostal Emeka Nwankpa (1994) suggests a number of strategies Christians can employ to 'redeem the land' from the hand of Satan, partly gleaned from American Pentecostal literature.[13] There is a strong ethical element in this teaching, reflected in an emphasis on holiness and reconciliation as necessary conditions for effective intercession. Nwankpa promotes a violent form of spiritual warfare to wrest control over governments from malign spirits, and believes that ordinary Christians can change the destinies of nations through 'prophetic' prayer. 'When you pray prophetically, you are in the place of governmental authority . . . Prophetic praying is very powerful. It can change laws. It can cancel what politicians have said' (Nwankpa 1994, pp. 65, 69). There is also a strong emphasis on predictive prophecy in these methodologies. Fellow Nigerian Pentecostal Mosy Madugba (2000, pp. 1, 16–17) refers to a prophecy given during a prayer meeting in 1998 predicting the removal of two prominent political leaders. Within three weeks the incumbent President General Sani Abacha died suddenly in his sleep, and a month later Chief Abiola, winner of the annulled 1993 Presidential election, died in prison.[14]

Nigerian Pentecostals believe that by employing such strategies they are able to change society for the better. Yet claims of this nature are difficult to prove, even though they may be consistent with African and biblical cosmologies and supported by anecdotal evidence. Gifford (2004, p. 172) takes issue with scholars, such as Ruth Marshall, Stephen Ellis and Gerrie ter Haar, for making unsubstantiated claims that Pentecostal deliverance strategies are actually transforming African societies in practical ways (see Marshall 1993, p. 242). He suggests that spiritualizing

---

13 Especially popular are the writings of C. Peter Wagner and George Otis Jr, leading proponents of 'Strategic-level spiritual warfare'; see for example Wagner (ed.) 1991. Strategies include identificational repentance, spiritual mapping, breaking covenants and prophetic prayer.

14 It is perhaps significant that both Abacha and Abiola were Muslims with a strong Islamic agenda.

politics contributes little to debate on modern government. Rather it di-
verts attention from 'the mundane plane on which political issues have
been most fruitfully addressed', discouraging a life of activism in politics
(Gifford 2004, p. 169). However, given their particular theological beliefs and restricted access to the corridors of power, there is an inner logic
to Pentecostal preferences for prayer as the principal tool for political engagement, which belies the movement's acquiescent image. As Ogbu Kalu
(2008, pp. 199–200) notes, it is important for commentators to be attentive to the magical substratum that underpins Africa's political culture,
where it is commonplace for political aspirants to draw upon traditional
religious resources to acquire and maintain political power.

The search for criteria of orthodoxy

One of the challenges for intercultural theology is how to assess the val-
idity of particular local theological expressions. For Hollenweger (1997,
pp. 132–41), all forms of Christianity, including biblical versions, are
syncretistic because they mix gospel with culture. He calls for a theologically responsible syncretism, following the pattern of the biblical authors who took seriously the religious context of their time. Yet how
does one ensure that what is proposed is in fact theologically responsible?
Stephen Bevans (2007, p. 22–3) refers to the danger in contextualization
of mixing gospel and culture in ways that undermine, rather than enhance, Christianity. He suggests that the contemporary pluralism in theology challenges theologians to search for criteria of orthodoxy. Robert
Schreiter (1985, pp. 117–21) identifies five such criteria for establishing
Christian identity. First, a theology must have inner consistency; it must
be consistent with the basic movement of Christianity. This is similar to
Volker Küster's (1999, p. 26) criterion of identity, by which he means
that any contextual theology must be compatible with the gospel. Second, it must be able to be translated into worship. How does a particular
theology develop in the communal prayer of the Church? Here Schreiter
refers to the importance of the worshipping context being safeguarded
by the place accorded to the Scriptures in that context. The third measure is the criterion of orthopraxis. A genuinely contextual theology must
lead to Christian behaviour that is consistent with biblical parameters.
Thus a theology of liberation that justifies violent action against oppres-
sors would be wrong. Fourth, it should be open to criticism from other
Churches rather than defensive and parochial. This is what Küster (1999,
p. 28) refers to as the criterion of dialogue: 'Any contextual theology

must be open to discussion in the ecumenical forum.' Fifth, it should have the strength to challenge other theologies by contributing positively to dialogue among contextual theologians. However, a particular theological expression may satisfy all these criteria yet have little practical value in terms of addressing the needs of local communities. Küster (1999, p. 26) proposes a criterion of relevance, whether the contextual theology is relevant in each situation.

How does Nigerian Pentecostal theology measure up to these criteria? If we take prosperity teaching as an example, there are both continuities and discontinuities with Christian tradition. In as much as it encourages hard work and honest and disciplined living, which in turn may lead to wealth accumulation, it resonates with the classic Protestant work ethic. However, its 'magical' approach to money, which links faith and prayer to the expectation of wealth and success, represents a departure from this tradition. Prosperity teaching can also encourage a self-centred approach to worship, whereby Pentecostals engage in prayer for their own personal benefit rather than as an expression of their devotion to God. It can also encourage personal enrichment at the expense of others who are less fortunate, thus undermining social justice. On the other hand, Nigerian Pentecostal worship is often accompanied by strong expressions of gratitude to God for his bountiful gifts. Moreover there is often a culture of generosity and altruism towards others that belies this self-serving image. Finally, prosperity churches are sometimes reluctant to engage in dialogue with other church traditions and submit their theologies to ecumenical scrutiny. However, the popularity of prosperity teaching, especially among the urban poor, is evidence of its practical relevance. In a context such as Nigeria where unemployment and deprivation are rife and access to public funds is severely restricted, the focus on the role of faith in poverty alleviation and economic mobility is for many a welcome addition to the religious repertoire.

When we turn to Nigerian deliverance theologies we find similar continuities and ruptures with Christian tradition. While there has existed a continuing belief in demons and exorcism throughout the history of Christianity, the devil and his works were generally kept in their place, seldom becoming the centre of attention. According to Andrew Walker (1993, p. 88), this was because a 'sound psychology of the spiritual life developed that distinguished between God's acts, the devil's ploys, and the normal processes of the natural world'. However, Nigerian deliverance theologies are based on a heightened dualism that divides reality into God and Satan, good and evil, thus eclipsing the realm of the natural. In the case of MFM, an unhealthy preoccupation with demons has resulted in undue attention being given to the devil in Pentecostal worship and prayer. An overemphasis on demonic agency has also encouraged a diminished sense of responsibility with respect to individual and corporate sin, and discouraged public criticism of political structures. Finally, a lack of openness to criticism from other church traditions has allowed certain excesses to go unchecked. Nigerian Pentecostals are rightly critical of the influence of secularism on Western Christianity. However, they themselves are sometimes unaware of their own (over)dependence on traditional religious categories in shaping their theology. A concern for contextualization and practical relevance has meant that deliverance strategies are often based on questionable biblical and theological foundations. Thus Churches such as MFM run the risk of mixing gospel and culture in ways that are not theologically responsible.

Conclusion

This chapter has been an exercise in intercultural theology. We began with a reference to Schreiter's call for a stronger sense of intercultural exchange and communication given the challenges of globalization and late modernity, and the need to hold disparate theologies together in tension as contributing to the whole (Schreiter 1997, pp. 127–8). An intercultural approach insists that for authentic communication to take place, different theological expressions must be understood within their particular cultural and social settings. By exploring popular theological themes within Nigerian Pentecostalism, we have shown the way that participants engage in a bargaining process of accommodation and resistance with respect to local culture and context. Thus deliverance theology, as practised by Nigerian Pentecostals, reinforces traditional conceptions of cosmology and spiritual power while simultaneously urging the severance of ties with social and religious pasts. The importance of context is also evident in the range of political postures adopted by Nigerian Pentecostals in response to changing socio-political and economic landscapes. The investigation of the role of context in the production of local theologies allows for a greater degree of mutual understanding, especially between the new faces of Christianity in the global South and the former Christian heartlands of North America and Western Europe.

One of the values of intercultural theology, as noted by Wijsen (2001, pp. 221–3), is the space it allows for mutual enrichment and critical interrogation. Returning to the question posed at the beginning of the chapter, I suggest that Nigerian Pentecostalism can contribute to intercultural theology in a number of ways. First, Nigerian Pentecostal theologies, with their practical orientation, their sensitivity to local culture and context and their openness to the power of the Spirit, present a challenge to the more rationalistic and systematic theologies of the global North. Deliverance and success-orientated theologies, while they remain open to abuse, provide a means for individuals to leave behind the influences of their pasts and build new identities for themselves. In this sense they offer hope to those struggling with sin, sickness and adverse economic circumstances. They also empower individuals and church communities, such as those on the African continent, who feel marginalized in the political process. Their theology of the cross is a *theologia gloriae*, which celebrates Christ as the *Christus victor*. Nigerian Pentecostals believe that Christ's incarnation, death and resurrection liberates humanity from sin and all its material and social consequences, whether sickness, social alienation, poverty or political oppression. This theological pragmatism is actually not far removed from theology as it was traditionally conceived. As Elaine Graham et al. (2005, p. 10) suggest, historically, theology emerged in response to three key tasks in relation to practical circumstances: to form individual character, to build the collective identity of Christians and to enable the faith community to relate to the surrounding culture and communicate its faith to the wider world. As this chapter has shown, while the practical concerns of Nigerian Pentecostals tend to focus on issues such as healing, economic security and fertility, their theologies also reflect a concern for character formation, identity construction and contextual relevance. However, it is this pragmatic focus, combined with a reluctance to engage with broader Christian traditions, that has made Nigerian Pentecostalism vulnerable to heterodoxy by combining gospel and culture in ways that have sometimes undermined the credibility of the Christian faith.

Second, the readiness of contemporary Nigerian Pentecostals to engage with socio-political realities presents a challenge to the dominant secular model of late modernity, which separates Church and state and opposes the involvement of religion in the public sphere. The emphasis of Nigerian Pentecostals on the role of prayer as a legitimate means of political engagement is an important corrective to the tendency of Liberation theologians and advocates of Western liberal theology to deny the ontological reality of the powers behind material events. A post-secular age demands that we reconsider the role of religion in politics without necessarily seeking to merge the domains of the political and religious at an institutional level. However, the feasibility of a political ecclesiology whereby the Church rather than the state assumes responsibility for addressing the social ills of a nation remains open to question. Perhaps a more realistic scenario is for Pentecostal churches to continue to function as alternative forms of socio-political and economic solidarity for those on the margins of society, while simultaneously endeavouring to address the social problems in the wider community left untouched by government institutions.

Bibliography

Adeboye, E. A., 1999, *A New Beginning: The Holy Spirit in the Life of Peter*, Lagos: C. R. M. Press.

Adeboye, E. A., 2002, *Sermons of the 2001 Holy Ghost Services*, Lagos: The Book Ministry.

Adogame, A., 2005, 'Dealing with Local Satanic Technology: Deliverance Rhetoric in the Mountain of Fire and Miracles Ministry', unpublished paper presented at the CESNUR International Conference 'Religious Movements, Globalization and Conflict: Transnational Perspectives' held in Palermo, Sicily, June 2005.

Adorno, T. and Horkheimer, M., [1944] 1989, *Dialectic of Enlightenment*, trans. John Cumming, London and New York: Verso.

Agamben, G., 2005, *The Time that Remains: A Commentary on the Letter to the Romans*, trans. P. Dailey, Stanford, CA: Stanford University Press.

Ahrens, T. et al. (eds), 1992, *Hans Jochen Margull: Zeugnis und Dialog: Ausgewählte Schriften*, Ammersbek: Verlag an der Lottbek.

All Christians Fellowship Mission, 2001, *Teaching the Whole Counsel of God: New Life Sunday School*, Abuja: Christian Education Department, All Christians Fellowship Mission.

Anderson, A., 1991, *Moya: The Holy Spirit in an African Context*, Pretoria: Unisa Press.

Anderson, A., 1992a, *African Pentecostalism in a South African Urban Environment: A Missiological Evaluation*, DTh thesis, University of South Africa.

Anderson, A., 1992b, *Bazalwane: African Pentecostals in South Africa*, Pretoria: Unisa Press.

Anderson, A., 1993, *Tumelo: The Faith of African Pentecostals in South Africa*, Pretoria: Unisa Press.

Anderson, A., 2000, *Zion and Pentecost: The Spirituality and Experience of Pentecostal and Zionist/Apostolic Churches in South Africa*, Pretoria: Unisa Press.

Anderson, A., 2001, *African Reformation: African Initiated Christianity in the Twentieth Century*, Trenton, NJ and Asmara, Eritrea: Africa World Press.

Anderson, A., 2003, 'Healing in the Zion Christian Churches in Southern Africa', in Cuthbertson, G., Pretorius, H. and Robert, D. (eds), *Frontiers in African Christianity: Essays in Honour of Inus Daneel*, Pretoria: Unisa Press, pp. 103–19.

Anderson, A., 2004, *An Introduction to Pentecostalism: Global Charismatic Christianity*, Cambridge: Cambridge University Press.

Anderson, A., 2009, 'Varieties, Definitions and Taxonomies in the Study of Global Pentecostalism', in Anderson, A., Bergunder, M., Droogers, A. and Laan, C. van der (eds), *Studying Global Pentecostalism: Theories and Methods*, Berkeley, CA: University of California Press, pp. 13–29.

Aquinas, T., 1953, *Truth (De veritate)*, trans. McGlynn, J. V., SJ, Chicago: Henry Regnery.

Archer, K. J., 2004, *A Pentecostal Hermeneutic for the Twenty-First Century: Spirit, Scripture and Community*, London: T & T Clark.

Archer, K. J., 2007, 'A Pentecostal Way of Doing Theology: Method and Manner', *International Journal of Systematic Theology* 9.1, pp. 1–14.

Arellano, L. B., 1988, 'Women's Experience of God in Emerging Spirituality', in Fabella, Virginia and Oduyoye, Mercy Amba (eds), *With Passion and Compassion: Third World Women Doing Theology*, Maryknoll, NY: Orbis Books, pp. 135–50.

Ariarajah, W., 2003, 'Interreligious Dialogue as an Intercultural Encounter', in Frederiks, Dijkstra and Houtepen (eds), *Towards an Intercultural Theology*, pp. 55–66.

Arnold, M., 1867, *New Poems*, London: Macmillan.

Asamoah-Gyadu, J. K., 2000, 'Renewal within African Christianity: A Study of Some Current Historical and Theological Developments within Independent Indigenous Pentecostalism in Ghana', PhD thesis, University of Birmingham.

Asamoah-Gyadu, J. K., 2006, *African Charismatics: Current Developments within Independent Indigenous Pentecostalism in Ghana*, Leiden: Brill.

Ashimolowo, M., 2007, *What is Wrong with Being Black? Celebrating our Heritage, Confronting our Challenges*, Shippensburg, PA: Destiny Image Publishers.

Astley, J., 2002, *Ordinary Theology: Looking, Listening and Learning Theology*, Aldershot: Ashgate.

Awolalu, J. O., 1979, *Yoruba Beliefs and Sacrificial Rites*, London: Longman.

Barrett, D., Kurian, G. T. and Johnson, T. M. (eds), 2001, *World Christian Encyclopedia*, 2nd edn, Oxford and New York: Oxford University Press.

Barrett, D. B. (ed.), 1982, *World Christian Encyclopedia*, Nairobi, Oxford and New York: Oxford University Press.

Becher, J. (ed.), 1990, *Women, Religion and Sexuality: Studies on the Impact of Religious Teachings on Women*, Geneva: WCC Publications.

Bediako, K., 1996, 'Types of African Theology', in Fyfe, Christopher and Walls, Andrew F. (eds), *Christianity in Africa in the 1990s*, University of Edinburgh: Centre of African Studies, pp. 56–69.

Benjamin, C. R., 1993, 'Aladura Christianity', *Journal of Religion in Africa* 23.3, pp. 266–91.

Bevans, S. B., 1992, *Models of Contextual Theology*, Maryknoll, NY: Orbis Books.

Bevans, S. and Shroeder, R. P., 2004, *Constants in Context: A Theology of Mission for Today*, Maryknoll, NY, Orbis Books.

Bevans, S., 2007, *Models of Contextual Theology*, revised edn, Maryknoll, NY: Orbis Books.

Bevis, K., 2007, 'Dwelling, Ambivalence and the Maternal Body: The "Sensible Transcendent" in Lévinas', unpublished paper.

Bhabba, H. K., 1994, *The Location of Culture*, New York: Routledge.

Bingemer, M. C., 1994, 'Women in the Future of the Theology of Liberation', in King, Ursula (ed.), *Feminist Theology from the Third World*, pp. 308–17.

Bittlinger, A., 1977, 'Papst und Pfingstler: Der römisch katholische/pfingstliche Dialog und seine ökumenische Relevanz', PhD thesis, University of Birmingham.

Bosch, D. J., 1991, *Transforming Mission*, Maryknoll, NY: Orbis Books.

Bosch, D. J., 1995, *Believing in the Future: Towards a Missiology of Western Culture*, Leominster: Gracewing.

Brandon, S. G. F., 1967, *Jesus and the Zealots*, New York: Scribner.

Brown, T. (ed.), 2006, *Other Voices, Other Worlds: The Global Church Speaks Out on Homosexuality*, London: Darton, Longman & Todd.

Brück, M. von, 1992, 'Religionswissenschaft und interkulturelle Theologie', *Evangelische Theologie* 52, 3, pp. 245–61.

Burgess, R. J., 2008, *Nigeria's Christian Revolution: The Civil War Revival and its Pentecostal Progeny (1967–2006)*, Carlisle: Regnum/Paternoster.

Burgess, R. J., 2004, 'The Civil War Revival and its Pentecostal Progeny: A Religious Movement among the Igbo People of Eastern Nigeria (1967–2002)', PhD thesis, University of Birmingham.

Burnard, P., 1991, 'A Method of Analysing Interview Transcripts in Qualitative Research', *Nurse Education Today* 11.6, pp. 461–6.

Byrne, L. (ed.), 1993, *The Hidden Journey: Missionary Heroines in Many Lands*, London: SPCK.

Byrne, L. (ed.), 1995, *The Hidden Voice: Christian Women and Social Change*, London: SPCK.

Caipora Women's Group, 1993, *Women in Brazil*, London: Latin America Bureau.

Cantwell Smith, W., 1989, *Towards a World Theology: Faith and the Comparative History of Religion*, London: Macmillan.

Cartledge, M., 2003, *Practical Theology: Charismatic and Imperical Perspectives*, Carlisle: Paternoster.

Cartledge, M., 2004, 'Trinitarian Theology and Spirituality: An Empirical Study of Charismatic Christians', *Journal of Empirical Theology* 17.1, pp. 76–84.

Cartledge, M., 2006, *Encountering the Spirit: The Charismatic Tradition*, London: Darton, Longman & Todd, and 2007, Maryknoll, NY: Orbis Books.

Chandran, J. R., 'The Development of Christian Theology in India', in Sugirtharajah, R. S. and Hargreaves, C. (eds), 1993, *Readings in Indian Christian Theology, Vol. 1*, London: SPCK, pp. 4–13.

Chant, S. with Craske, N., 2003, *Gender in Latin America*, New Brunswick, NJ: Rutgers University Press.

Cheetham, D., 2008, 'Comparative Philosophy of Religion', in Cheetham and King (eds), *Contemporary Practice and Method in the Philosophy of Religion*, pp. 101–116.

Cheetham, D. and King, R. (eds), 2008, *Contemporary Practice and Method in the Philosophy of Religion*, London: Continuum.

Cheetham, D., (forthcoming), 'Contextual Theology', in Kurian, G. (ed.), *Encyclopedia of Christian Civilization*, Oxford: WileyBlackwell.

Chopp, R. S., 1997, 'Latin American Liberation Theology', in Ford, David F. (ed.), 1997, *The Modern Theologians: An Introduction to Christian Theology of the Twentieth Century*, Oxford: Blackwell, pp. 409–25.

Chung, H. K., 1990, *Struggle to be the Sun Again: Introducing Asian Women's Theology*, London: SCM Press.

Chung, H. K., 1991, 'Come Holy Spirit – Renew the Whole Creation', in Kinnamon, M. (ed.), *Signs of the Spirit: Official Report of the Seventh Assembly of the World Council of Churches, Canberra, 1991*, Geneva: WCC Publications, pp. 37–47.

Chung, H. K., 1994. 'Ecology, Feminism and African and Asian Spirituality: Towards a Spirituality of Eco-Feminism', in Hallman, D. G. (ed.), *Ecotheology: Voices from South and North*, Geneva: WCC Publications, pp. 175–8.

Clarke, C. R., 2003, 'Faith in Christ in Post-Missionary Africa: Christology among Akan African Indigenous Churches in Ghana', PhD thesis, University of Birmingham.

Clements, K., 1999, *Faith on the Frontier: A Life of J. H. Oldham*, Edinburgh and Geneva: T & T Clark and WCC.

Clooney, F. X., 1995, 'The Emerging Field of Comparative Theology: A Bibliographical Review (1989–1995)', *Theological Studies* 56.3, pp. 521–550.

Clooney, F. X., 2010, *Comparative Theology: Deep Learning Across Religious Borders*, Oxford: WileyBlackwell.

Colletti, J., 1990, 'Ethnic Pentecostalism in Chicago 1890–1950', PhD thesis, University of Birmingham.

Conn, J. W., 1986, *Women's Spirituality: Resources for Christian Development*, Mahwah, NJ: Paulist Press.

Cox, H., 1996, *Fire from Heaven: The Rise of Pentecostal Spirituality and the Reshaping of Religion in the Twenty-First Century*, London: Cassell.

Critchley, S., 1999, *Ethics of Deconstruction: Derrida and Levinas*, 2nd edn, Edinburgh: Edinburgh University Press.

Cross, F. L., et al. (eds), 1997, *The Oxford Dictionary of the Christian Church*, 3rd edn, Oxford: Oxford University Press.

Cruchley-Jones, P. (ed.), 2008, *God at Ground Level*, Frankfurt am Main: Peter Lang.

Cullmann, O., 1956, *The State in the New Testament*, New York: Scribner.

Daly, M., 1986, *Beyond God the Father: Toward a Philosophy of Women's Liberation*, London: The Women's Press.

Damasio, A., 2000. *The Feeling of What Happens: Body and Emotion in the Making of Consciousness*, London: Harvest Books.

Daneel, M. L., 1974, *Old and New in Southern Shona Independent Churches*, Vol. 2, The Hague: Mouton.

Daneel, M. L., 1988, *Old and New in Southern Shona Independent Churches*, Vol. 3, Gweru: Mambo Press.

Daneel, M. L., 1989, *Christian Theology of Africa*, Pretoria: Unisa Press.

Daneel, M. L., 1998, *African Earthkeepers: Interfaith Mission in Earth-care*, Vol. 1, Pretoria: Unisa Press.

Daneel, M. L., 1999, *African Earthkeepers: Environmental Mission and Liberation in Christian Perspective*, Vol. 2, Pretoria: Unisa Press.

Daneel, M. L., 2007, *All Things Hold Together: Holistic Theologies at the African Grassroots*, Pretoria: Unisa Press.

Davie, G., 2002, *Religion in Modern Europe: A Memory Mutates*, Oxford: Oxford University Press.

Dempster, M. W., 1993, 'Christian Social Concern in Pentecostal Perspective: Reformulating Pentecostal Eschatology', *Journal of Pentecostal Theology* 2, pp. 51–64.

Derrida, J., 1995, *Gift of Death*, trans. Wills, D., Chicago: University of Chicago Press.

Derrida, J., 1997, *De l'hospitalité*, Paris: Calman-Lévy.

Dube, M. W. (ed.), 2001, *Other Ways of Reading: African Women and the Bible*, Atlanta, GA: Society of Biblical Literature.

Ehrenreich, B., 2009, *Smile or Die: How Positive Thinking Fooled America and the World*, London: Granta.

Eliot, T. S., 1939, *The Idea of a Christian Society*, London: Faber.

Ellis, S. and Haar, G. T., 2004, *Worlds of Power: Religious Thought and Political Practice in Africa*, London: Hurst & Co.

Esquivel, J., 1990, 'Conquered and Violated Women', in Boff, L. and Elizondo, V. (eds), *1492–1992: The Voice of the Victims*, London: SCM Press, pp. 68–77.

Evans, M. J., 1983, *Woman in the Bible*, Downers Grove, IL: InterVarsity Press.

Fabella, V. and Mercy, A. O. (eds), 1988, *With Passion and Compassion: Third World Women Doing Theology*, Maryknoll, NY: Orbis Books.

Fabella, V., 1988, 'A Common Methodology for Diverse Christologies?', in Fabella, V. and Mercy, A. O. (eds), *With Passion and Compassion: Third World Women Doing Theology*, Maryknoll, NY: Orbis Books, pp. 108–17.

Faupel, D. W., 1989, 'This Gospel of the Kingdom: The Significance of Eschatology in the Development of Pentecostal Thought', PhD thesis, University of Birmingham.

Fiorenza, E. S., 1983, *In Memory of Her: A Feminist Theological Reconstruction of Christian Origins*, London: SCM Press

Flannery, A. (ed.), 1996, *Vatican Council II: The Basic Sixteen Documents; Constitutions, Decrees, Declarations – A Completely Revised Translation in Inclusive Language*, New York: Costello; and Dublin: Dominican.

Ford, D., Quash, B. and Soskice, J. M. (eds), 2005. *Fields of Faith: Theology and Religious Studies for the Twenty-First Century*, Cambridge: Cambridge University Press.

Ford, D., 1999, *Self and Salvation: Being Transformed*, Cambridge: Cambridge University Press.

Fredericks, J., 2004, *Buddhists and Christians: Through Comparative Theology to Solidarity*, Maryknoll, NY: Orbis Books.

Frederiks, M., Dijkstra, M. and Houtepan, A. (eds), 2003, *Towards an Intercultural Theology: Essays in Honour of Jan A.B. Jongeneel*, Zoetarmeer: Vitgeverij Meinenia.

Freston, P., 2001, *Evangelicals and Politics in Asia, Africa and Latin America*, Cambridge: Cambridge University Press.

Friedli, R., 1974, *Fremdheit als Heimat: Auf der Suche nach einem Kriterium für den Dialog zwischen den Religionen*, Freiburg: Universitätsverlag.

Friedli, R., 1982a, *Mission oder Demission: Konturen einer lebendigen, weil missionarischen Gemeinde*, Freiburg: Universitätsverlag.

Friedli, R., 1982b, 'Zum Dank an Prof. Hans-Jochen Margull' [obituary], *Zeitschrift für Missionswissenschaft und Religionswissenschaft 66*, p. 293.

Friedli, R., 1987, 'Interkulturelle Theologie', in Müller, K. and Sundermeier, T. (eds), *Lexikon Missionstheologischer Grundbegriffe*, Berlin: Reimer, pp. 181–5.

Friedli, R., 1991, 'Kultur und kulturelle Vielfalt: Bemerkungen zur interkulturellen Übersetzung von Ex. 3,14', in Sundermeier, T. and Ustorf, W. (eds), *Begegnung mit dem Anderen: Plädoyers für eine interkulturelle Hermeneutik*, Gütersloh: Gerd Mohn, pp. 29–38.

Friedli, R., 1995, 'Synkretismus als Befreiungspraxis: Asiatische und afrikanische Modelle im Dialog', *Dialog der Religionen* 5, pp. 42–66.

Friedli, R., 1997, 'Intercultural Theology', in Müller et al. (eds), *Dictionary of Mission*, pp. 219–22.

Friedli, R., 2000, 'Mission–Religionen–Religionswissenschaft: Erfahrungen mit universitären Neukompositionen', in Becker, D. (ed.), *Mit dem Fremden leben*, Vol. 2, Erlangen: Erlanger Verlag, pp. 185–91.

Gadamer, H.-G., 2004, *Truth and Method*, 2nd edn, trans. Weinsheimer, J. and Marshall, D. G., London: Continuum.

Gaxiola-Gaxiola, M. J., 1990, 'Mexican Pentecostalism: The Struggle for Identity and Relevance in a Pluralistic Society', PhD thesis, University of Birmingham.

Gebara, I. and Bingemer, M. C., 1994, 'Mary – Mother of God, Mother of the Poor', in King, U. (ed.), *Feminist Theology from the Third World*, pp. 275–82.

Gerloff, R. I. H., 1992, *A Plea for British Black Theologies: The Black Church Movement in Britain*, Frankfurt am Main: Peter Lang.

Giddens, A., 1991, *Modernity and Self-Identity: Self and Society in the Late Modern Age*, Cambridge: Polity Press.

Giddens, A., 2001, *Sociology*, 4th edn, Cambridge: Polity Press.

Gifford, P., 1990, 'Prosperity: A New and Foreign Element in African Christianity', *Religion*, 20, pp. 373–88.

Gifford, P., 1998, *African Christianity: Its Public Role*, London: Hurst and Co.

Gifford, P., 2004, *Ghana's New Christianity: Pentecostalism in a Globalizing African Economy*, Bloomington and Indianapolis: Indiana University Press.

Gifford, P., 2008, 'The Bible in Africa: A Novel Usage in Africa's New Churches', *Bulletin of SOAS* 71.2, pp. 203–19.

Gill, K. D., 1994, *Towards a Contextualized Theology for the Third World: The Emergence and Development of Jesus' Name Pentecostalism in Mexico*, Frankfurt am Main: Peter Lang.

Gnanadason, A., 1993, 'Towards a Feminist Eco-Theology for India', in Kumari, P. (ed.), *A Reader in Feminist Theology*, pp. 95–105.

Gnanadason, A., 1994, 'Women and Spirituality in Asia', in King, U. (ed.), *Feminist Theology from the Third World*, pp. 351–60.

Gnanadason, A., Kanyoro, M. and McSpadden, L. A. (eds), 1996, *Women, Violence and Nonviolent Change*, Geneva: WCC Publications.

Goodchild, P., 2007, *The Theology of Money*, London: SCM.

Gorringe, T., 2004, *Furthering Humanity: A Theology of Culture*, Aldershot: Ashgate.

Graham, E., 1995, *Making the Difference: Gender, Personhood and Theology*, London: Continuum.

Graham, E., 2007, 'Feminist Theology, Northern', in Scott, P. and Cavanaugh, W. T. (eds), *Political Theology*, Oxford: Blackwell, pp. 210–26.

Graham, E., Walton, H. and Ward, F., 2005 (eds), *Theological Reflection: Methods*, London: SCM Press.

Grey, M., 2001, *Introducing Feminist Images of God*, Sheffield: Sheffield Academic Press.

Grey, M., 2004, *The Unheard Scream: The Struggles of Dalit Women in India*, New Delhi: Centre for Dalit Studies.

Gross, R. M., 2005, 'Where Have We Been? Where Do We Need to Go? Women's Studies and Gender in Religion and Feminist Theology', in King, Ursula and Beattie, Tina (eds), *Gender, Religion and Diversity*, pp. 17–27.

Hare, D., 2009, 'The Decade of Looking Away', *Guardian Magazine*, 17 October.

Harris, H., 2006, *Yoruba in Diaspora: An African Church in London*, New York: Palgrave Macmillan.

Hastings, A., 1979, *A History of African Christianity 1950–1975*, Cambridge: Cambridge University Press.

Hauerwas, S., 1983, *The Peaceable Kingdom*, Notre Dame: University of Notre Dame Press; and London: SCM Press.

Hengel, M., 1961, *Die Zeloten*, Leiden: Brill.

Hick, J., 1995, *The Rainbow of Faiths: Critical Dialogues on Religious Pluralism*, London: SCM Press.

Hick, J., 2004, *An Interpretation of Religion*, 2nd edn, London: Palgrave Macmillan.

Hintersteiner, N., 2001, 'Interkulturelle Traditionshermeneutik: Zur grenzüberschreitenden Kommunikation der christlichen Tradition bei Robert J. Schreiter', *Zeitschrift für Missions und Religionswissenschaft* 85.4, pp. 290–314.

Hintersteiner, N. (ed.), 2007a, *Naming and Thinking God in Europe Today: Theology in Global Dialogue*, Amsterdam: Rodopi.

Hintersteiner, N., 2007b, 'Intercultural and Interreligious (Un)Translatibility and the Comparative Theology Project', in Hintersteiner, N., *Naming and Thinking God*, pp. 465–492.

Hocken, P., 1984, 'Baptised in the Spirit: The Origins and Early Development of the Charismatic Movement in Great Britain', PhD thesis, University of Birmingham.

Hollenweger, W. (ed.), 1967, *The Church for Others*, Geneva: WCC Publications.

Hollenweger, W., 1969, *Enthusiastisches Christentum: Die Pfingstbewegung in Geschichte und Gegenwart*, Zürich: Zwingli-Verlag; and Wupperthal: Theol. Verlag R. Brockhaus.

Hollenweger, W., 1972, *The Pentecostals*, London: SCM Press.

Hollenweger, W., 1973. *Marxist and Kimbanguist Mission: A Comparison* (inaugural lecture, 23 November 1972), Birmingham: University of Birmingham.

Hollenweger, W., 1978a, 'Intercultural Theology', in Gordon Davies, J. (ed.), *Research Bulletin 1978*, Birmingham: University of Birmingham, pp. 90–104.

BIBLIOGRAPHY

Hollenweger, W., 1978b, 'Intercultural Theology', *Theological Renewal* 10, pp. 2–14.

Hollenweger, W., 1979, 1982, 1988, *Interkulturelle Theologie*, three vol, Munich: Kaiser.

Hollenweger, W., 1986, 'Intercultural Theology', *Theology Today* 43.1, pp. 28–35.

Hollenweger, 1987, 'Towards an Intercultural History of Christianity', in *International Review of Mission* 76, pp. 526–56.

Hollenweger, W., 1989, *The Future of Mission and the Mission of the Future*, Birmingham: Selly Oak Colleges Occasional Paper.

Hollenweger, W., 1997, *Pentecostalism: Origins and Developments Worldwide*, Peabody, MA: Hendrickson.

Hollenweger, W., 2003, 'Intercultural Theology: Some Remarks on the Term', in Frederiks, Dijkstra, and Houtepen (eds), *Towards an Intercultural Theology*, pp. 89–96.

Hopewell, J., 1987, *Congregation: Stories and Structures*, Philadelphia: Fortress Press.

Horton, R., 1971, 'African Conversion', *Africa* 41.2, pp. 91–112.

Hunt, A., 2005, *Trinity: Nexus of the Mysteries of the Christian Faith*, Maryknoll, NY: Orbis Books.

Hunt, S., 1998, 'Managing the Demonic: Some Aspects of the Neo-Pentecostal Deliverance Ministry', *Journal of Contemporary Religion* 13.2, pp. 215–30.

Ikenga-Metuh, E. E., 1981, *God and Man in African Religion: A Case Study of the Igbo of Nigeria*, London: Geoffrey Chapman.

Isasi-Diaz, A. D., 1996, *Mujerista Theology: A Theology for the Twenty-First Century*, Maryknoll, NY: Orbis Books.

Jehu-Appiah, J. H., 2001, 'The African Indigenous Churches in Britain: An Investigation into their Theology with Special Reference to the Musama Disco Christo Church and the Church of the Lord (Brotherhood)', PhD thesis, University of Birmingham.

Jenkins, P., 2002, *The Next Christendom: The Coming of Global Christianity*, Oxford and New York: Oxford University Press.

Jenkins, P., 2006, *The New Faces of Christianity: Believing the Bible in the Global South*, Oxford and New York: Oxford University Press.

Jenkins, P., 2007, *God's Continent: Islam and Europe's Religious Crisis*, Oxford and New York: Oxford University Press.

Johnson, E. A., 1992, *She Who Is: The Mystery of God in Feminist Theological Discourse*, New York: Crossroad Herder.

Jongeneel, J. A. B. et al. (eds), 1992, *Pentecost, Mission and Ecumenism: Essays on Intercultural Theology. Festschrift for W. J. Hollenweger*, Frankfurt am Main/ Bern: Peter Lang.

Jongeneel, J. A. B., 1994 [revised edn, 2002], and 1997, *Philosophy, Science and Theology of Mission in the 19th and 20th Centuries,* two vols., Frankfurt am Main: Peter Lang.

Kalu, O. U., 2008, *African Pentecostalism: An Introduction*, Oxford: Oxford University Press.

Kang, N., 2008, 'Reconstructing Asian Feminist Theology: Toward a Glocal Feminist Theology in an Era of Neo-Empires', in Kim, S. C. H. (ed.), *Christian Theology in Asia*, Cambridge: Cambridge University Press, pp. 205–26.

Kanyoro, M. R. A., 2001, 'Cultural Hermeneutics: An African Contribution', in Dube, Musa W. (ed.), *Other Ways of Reading: African Women and the Bible*, Atlanta, GA: Society of Biblical Literature, pp. 101–13.

Kaplan, R. B., 1966, 'Cultural Thought Patterns in Intercultural Education', *Language Learning* 16, pp. 1–20.

Katoppo, M., 1979, *Compassionate and Free: An Asian Woman's Theology*, Geneva: WCC Publications.

Kerr, D. A., 1991, 'Come Holy Spirit – Renew the Whole Creation: The Canberra Assembly and Issues of Mission', *International Bulletin of Missionary Research* 15, pp. 98–104.

Kim, K., 2004, 'Spirit and "spirits" at the Canberra Assembly of the World Council of Churches, 1991', *Missiology: An International Review* 32/3 (July), pp. 349–65.

Kim, K., 2007, *The Holy Spirit in the World: A Global Conversation*, Maryknoll, NY: Orbis Books.

King, U. (ed.), 1994, *Feminist Theology from the Third World: A Reader*, London: SPCK.

King, U. and Beattie, T. (eds), 2005, *Gender, Religion and Diversity: Cross-Cultural Perspectives*, London: Continuum.

Klostermaier, K., 1993, 'What Do Men Say About The Son of Man?', in Sugirtharajah, R. S. and Hargreaves, C. (eds), *Readings in Indian Christian Theology*, pp. 116–27.

Knitter, P., 1996, *Jesus and the Other Names. Christian Mission and the Global Responsibility*, Oxford: Oneworld.

Knitter, P., 2002, *Introducing Theologies of Religion*, Maryknoll, NY: Orbis Books.

Köstenberger, A. J. and Schreiner, T. R., 2005, *Women in the Church: An Analysis and Application of 1 Timothy 2:9–15*, 2nd edn, Grand Rapids, MI: Baker Academic.

Kraemer, H., 1938, *The Christian Message in a Non-Christian World*, London: Edinburgh House Press.

Kroeger, R. C. and Kroeger, C. C., 1992, *I Suffer Not a Woman: Rethinking 1 Timothy 2:11–15 in Light of Ancient Evidence*, Grand Rapids, MI: Baker Book House.

Kumari, P. (ed.), 1993, *A Reader in Feminist Theology*, Gurukul, Madras: Gurukul Lutheran Theological College and Research Institute.

Küster, V., 1999, *The Many Faces of Jesus Christ: Intercultural Christology*, Maryknoll, NY: Orbis Books.

Küster, V., 2001a, 'Interkulturelle Theologie', in *Religion in Geschichte und Gegenwart*, Vol. 4, Tübingen: Mohr Siebeck, pp. 197–9. (The English version of this dictionary is currently published by Brill/Leiden under the title *Religion Past and Present*.)

Küster, V., 2001b, *The Many Faces of Jesus Christ: Intercultural Christology*, London: SCM Press.

Küster, V., 2003, 'Von der lokalen Theologie zur neuen Katholizität', *Evangelische Theologie* 63, pp. 362–74.

Küster, V., 2005, 'The Project of an Intercultural Theology', *Swedish Missiological Themes* 93, pp. 417–32.

Kwok P., 1995, *Discovering the Bible in the Non-Biblical World*, Maryknoll, NY: Orbis Books.

Kwok P., 2000, *Introducing Asian Feminist Theology*, Sheffield: Sheffield Academic Press.

Kwok P., 2002, 'Feminist Theology as Intercultural Discourse', in Parsons, S. F. (ed.), *Cambridge Companion to Feminist Theology*, Cambridge: Cambridge University Press, pp. 23–39.

Kwok P., 2007, 'Feminist Theology, Southern', in Scott, P. and Cavanaugh, W. T. (eds), *Political Theology*, Oxford: Blackwell, pp. 194–209.

Laan, C., 1987, 'Gerrit Polman: Sectarian Against his Will. Birth of Pentecostalism in the Netherlands', PhD thesis, University of Birmingham.

Laan, P., 1988, 'The Question of Spiritual Unity: The Dutch Pentecostal Movement in Ecumenical Perpective', PhD thesis, University of Birmingham.

LaCugna, C. M., 1991, *God for Us: The Trinity and Christian Life*, New York: HarperCollins.

Land, S. J., 1993, *Pentecostal Spirituality: A Passion for the Kingdom*, Sheffield: Sheffield Academic Press.

Lartey, E., 2007, 'An Intercultural Approach to Pastoral Care', in Jagessar, M. N. and Reddie, A. G., *Black Theology in Britain: A Reader*, London: Equinox, pp. 271–9.

Lee, M., 2008, 'Reading the Bible in the Non-Western Church: An Asian Dimension', in Walls, A. and Ross, C. (eds), 2008, *Mission in the 21st Century: Exploring the Five Marks of Global Mission*, London: Darton, Longman & Todd.

Lévinas, E., 1981, *Otherwise than Being or Beyond Essence*, trans. Lingis, A., The Hague: Martinus Nijhoff.

Loades, A., 2001, *Feminist Theology: Voices from the Past*, Oxford: Polity.

Locke, K. A., 2009, *The Church in Anglican Theology: A Historical, Theological and Ecumenical Exploration*, Farnham: Ashgate.

Lossky, N. et al. (eds), 1991, *Dictionary of the Ecumenical Movement*, Geneva: WCC Publications; and Grand Rapids, MI: Eerdmans.

Luzbetak, L., 1988 [1963], *The Church and Cultures*, Maryknoll, NY: Orbis Books.

Lynch, T., 1998, *The Undertaking: Life Studies from the Dismal Trade*, New York, Penguin.

Macchia, F., 2002, 'African Enacting Theology: A Rediscovery of an Ancient Tradition?', *Pneuma: The Journal of the Society for Pentecostal Studies* 24.2, pp. 105–9.

McConnell, D. R., 1990, *The Promise of Health and Wealth: A Historical and Biblical Analysis of the Modern Faith Movement*, London: Hodder & Stoughton.

McConnell, D. R., 2004, 'Christianity in Africa: From African Independent to Pentecostal-Charismatic Churches', *Annual Review of Anthropology* 33, pp. 447–74.

McFague, S., 1993, *The Body of God: An Ecological Theology*, London: SCM Press.

Mackie, S., 1970, *Can Churches be Compared?* Geneva: WCC, and New York: Friendship.

McRobert, I., 1989, 'Black Pentecostalism: Its Origins, Functions and Theology with Special Reference to a Midlands Borough', Ph.D. thesis, University of Birmingham.

Madugba, M. U., 2000, *Africa's Time of Recovery*, Port Harcourt: Spiritual Life Publications.

Maluleke, T. S., 1993, 'Review of *Bazalwane*', in *Missionalia* 21.2, pp. 186–7.

Maluleke, T. S., 1994, 'Review of *Tumelo*', in *Missionalia* 22.1, pp. 61–2.

Maluleke, T. S., 1996, 'Research Methods on AICs and other Grass-Root Communities', *Journal of Black Theology in South Africa* 10.1, pp. 29–48.

Margull, H. J., 1962a, *Hope in Action*, Philadelphia: Mühlenberg Press.

Margull, H. J., 1962b, *Aufbruch zur Zukunft: Chiliastisch-messianische Bewegungen in Afrika und Südostasien*, Gütersloh: Mohn.

Margull, H. J., 1970, 'Mission '70 – riskanter denn je', *Der Überblick* 6, pp. 7–10.

Margull, H. J., 1971, 'Überseeische Christenheit: Markierungen eines Forschungsbereiches anhand der letztjährigen Literatur', *Verkündigung und Forschung* 16, pp. 2–54.

Margull, H. J., 1972, 'Der Dialog von Ajaltoun/Beirut', in Margull, H. J. and Samartha, S. J. (eds), *Dialog mit anderen Religionen*, Frankfurt am Main: Lembeck, pp. 74–89.

Margull, H. J., 1973, 'Ethos des Dialogs' *Missionsjahrbuch der Schweiz*, pp. 101–4.

Margull, H. J., 1974a, 'Überseeische Christenheit II: Vermutungen zu einer Tertiaterranität des Christentums', *Verkündigung und Forschung* 19, pp. 56–103.

Margull, H. J., 1974b, 'Verwundbarkeit: Bemerkungen zum Dialog', *Evangelische Theologie* 34, pp. 410–20.

Margull, H. J., 1980, 'Der "Absolutheitsanspruch" des Christentums im Zeitalter des Dialogs', *Theologia Practica* 1, pp. 67–75.

[Mission 2008], The Religious Studies and Mission Studies Section of the Academic Association for Theology (WGTh) and the Administrative Board of the German Association for Mission Studies. 2008. '"Mission Studies as Intercultural Theology and its Relationship to Religious Studies", Declaration dated 21 September 2005', *Mission Studies* 25, pp.103–8.

Marshall, R., 1993, 'Power in the Name of Jesus: Social Transformation and Pentecostalism in Western Nigeria "Revisited"', in Ranger, T. O. and Vaughan, O. (eds), *Legitimacy and the State in Twentieth-Century Africa*, London: Macmillan, pp. 213–46.

Marshall-Fratani, R., 1995, '"God is not a Democrat": Pentecostalism and Democratization in Nigeria', in Gifford, Paul (ed.), *The Christian Churches and the Democratisation of Africa*, Leiden: J. Brill, pp. 239–60.

Marshall-Fratani, R., 1998, 'Mediating the Global and the Local in Nigerian Pentecostalism', *Journal of Religion in Africa* 28.3, pp. 278–315.

Marshall, R., 2009, *Political Spiritualities: The Pentecostal Revolution in Nigeria*, Chicago: University of Chicago Press.

Martin, F., 1994, *The Feminist Question: Feminist Theology in the Light of Christian Tradition*, Grand Rapids, MI: Eerdmans.

Massey, R. D.,1987, 'A Sound and Scriptural Union: An Examination of the Origins of the Assemblies of God of Great Britain and Ireland during the years 1920–1925', PhD thesis, University of Birmingham.

Maximus the Confessor, 1955, *The Ascetic Life: Four Centuries on Charity*, trans. Sherwood, P., London: Longmans.

Maxwell, D., 2002. 'Introduction: Christianity and the African Imagination', in Maxwell, David with Lawrie, Ingrid (eds), *Christianity and the African Imagination: Essays in Honour of Adrian Hastings*, Leiden: Brill, pp. 1–24.

Meyer, B., 1998, '"Make a Complete Break with the Past": Memory and Postcolonial Modernity in Ghanaian Pentecostal Discourse', in Werbner, R. (ed.), *Memory and the Postcolony: African Anthropology and the Critique of Power*, London and New York: Zed Books, pp. 182–208.

Meyer, B., 2004, 'Christianity in Africa: From African Independent to Pentecostal-Charismatic Churches', *Annual Review of Anthropology*, 33, pp. 447–74.

Miller, D. E. and Yamamori, T., 2007, *Global Pentecostalism: The New Face of Christian Social Engagement*, Berkeley and Los Angeles, CA: University of California Press.

Moltmann, J., 1992, *The Spirit of Life: A Universal Affirmation*, London: SCM Press.

Muers, R., 1997, 'Feminism, Gender, and Theology', in Ford, David F. (ed.), 1997, *The Modern Theologians: An Introduction to Christian Theology*, Oxford: Blackwell, pp. 431–50.

Müller, K., Sundermeier, T., Bevans, S. B. and Bliese, R. H. (eds), 1997, *Dictionary of Mission: Theology, History, Perspectives*, Maryknoll, NY: Orbis Books.

Nelson, D. J., 1981, 'Such a Time as This: The Story of William J. Seymour and the Azusa Street Revival', PhD thesis, University of Birmingham.

Newbigin, L., 1963, *Trinitarian Doctrine for Today's Mission*, London: Edinburgh House Press.

Newlands, G., 2004, *The Transformative Imagination: Rethinking Intercultural Theology*, Aldershot: Ashgate.

Nida, E. and Taber, C., 1969, *The Theory and Practice of Translation*, Leiden: Brill.

Niebuhr, R., 1951, *Christ and Culture*, New York: Harper & Row.

Nwankpa, E., 1994, *Redeeming the Land: Interceding for the Nations*, Achimota, Ghana: Africa Christian Press.

Njoroge, N. J., 2001, 'The Bible and African Christianity: A Curse or a Blessing?', in Dube, Musa W. (ed.), *Other Ways of Reading: African Women and the Bible*, Atlanta, GA: Society of Biblical Literature, pp. 207–36.

Oborji, F. A., 2008, 'Missiology in its Relation to Intercultural Theology and Religious Studies', *Mission Studies* 25, pp. 113–14.

Oduyoye, M. A., 1986, *Hearing and Knowing: Theological Reflections on Christianity in Africa*, Maryknoll, NY: Orbis Books.

Oduyoye, M. A., 1994, 'The Empowering Spirit of Religion', in King, U. (ed.), *Feminist Theology from the Third World*, pp. 361–76.

Oduyoye, M. A., 2001, *Introducing African Women's Theology*, Sheffield: Sheffield Academic Press.

Oduyoye. M. A., 2002, *Beads and Strands: Reflections of an African Woman on Christianity in Africa*, Oxford: Regnum–Paternoster.

Ojo, M. A., 1996, 'Charismatic Movements in Africa', in Fyfe, Christopher and Walls, Andrew F. (eds), *Christianity in Africa in the 1990s*, University of Edinburgh: Centre of African Studies, pp. 92–110.

Ojo, M. A., 2006, *The End-Time Army: Charismatic Movements in Modern Nigeria*, Trenton, NJ: Africa World Press Studies.

Okorocha, C. C., 1987, *The Meaning of Religious Conversion in Africa: The Case of the Igbo of Nigeria*, Aldershot: Avebury.

Okure, T., 1988, *The Johannine Approach to Mission: A Contextual Study of John 4.1–42*, Tübingen: J. C. B. Mohr.

Olaniyi, M., 2007, 'The Meaning of Religious Conversion in the Christ Apostolic Church of Nigeria: Towards the Incarnation of Christianity in Yorubaland', PhD thesis, University of Birmingham.

Olukoya, D. K., 1999a, *Violent Prayers to Disgrace Stubborn Problems*, Lagos: The Battle Cry Christian Ministries.

Olukoya, D. K., 1999b, *Prayer Rain*, Lagos: MFM Ministries.

Olukoya, D. K., 1999c, *Overpowering Witchcraft*, Lagos: MFM Ministries.

Onyinah, O., 2002, 'Akan Witchcraft and the Concept of Exorcism in the Church of Pentecost', PhD thesis, University of Birmingham.

Orevillo-Montenegro, M., 2006, *The Jesus of Asian Women*, Maryknoll, NY: Orbis Books.

Ositelu, P. and G., 1998, *African Initiatives in Christianity: The Growth, Gifts and Diversities of Indigenous African Churches – A Challenge to the Ecumenical Movement*, Geneva: WCC Publications.

Ott, C., 2007, 'Conclusion: Globalising Theology', in Ott and Netland (eds), *Globalizing Theology*, pp. 309–36.

Ott, C. and Netland, H. (eds), 2007, *Globalizing Theology: Belief and Practice in an Era of World Christianity*, Nottingham: Apollos.

Oyewole, O. and Ebofin, O., 2000, *Poverty Must Die*, Lagos: The Battle Cry Ministries.

Padwick, T. J., 2003, 'Spirit, Desire and the World: Roho Churches of Western Kenya in the Era of Globalization', PhD thesis, University of Birmingham.

Park, J. C., 1998, *Crawl with God, Dance in the Spirit! A Creative Formation of Korean Theology of the Spirit*, Nashville, TN: Abingdon Press.

Park, B.-K., 2005, 'A Pneumatocentric Soteriology: A Study of the Christ Apostolic Church Against the Background of the Church Missionary Society in Yorubaland, Nigeria', PhD thesis, University of Birmingham.

Parratt, J., 1995, *Reinventing Christianity: African Theology Today*, Grand Rapids, MI: Eerdmans.

Parsons, S. F. (ed.), 2002, *Cambridge Companion to Feminist Theology*, Cambridge: Cambridge University Press.

Peel, J. D. Y., 2000, *Religious Encounter and the Making of the Yoruba*, Bloomington and Indianapolis: Indiana University Press.

Percy, M., 2005, *Engaging with Contemporary Culture: Christianity, Theology and the Concrete Church*, Aldershot: Ashgate.

Perriman, A. (ed.), 2003, *Faith, Health and Prosperity: A Report on 'Word of Faith' and 'Positive Confession' Theologies*, Carlisle: Paternoster.

Peterson, D., 1996, *Not by Might Nor by Power: A Pentecostal Theology of Social Concern in Latin America*, Oxford: Regnum.

Petter, F. A., 2002, *Profanum et Promissio. Het begrip wereld in de missionaire ecclesiologien. van Hans Hoekendijk, Hans Jochen Margull en Ernst Lange*, Groningen: Proefschrift University of Groningen.

Podmore, C., 2005, *Aspects of Anglican Identity*, London: Church House Publishing.

Pranger, J. H., 2003, *Redeeming Tradition: Inculturation, Contextualization, and Tradition in a Postcolonial Perspective*, Groningen: Proefschrift University of Groningen.

Price, L., 1996, *Faithful Uncertainty: Leslie D. Weatherhead's Method of Creative Evangelism*, Frankfurt am Main: Peter Lang.

Price, L., 2002, *Theology out of Place: A Theological Biography of Walter J. Hollenweger*, Sheffield: Sheffield Academic Press.

Radner, E. and Turner, P., 2006, *The Fate of Communion: The Agony of Anglicanism and the Future of a Global Church*, Grand Rapids, MI, Eerdmans.

Raj, P. S., 1986, *Christian Folk Religion in India: A Study of the Small Church Movements in Andhra Pradesh, South India*, Frankfurt am Main: Peter Lang.

Rapu, T., 2006a, 'Where will we be in 15 years?' *This Day*, June.

Rapu, T., 2006b, 'The Next Frontier', *This Day*, July.

Rapu, T., 2007, 'The Joshua Generation', *This Day*, February.

Ray, B. C., 1993, 'Aladura Christianity', *Journal of Religion in Africa*, 23.3, pp. 266–91.

Reat, R. and Perry, E., 1991, *A World Theology: The Central Spiritual Reality of Humankind*, Cambridge: Cambridge University Press.

Reed, B., 1978, *The Dynamics of Change: Process and Movement in Christian Churches*, London, Darton, Longman & Todd.

Ricœur, P., 1986, 'L'idéologie et l'utopie: deuz expressions de l'imaginaire social', in Ricœur, P., *Du texte à la l'action: Essais d'herméneutique*, Paris: Éditions du Seuil, pp. 79–92.

Ricœur, P., 1992, *Oneself as Another*, Chicago: University of Chicago Press.

Robbins, J., 2004, 'The Globalization of Pentecostal and Charismatic Christianity', *Annual Review of Anthropology* 33, pp. 117–43.

Roberts, O., 1970, *Miracle of Seed-Faith*, Tulsa, OK: Revell.

Robinson, G., 2008, *In the Eye of the Storm*, Norwich: Canterbury Press.

Robinson, M., 1987, 'To the Ends of the Earth: The Pilgrimage of an Ecumenical Pentecostal, David J. du Plessis 1905–1987', PhD thesis, University of Birmingham.

Roszak, T., 2000, *The Making of a Counter Culture*, London: Faber.

Ruether, R. R., 1975, *New Woman, New Earth: Sexist Ideologies and Human Liberation*, New York: Seabury Press.

Ruether, R. R., 1983, *Sexism and God-Talk: Toward a Feminist Theology*, London: SCM Press.

Ruether, R. R., 1994, *Gaia and God: An Ecofeminist Theology of Earthkeeping*, New York: HarperCollins.

Ruether, R. R., 1998, *Women and Redemption: A Theological History*, Minneapolis, MN: Augsburg Fortress.

Ruether, R. R., 2002, 'The Emergence of Christian Feminist Theology', in Susan Frank Parsons (ed.), *The Cambridge Companion to Feminist Theology*, Cambridge: Cambridge University Press, pp. 3–22.

Russell, L. M., 1974, *Human Liberation in Feminist Perspective: A Theology*, Philadelphia: The Westminster Press.

Sachs, W. L., 2009, *Homosexuality and the Crisis of Anglicanism*, Cambridge: Cambridge University Press.

Samartha, S., 1973, 'Ethos des Dialogs', *Missionsjahrbuch der Schweiz*, pp. 101–4.

Samartha, S., 1974a, 'Überseeische Christentheit II: Vermutungen zu einer Tertiaterranität des Christentums', *Verkündigung und Forschung* 19, pp. 56–103.

Samartha, S., 1974b, 'Verwundbarkeit: Bemerkungen zum Dialog', *Evangelische Theologie* 34, pp. 410–20.

Samartha, S., 1980, 'Der "Absolutheitsanspruch" des Christentums im Zeitalter des Dialogs', *Theologia Practica* 1, pp. 67–75.

Sandel, M., 2009, *Justice*, London: Allen Lane.

Saracco, J. N., 1990, 'Argentine Pentecostalism: Its History and Theology', PhD thesis, University of Birmingham.

Sawyer, D. F., 2002, *God, Gender and the Bible*, London: Routledge.

Schmidt-Leukel, P., 2005, *Gott ohne Grenzen: Eine christliche und pluralistische Theologie der Religionen*, Gütersloh: Gütersloher Verlagshaus.

Schmidt-Leukel, P., 2009, *Transformation by Integration: How Inter-faith Encounter Changes Christianity*, London: SCM Press.

Schreiter, R., 1985, *Constructing Local Theologies*, Maryknoll, NY: Orbis.

Schreiter, R., 1996, 'The Changing Context of Intercultural Theology: A Global View', *Studia Missionalia* 46, pp. 359–80.

Schreiter, R., 1997, *The New Catholicity*, Maryknoll, NY: Orbis Books.

Schreiter, R., 2003, 'Theology, Culture and Dialogue in a New Millennium', *Studies in Interreligious Dialogue* 13.1, pp. 30–40.

Scott, P. and Cavanaugh, W. T. (eds), 2007, *Political Theology*, Oxford: Blackwell.

Sen, A., 2009, *The Idea of Justice*, London: Allen Lane.

Sharma, A. and Young, K. K. (eds), 1998, *Feminism and World Religions*, Albany, NY: State University of New York Press.

Sharpe, E., 1986, *Comparative Religion: A History*, 2nd edn, London: Duckworth.

Shorter, A., 1994, *Towards a Theology of Inculturation*, Maryknoll, NY: Orbis Books.

Skaggs, R., 2004, *The Pentecostal Commentary on 1 Peter, 2 Peter, Jude*, London: T & T Clark.

Smail, T., Walker, A. and Wright, N., 1994, '"Revelation Knowledge" and Knowledge of Revelation: The Faith Movement and the Question of Heresy', *Journal of Pentecostal Theology* 5, pp. 57–77.

Smart, N. and Konstantine, S., 1991, *Christian Systematic Theology in a World Context*, London: Harper Collins.

Smith, D. J., 2001, '"The Arrow of God": Pentecostalism, Inequality, and the Supernatural in South-Eastern Nigeria', *Africa* 71.4, pp. 587–613.

Sölle, D., 1968, *Atheistisch an Gott glauben*, Munich: Deutscher Taschenbuch Verlag.

Sölle, D., 1984, *The Strength of the Weak: Toward a Christian Feminist Identity*, Philadelphia: Westminster Press.

Sørensen, J. S., 2007, *Missiological Mutilations – Prospective Paralogies: Language and Power in Contemporary Mission Theory*, Frankfurt am Main: Peter Lang.

Soskice, J. M. and Lipton, D. (eds), 2003, *Feminism and Theology: Oxford Readings in Feminism*, Oxford: Oxford University Press.

Stackhouse, M. L., 2007, *Globalization and Grace* (God and Globalization, Vol. 4), New York and London: Continuum.

Studies in the Intercultural History of Christianity 1975 ff. (over 150 vols), Frankfurt am Main, Bern, later New York and other places: Peter Lang; Margull, H. J., Hollenweger, W. J. and Friedli, R. were founding eds. Later joined Sundermeier, T., Jongeneel, J. A. B., Ustorf, W. and Koschorke, K.

Sugirtharajah, R. S. and Hargreaves, C. (eds), 1993, *Readings in Indian Christian Theology, Vol. 1*, Delhi: ISPCK.

Sugirtharajah, R. S., 1995, 'Afterword. Cultures, Texts and Margins: A Hermeneutical Odyssey', in Sugirtharajah, R. S. (ed.), *Voices from the Margin: Interpreting the Bible in the Third Word*, Maryknoll, NY: Orbis, pp. 457–75.

Sugirtharajah, R. S., 1999, *Vernacular Hermeneutics*, Sheffield: Sheffield Academic Press.

Sugirtharajah, R. S., 2002, *Postcolonial Criticism and Biblical Interpretation*, Oxford: Oxford University Press.

Sundermeier, T., 1985, *Das Kreuz als Befreiung: Kreuzesinterpretationen in Asien und Afrika*, Munich: Kaiser.

Sundermeier, T., 1986, 'Konvivenz als Grundstruktur ökumenischer Existenz heute', in Huber, W., Ritschl, D. and Sundermeier, T., *Ökumenische Existenz heute, Vol. 1*, Munich: Kaiser, pp. 49–100.

Sundermeier, T. and Küster, V. (eds), 1991, *Das schöne Evangelium: Christliche Kunst im balinesischen Kontext*, Steyl: Steyler Verlagsbuchhandlung.

Sundermeier, T. and Ustorf, W. (eds), 1991, *Begegnung mit dem Anderen: Plädoyers für eine interkulturelle Hermeneutik*, Gütersloh: Gerd Mohn.

Sundermeier, T., 1992, *A Theology of Religions*, Special Issue (S 10) of *Scriptura: Journal of the Bible and Theology in Southern Africa*.

Sundermeier, T., 1996, *Den Fremden verstehen: Eine praktische Hermeneutik*, Göttingen: Vandenhoeck & Ruprecht.

Sundermeier, T., 1999, *Was ist Religion?* Gütersloh: Kaiser.

Sundkler, B. G. M, 1961, *Bantu Prophets in South Africa*, Oxford: Oxford University Press.

Tamez, E., 1982, *The Bible of the Oppressed*, Maryknoll, NY: Orbis Books.

Tanner, K., 1997, *Theories of Culture: A New Agenda for Theology*, Minneapolis, MN: Fortress Press.

Tanner, K., 2005, *Economy of Grace*, Minneapolis, MN: Fortress Press.

Taylor, C., 2007, *A Secular Age*, London: Belknap Press of Harvard University.

Thomas, J. C., 1994, 'Women, Pentecostals and the Bible: An Experiment in Pentecostal Hermeneutics', *Journal of Pentecostal Theology* 5, pp. 41–56.

Thomas, J. C., 2000, 'Reading the Bible from within our Traditions: A Pentecostal Hermeneutic as a Test Case', in Green, J. B. and Turner, M. (eds), *Between Two Horizons: Spanning New Testament and Systematic Theology*, Grand Rapids, MI: Eerdmans, pp. 108–22.

Thomas, J. C., 2004, *The Pentecostal Commentary on 1 John, 2 John, 3 John*, London: T & T Clark.

Tienou, T., 2007, 'Christian Theology in an Era of World Christianity', in Ott and Netland (eds), *Globalizing Theology*, pp. 37–51.

Tiwari, Y. D., 1993, 'From Vedic Dharma to the Christian Faith', in Sugirtharajah and Hargreaves (eds), *Readings in Indian Christian Theology*, pp. 132–38.

Tomasi, J., 2001, *Liberalism Beyond Justice: Citizens, Societies and the Boundaries – a Political Theory*, Princeton: Princeton University Press.

Tooker, D. E., 1992, 'Identity Systems of Highland Burma: "Belief", Akha Zan, and a Critique of Interiorized Notions of Ethno-Religious Identity', *Man*, New Series 27.4, pp. 799–819.

Townes, E., 1993, *A Troubling in my Soul: Womanist Perspectives on Evil and Suffering*, Maryknoll, NY: Orbis Books.

Tracy, D., 1987, 'Comparative Theology', in Eliade, M. (ed.), *Encyclopedia of Religion, Vol. 14*, New York: Collier Macmillan, pp. 446–55.

Tremlett, P.-F., 2006, 'Cosimo Zene, *The Rishi of Bangladesh: A History of Christian Dialogue*', *Bulletin of the School of Oriental and African Studies*, Reviews 63, pp. 481–3.

Tremlett, P.-F., 2007, 'The Ethics of Suspicion in the Study of Religions', *DISKUS* 8 www.basr.ac.uk/diskus/diskus8/Tremlett.htm (accessed 20 February 2011).

Trible, P., 1984, *Texts of Terror: Literary-Feminist Readings of Biblical Narratives*, London: SCM Press.

Turner, H. W., 1979, *Religious Innovation in Africa*, Boston: G. K. Hall.

Ukpong, J. S., 1984, 'Current Theology: The Emergence of African Theologies', *Theological Studies* 45, pp. 501–536.

Ustorf, W., 1989. 'Das Heidelberger Projekt einer interkulturellen Theologie', in Rudolph, K. and Rinschede, G. (eds), *Beiträge zur Religion/Umwelt-Forschung I*, Berlin: Reimer, pp. 177–90.

Ustorf, W., 1990, 'Review of Hollenweger's third volume on intercultural theology', *International Review of Mission*, 79.314, April, pp. 227–9.

Ustorf, W., 1992, 'Warum Margull lesen?' in Ahrens, T. et al. (eds), *Hans Jochen Margull: Zeugnis und Dialog*, Ammersbek bei Hamburg: Verlag and der Lottbek, pp. 9–15.

Ustorf, W., 2000, *Sailing on the Next Tide: Missions, Missiology, and the Third Reich*, Frankfurt am Main: Peter Lang.

Ustorf, W., 2004, 'Wissenschaft, Africa and the Cultural Process according to Johann Gottfried Herder (1744–1803)', in Ludwig, F. and Adogame, A. (eds), *European Traditions in the Study of Religion in Africa*, Wiesbaden: Harrassowitz, pp. 117–27.

Ustorf, W., 2008a, 'The Cultural Origins of "Intercultural Theology"', *Mission Studies* 25, pp. 229–51.

Ustorf, W., 2008b, 'The Missiological Roots of the Concept of "Political Religion"', in Mallett, R. et al. (eds), *The Sacred in Twentieth-Century Politics*, Basingstoke and New York: Palgrave Macmillan, pp. 36–50.

Ustorf, W., 2010, 'The "Beast from the South" und das "Ende des liberalen Christentums"', *Berliner Theologische Zeitschrift* 27.1, pp. 36–69.

Ustorf, W. and McLeod, H. (eds), 2003, *The Decline of Christendom in Western Europe, 1750–2000*, Cambridge: Cambridge University Press.

Vandana, M. (ed.), 1995, *Shabda Shakti Sangam*, Rishikesh: Vandana Mataji.

Vandana, M. 1987, *Jesus the Christ: Who is He? What was His Message?* Jaiharikhal: Vandana Mataji.

Vandana, M. 1989, *Waters of Fire*, Bangalore: Asian Trading Corporation.

Vanhoozer, K., 2005, *The Drama of Doctrine: A Canonical-Linguistic Approach to Christian Theology*, Louisville, KY: Westminster John Knox Press.

Vanhoozer, K., 2007, '"One Rule to Rule them All?" Theological Method in an Era of World Christianity', in Ott and Netland (eds), *Globalizing Theology*, pp. 85–105.

Wagner, C. P. (ed.), 1991, *Territorial Spirits: Insights on Strategic-Level Spiritual Warfare from Nineteen Christian Leaders*, Chichester: Sovereign World.

Walker, A., 1993. 'The Devil You Think You Know: Demonology and the Charismatic Movement', in Smail, T., Walker, A. and Wright, N., *Charismatic Renewal: The Search for a Theology*, London: SPCK, pp. 86–105.

Ward, G., 1999, 'Bodies: The Displaced Body of Jesus Christ', in Milbank, J., Pickstock, C. and Ward, G. (eds), *Radical Orthodoxy*, London: Routledge, pp. 163–81.

Ward, G., 2005, *Christ and Culture,* Oxford: Blackwell.

Ward, K., 1994, *Religion and Revelation: A Theology of Revelation in the World's Religions*, Oxford: Clarendon.

Ward, K., 1996, *Religion and Creation*, Oxford: Clarendon.

Ward, K., 1998, *Religion and Human Nature*, Oxford: Clarendon.

Ward, K., 1999, *Religion and Community*, Oxford: Clarendon.

Ward, K., 2007, 'The Idea of God in Global Theology', in Hintersteiner, N. (ed.), *Naming and Thinking God*, pp. 377–388.

Warner, M., 1985, *Alone of All Her Sex: The Myth and Cult of the Virgin Mary*, London: Picador.

Warren, R., 1995, *The Purpose-Driven Church*, Grand Rapids, MI: Zondervan.

Warren, R., 2002, *The Purpose-Driven Life*, Grand Rapids, MI: Zondervan.

Warrier, M. and Oliver, S. (eds), 2008, *Theology and Religious Studies: An Exploration of Disciplinary Boundaries*, London: T & T Clark.

Whiteman, D., 2007, 'Anthropological Reflections on Contextualising Theology in a Globalising World', in Ott and Netland (eds), *Globalizing Theology*, pp. 52–69.

Wijsen, F., 2001, 'Intercultural Theology and the Mission of the Church', *Exchange* 30.3, pp. 218–28.

Wijsen, F., 2003, 'New Wine in Old Wineskins: Intercultural Theology instead of Missiology', in Frederiks, Dijkstra and Houtepen (eds), *Towards an Intercultural Theology*, pp. 39–54.

Wijsen, F. and Schreiter, R. (eds), 2007, *Global Christianity: Contested Claims*, Amsterdam: Rodopi.

Williams, D. S., 1993, *Sisters in the Wilderness: The Challenge of Womanist God-Talk*, Maryknoll, NY: Orbis Books.

Williams, R., 2004, *Anglican Identities*, London: Darton, Longman & Todd.

Yates, T. (ed.), 2005, *Mission and the Next Christendom*, Sheffield: Cliff College Publishing.

Yoder, J. H., 1972, *The Politics of Jesus*, Grand Rapids, MI: Eerdmans.

Yong, A., 2002, *Spirit–Word–Community: Theological Hermeneutics in Trinitarian Perspective*, Aldershot: Ashgate.

Yong, A., 2003, *Beyond the Impasse: Towards a Pneumatological Theology of Religions*, Grand Rapids, MI: Baker Academic.

Yong, A., 2005, *The Spirit Poured Out on All Flesh: Pentecostalism and the Possibility of Global Theology*, Grand Rapids, MI: Baker Academic.

Yoo, B., 1988, *Korean Pentecostalism: Its History and Theology*, New York: Peter Lang.

Young, J. U., 1993, *African Theology: A Critical Analysis and Annotated Bibliography*, Westport, CT: Greenwood Press.

Zene, C., 2002, *The Rishi of Bangladesh: A History of Christian Dialogue*, London: Routledge/Curzon.

Žižek, S., 2001, *On Belief*, London: Routledge.

Index

Adeboye, E.A. 129, 149, 154, 156, 158, 169
Adogame, A. 153, 169, 186
Adorno, T. 20, 169
African Independent Churches (AIC) 133–144, 179
Agamben, G. 36, 169
Ahrens,T. 11, 169, 185
Alterity 8, 93 –97, 109
Anderson, A. 3, 9, 63, 128, 129, 132–137, 143, 169
Anglican 8, 9, 42, 55, 81, 112–128, 146, 178, 182, 183, 187
Aquinas, T. 33, 37, 39, 170
Archer, K.J. 7, 64–67, 72, 170
Arellano, L.B. 83, 170
Ariarajah, W. 48, 170
Arnold, M. 24, 170
Arrup, P. 96
Asamoah-Gyadu, J. K. 132, 150, 152, 158, 170
Ashimolowo, M. 155, 156, 170
Astley, J. 146, 170
Augustine 34
Awolalu, J. O. 159, 170

Barrett, D. B. 13, 131, 170
Beattie, T. 75, 175, 177
Becher, J. 75, 170
Bediako, K. 146, 170
Benjamin, C. R. 170
Bevans, S. 53, 94, 150, 164, 170, 180
Bevis, K. 111, 170
Bhabha, H. K. 22, 171
Bible 4, 46, 65, 67, 68, 70, 72, 73, 76, 77, 79, 81–83, 88, 119, 130,
142, 146 –150, 153, 154, 156, 157, 159, 173, 174, 176–178, 180, 183–185
Bingemer, M.C. 82, 171, 174
Bittlinger, A. 131, 171
Boff, L. 173
Book of Common Prayer 39
Bosch, D. 14, 94, 171
Brandon, S.G.F. 41, 171
Brown, T. 173
Brück, M. Von, 19, 171
Buddhism 12, 27, 37, 85, 87, 89, 101, 108, 109
Buddhists 8, 19, 23, 27, 88, 100–105, 108, 109, 111, 173
Burgess, R. J. 3, 9, 132, 157, 161, 171
Burnard, P. 101, 171
Byrne, L. 76, 171

Cantwell Smith, W. 44, 56, 171
Carey, G. 120
Cartledge, M.J. 3, 7, 63, 72, 74, 171
Catholic, Roman 8, 12, 24, 31, 42, 52, 56, 63, 76, 78–81, 89, 91, 94, 95, 97, 99, 100, 107, 118, 128, 145, 146
Catholicity 4, 8, 9, 18, 112, 113, 117 –119, 121, 123, 124, 126, 127, 132, 145, 183
Cavanaugh, W.T. 83, 175, 178, 183
Chandran, J.R. 52, 171
Chant, S. 82, 171
Charismatic 63, 73, 74, 128, 143, 147, 157, 169, 170, 171, 175, 179, 180–182, 186
Cheetham, D. 3, 5–7, 44, 59, 171

Chopp, R.S. 83, 171
Christology 18, 52, 72, 84, 87, 172, 177, 178
Clarke, C.R. 132, 172
Clements, K. 20, 172
Clooney, F.X. 56–58, 172
Colletti, J. 131, 172
Colonialism 46, 85, 86, 91, 146, 155
Comparative religion 44, 54, 56, 58, 183
Comparative theology 45, 54–58, 172, 173, 175, 185
Confucianism 85, 89
Conn, J.W. 79, 172
Conservative 3, 44, 76, 83, 113, 117, 119, 121, 123, 124, 126, 139, 141, 147, 161
Contextual theology 32, 44, 46, 121, 139, 145, 150, 164, 165, 170, 171
Contextualization 14, 68, 94, 101, 135, 138, 164, 166, 182
Cox, H. 133 –135, 140, 144, 172
Craske, N. 171
Critchley, S., 96, 172
Cross, F.L. 13, 172
Cruchley-Jones, P. 26, 172
Cullmann, O. 41, 172

Daly, M. 78, 172
Damasio, A. 38, 172
Daneel, M.L. 135–140, 142, 143, 169, 172, 173
Davie, G. 26, 173
Decolonization 4, 9, 11, 43
Demonology 186
Depoliticization 31
Dempster, M.W. 160, 173
Derrida, J. 28, 111, 172, 173
Dialogue 3, 4, 8, 12, 19–21, 27, 29, 44, 47, 48, 51, 56, 57, 60, 64, 71, 73, 89, 91–98, 100, 109, 111, 131, 138, 146 –148, 156, 164, 165, 170, 175, 183, 185, 187
Diaspora 29, 154, 160, 175
Dijkstra, M. 170, 173, 176, 187
Discernment 49
Discipleship 5, 29, 30–34, 36–42, 114

Diversity 1, 4, 6, 17, 21, 22, 50, 53–55, 59, 62, 68, 71, 73, 115–118, 125, 126, 145, 157, 160, 175, 177
Dube, M.W. 77, 81, 173, 177, 180

Ebofin, O. 156, 181
Ecclesiology 7, 18, 36, 37, 67, 73, 110, 167
Ecumenism 4, 71, 118, 176
Ehrenreich, B. 114, 173
Eliot, T.S. 124, 125, 173
Elizondo, V. 173
Ellis, S. 160, 163, 173
Emerging Church 123, 124
Enculturation 8, 9, 112, 124
Enlightenment 35, 160, 169
post –Enlightenment 149
Epistemology 5, 21, 23, 25, 26, 53, 59, 73, 147
Eschatology 6, 23, 35–37, 40, 43, 47, 50, 60, 61, 67, 161, 173
Esquivel, J. 82, 173
Ethics 4, 8, 27, 53, 92–94, 96, 98, 99, 109, 110, 111, 115, 152, 155, 161, 163, 165, 172, 185
Evangelization 95
Evans, M.J. 77, 173

Fabella, V. 80, 81, 86, 170, 173
Faupel, D.W. 131, 173
Feminist theology 7, 8, 75–79, 80–92, 171, 173–178, 180, 181, 183–185
Fiorenza, E.S. 77, 173
Fellowship of Confessing Anglicans (FOCA) 117
Ford, D, 45, 50, 61, 173, 180
Fredericks, J. 56–58, 173
Frederiks, M. 170, 173, 176, 187
Friedli, R. 11–15, 18–20, 22–24, 27, 174, 184
Fresh expressions 9, 123, 124
Freston, P. 160, 173

Gadamer, H-G. 54, 97, 98, 174
Global Anglican Futures Conference (GAFCON) 117
Gaxiola-Gaxiola, M.J., 131, 174
Gebara, I. 82, 174

Gender 5, 7, 29, 31, 42, 75, 77–79, 81, 82, 84, 90, 91, 116, 127, 141, 144, 171, 175, 177, 180, 183
Gerloff, R.I.H. 131, 174
Giddens, A. 154, 155, 174
Gifford, P. 129, 146, 148, 152, 156–158, 160, 161, 163, 164
Gill, K.D. 131, 174
Globalization 1, 4, 6, 17, 21, 31, 37, 40, 43, 122, 129, 144, 145, 166, 169, 181, 182, 184
Gnanadason, A. 80, 85, 88, 174
Goodchild, P. 36, 175
Gospel 5, 34, 35, 37, 41, 43–49, 51, 59, 60, 65, 67, 72, 73, 77, 89, 95, 96, 101, 102, 111, 115, 118, 125, 129, 137, 145, 150, 152, 153, 155, 156, 164, 166, 167, 173
Graham, Billy 77, 79, 83, 85, 167
Graham, E. 77, 79, 83, 85, 167, 175
Grey, M. 79, 175
Gross, R.M. 75, 175

Haar, G.T. 160, 163, 173
Habermas, J. 98
Hare, D. 122, 175
Hargreaves, C. 171, 177, 184, 185
Harris, H. 151, 175
Hastings, A. 137, 175, 180
Hauerwas, S. 40, 175
Hengel, M. 41, 175
Hermeneutics 20, 26, 46, 65–67, 77, 147, 149, 150, 177, 184, 185, 187
Heterodoxy 167
Hick, J. 27, 56, 175
Hinduism 31, 88, 89
Hindus 18, 27, 30, 52, 55, 89, 90
Hintersteiner, N. 14, 59, 175, 186
Hocken, P. 131, 175
Hollenweger, W. 1, 4, 6, 7, 11–13, 18, 19, 22–24, 46, 48, 50, 51, 62, 64, 66, 69–73, 128–135, 139–141, 148, 150, 164, 175, 176, 182, 184, 185
Homophobia 113
Hopewell, J. 147, 176
Horkheimer, M. 20, 169
Horton, R. 151, 176

Houtepan, A. 173
Hunt, A. 79, 176
Hunt, S. 152, 176

Ikenga-Metuh, E.E. 176
Incarnation (see Christology) 5, 14, 23, 44, 51, 59, 60, 78, 87, 92, 96, 167, 181
Inculturation 1, 14, 28, 94, 96, 182, 183
Indigenization 45, 53, 137
Interreligious 3, 4, 6, 7, 12, 19–21, 24, 27, 43–45, 47, 48, 50, 51, 54–56, 58–61, 64, 95, 100, 139, 160, 170, 175, 183
Isasi-Díaz, A.D. 83, 176
Islam 31, 94, 148, 160, 161, 163, 176
  Muslims 19–21, 27, 30, 55, 163

Jehu –Appiah, J.H. 132, 176
Jenkins, P. 15, 50, 134, 149, 176
Jew 21, 30, 42, 55, 87
Jewish 29, 30, 36, 65
Johnson, E.A. 79, 89, 170, 176
Jongeneel, J.A.B. 11, 13, 131, 173, 176, 184

Kalu, O. U. 150, 157, 158, 160, 163, 164, 177
Kang, N. 81, 83, 84, 86, 87, 177
Kanyoro, M. R. A. 81, 174, 177
Kaplan, R.B. 11, 177
Katoppo, M. 79, 83, 85, 88, 90, 177
Kerr, D. A. 27, 177
Kim, K. 3, 7, 8, 80, 87, 89, 177
King, R. 171
King, U. 75, 79, 86, 171, 174, 175, 177, 181
Klostermaier, K. 51, 52, 177,
Knitter, P. 27, 56, 57, 177
Konstantine, S. 56, 184
Köstenberger, A.J. 76, 177
Kraemer, H. 94, 177
Kroeger, C.C. 77, 177
Kumari, P. 174, 177
Küster, V. 14, 20, 150, 164, 165, 177, 178, 184

Kwok P. 77, 80, 81, 83–89, 91, 178,
Kyung, C.H. 80, 87–90

Laan, C. 131, 170, 178
Laan, P. 131, 178
LaCugna, C.M. 79, 178
Land, S. J. 149, 178
Lartey, E. 148, 150, 160, 178
Lee, M. 94, 178
Levinas, E. 94, 96–98, 108, 111, 170, 172, 178
Liberal 3, 21, 24, 31, 32, 44, 55, 56, 64, 76, 113, 117, 119, 122, 126, 147, 153, 167
Liberation 5, 21, 22, 27, 46, 49, 54, 78, 79, 82, 83, 85, 88, 90, 91, 101, 111, 138, 143, 146, 149, 151, 162–164, 167, 171, 172, 182, 183
Lipton, D. 83, 184
Liturgy 9, 78, 132, 133, 135, 138, 140–143, 153
Loades, A. 79, 178
Locke, K.A. 118, 178
Lossky, N. 13, 178
Ludwig, F.186
Luzbetak, L.12, 178
Lynch, T.113, 178

Macchia, F.D. 66, 72, 178
Mackie, S. 16, 179
MacRobert, I. 131
Madugba, M. U. 163, 179
Mallett, R. 186
Maluleke, T.S, 137–140, 179
Margull, H. J. 6, 11, 12, 16–20, 22–24, 26–28, 169, 174, 179, 182, 184, 185
Marshall, R. 155, 158, 160–163, 174, 179, 180
Martin, D. 24, 76
Martin, F. 180
Massey, R.D. 131, 180
Maximus the Confessor 38, 39, 180
Maxwell, D. 148, 180
McConnell, D.R. 156, 178, 179
McFague, S. 79, 179
McLeod, H. 186

McSpadden, L.A. 80, 174
Mercy, A.O. 81, 170, 173
Methodism 81, 128
Meyer, B. 152, 160, 180
Milbank, J. 186
Miller, D.E. 160, 162, 180
Mission 4, 8, 11, 13–16, 19, 21 –23, 25, 27, 28, 30, 35, 47, 48, 62, 64, 69, 81, 93–98, 100, 101, 105, 109, 111, 119, 123, 124, 128, 130–132, 134, 137, 140, 142, 149, 169–172, 174–181, 184–187
Missiology 4, 14, 15, 19, 23, 27, 69, 94–96
Modernity 20, 28, 75, 113, 145, 166, 167, 174, 180
Moltmann, J. 72, 73, 180
Muers, R. 77, 78, 80, 83, 86, 91, 180
Multi-cultural 30–32, 38, 43, 44, 62, 71, 78, 91, 148, 153

Narrative 5, 7, 18, 35, 41, 47, 66, 67, 69–73, 89, 132, 141, 149
Nelson, D.J. 5, 7, 18, 35, 41, 47, 66, 67, 69–73, 89, 131, 132, 141, 149, 180
Netland, H. 181, 185–187
Newbigin, L. 94, 180
Newlands, G. 13, 44, 64, 180
Nida, E., 12, 180
Niebuhr, R. 47, 53, 60, 61, 180
Njoroge, N. J. 82, 180
Nwankpa, E. 163, 180

Obama, B. 9, 112–114, 126, 127
Oborji, F. A. 15, 180
Oduyoye, M.A. 81, 82, 170, 180, 181
Ojo, M. A. 157, 161, 181
Okorocha, C.C. 151, 159, 181
Okure, T. 81, 181
Olaniyi, M. 132, 181
Oliver, S. 45, 186
Olukoya, D. K. 152, 153, 181
Onyinah, O. 132, 181
Ordination 76, 85
Orevillo-Montenegro, M. 86–89, 181

Orthodoxy 15, 52–54, 66, 89, 92, 139, 164
Ositelu, P. and G. 138, 181
Ott, C. 43, 181, 185–187
Oyewole, O. 156, 181

Padwick, T.J. 132, 181
Park, B-K. 132, 181
Park, J.C. 86, 181
Park Sun Ai 79
Parratt, J. 84, 146, 181
Parsons, S.F. 178, 181, 183
Peel, J.D.Y. 151, 159, 182
Pentecostalism
  African 9, 128–138
  Nigerian 10, 145–168
Pentecostal Theology 7, 46, 49, 62–74, 128–168, 169–173, 176, 178–180, 182, 184, 185
Percy, M. 3, 8, 112–127, 147, 182
Perriman, A. 156, 182
Perry, E. 56, 182
Peterson, D. 182
Petter, F. A. 11, 182
Philosophy 51, 59, 78, 85, 96, 108, 171, 172, 176
Pickstock, C. 186
Pluralism 16, 18, 27, 164, 175
Pneumatology 72, 84, 89–92, 132, 134, 178, 181, 187
Plato 33, 34
Podmore, C. 122, 182
Politics 4, 9, 17, 31, 32, 34, 39–42, 84, 92, 115, 116, 127, 160–164, 167, 173, 186, 187
Political 15–18, 25, 29–31, 33, 35–42, 78, 79, 84–86, 88, 110, 113, 120, 132, 139, 146, 152, 155, 157, 158, 160–164, 166–168, 173, 175, 178, 180, 183, 185, 186
Pontificium Institutum pro Missionibus Exteris (PIME) 8, 93, 99–109, 111
Postmodern 5, 6, 46, 48, 72, 94–96, 110, 111, 149
Post-colonial 6, 14, 25, 26, 81, 85, 146, 149
Poverty 82, 83, 153, 156, 158, 159, 165, 167, 181

Price, L. 11, 12, 27, 69–71, 130, 182
Prosperity 129, 143, 148, 150–151, 153, 154, 156–159, 161, 165, 174, 182

Quash, B. 45, 173

Racism 37, 83, 86, 103, 132, 133, 142, 155
Radner, E. 120, 182
Raj, P.S. 131, 182
Rapu, T. 161, 162, 182
Reat, R. 56, 182
Reed, B. 126, 182
Reformed 11, 23, 115, 130, 136, 139
Ricoeur, P. 20, 40, 182
Robbins, J. 160, 182
Roberts, O. 157, 182
Robinson, G. 9, 113, 114, 116, 120, 122, 126, 182
Robinson, M. 182
Roszak, T. 124, 182
Ruether, R.R. 76–78, 81, 83, 85, 86, 182, 183
Russell, L.M. 79, 183

Sachs, W.L. 119–121, 183
Sacraments 44, 115
Samartha, S. 179, 183
Sandel, M. 120, 183
Saracco, J.N. 131, 183
Sawyer, D.F. 77, 183
Schmidt -Leukel, P. 27, 28, 56–58, 183
Schreiner T.R. 76, 177
Schreiter, R. 14, 49, 50, 53, 54, 64, 145, 150, 164, 166, 175, 183, 187
Scott, P. 83, 175, 178, 183
Scripture 2, 7, 41, 56, 65, 67, 70, 71, 116, 147–149, 170
Secular 10, 11, 16, 18, 21–26, 32, 35, 42, 78, 99, 142, 145, 155, 160, 167, 185
Secularization 16, 25, 123, 144, 152, 160
Sen, A. 120, 183
Sexuality 75, 115, 116, 119–122, 124, 127, 170
Shamanism 90

Sharma, A. 75, 183
Sharpe, E. 44, 183
Shorter, A. 96, 183
Shroeder, R.P. 94, 170
Skaggs, R. 67, 184
Smail, T. 156, 184, 186
Smart, N. 56, 184
Smith, D.J. 158, 184
Smith, W.C. 44, 56, 171
Sölle, D. 22, 184
Sørensen, J. S. 28, 184
Soskice, J. M. 45, 83, 173, 184
Soskice, J.M. 45, 83, 173, 184
Spirituality 4, 7, 9, 24, 53, 63, 67, 73, 74, 77, 79, 80, 83, 89, 99, 114, 123, 133, 136, 137, 144, 146, 149, 151, 160, 169–172, 174, 178
Stackhouse, M. L. 28, 184
Sugirtharajah, R.S. 26, 72, 149, 171, 177, 184, 185
Sundermeier, T. 14, 20, 21, 26, 174, 180, 184
Sundkler, B.G.M. 131, 136, 137, 139, 140, 164
Syncretism 27, 133, 136, 137, 139, 140, 164

Taber, C. 12, 30, 180
Taoism 85
Tamez, E. 77, 83, 185
Tanner, K. 2, 39, 110, 11, 185
Taylor, C. 35, 185,
Taylor, J.V. 23
Testimony 1, 7, 37, 40, 45, 46, 65, 72, 109, 141
Tertullian 47
Thomas, J.C. 7, 64, 65, 67, 113, 185
Tienou,T. 48, 185
Tiwari, Y.D. 52, 185
Tomasi, J. 120, 185
Tooker, D.E. 103, 185
Townes, E. 83, 185
Tracy, D. 55, 185
Tremlett, P.F. 98, 111, 185
Trible, P. 77, 185
Trinity 33, 67, 72, 79, 88, 117, 154, 176, 178
Trinitarian 34, 36, 171, 180, 187

Truth 19, 20, 21, 23–25, 28, 33, 34, 37, 43, 52, 54, 58, 59, 61, 71, 95, 111, 124, 162, 170, 174
Turner, H.W. 134, 185
Turner, M. 185
Turner, P. 120, 182

Ukpong, J.S. 138, 185
Ustorf, W. 1, 3–6, 11–28, 43, 48, 174, 184, 184–186

Vandana, M. 87–90, 186
Vanhoozer, K. 54, 56, 61, 186
Vatican II 76, 82, 94–96, 100, 145
Via Media 115–116

Wagner, C. P. 163, 186
Walker, A. 152, 156, 165, 184, 186
Walton, H. 175
Ward, F. 175
Ward, G. 4–6, 29–42, 186
Ward, K. 51, 55, 56, 58, 59, 186
Warner, M. 77, 186
Warren, R. 9, 112–114, 126, 186
Warrier M. 45, 186
Womanist 76, 83, 185, 187
World Council of Churches (WCC) 8, 11, 12, 16, 20, 21, 28, 73, 79, 80, 130, 170, 172, 174, 175, 177, 178, 179, 181
Whiteman, D. 43, 187
Wijsen, F. 2, 50, 64, 145, 166, 187
Williams, D.S. 83, 187
Williams, R. 118, 187
Wright, N. 156, 184, 186

Yates, T. 50, 187
Yamamori, T. 160, 162, 180
Yin-Yang 85, 86
Yoder, J.H. 41, 187
Yong, A. 49, 64, 74, 187
Yoo, B. 131, 187
Young, J.U. 146, 187
Young, K.K. 75, 183

Zene, C. 8, 93–99, 109, 110, 111, 185, 187
Zizek, S. 37, 187